Also by Tansy E. Hoskins

Stitched Up: The Anti-Capitalist Book of Fashion

TANSY E. HOSKINS

FOOT WORK

What Your Shoes Tell You
About Globalisation

First published in Great Britain in 2020 by Weidenfeld & Nicolson
This paperback edition published in 2022 by Weidenfeld & Nicolson
an imprint of The Orion Publishing Group Ltd
Carmelite House, 50 Victoria Embankment
London EC4Y 0DZ

An Hachette UK Company

1 3 5 7 9 10 8 6 4 2

A CIP catalogue record for this book is
available from the British Library.

ISBN (Mass Market Paperback) 978 1 4746 0986 9
ISBN (eBook) 978 1 4746 0987 6
ISBN (Audio) 978 1 4746 1833 5

Typeset by Input Data Services Ltd, Somerset

Printed and bound in Great Britain by Clays Ltd, Elcograf S.p.A.

www.weidenfeldandnicolson.co.uk
www.orionbooks.co.uk

Every morning I forget how it is.
I watch the smoke mount
In great strides above the city.
I belong to no one.

Then I remember my shoes,
How I have to put them on,
How bending over to tie them up
I will look into the earth.

Charles Simic, born 1938

To Bryn, for the journey

CONTENTS

AUTHOR'S NOTE

The names of the children and young people at Sneaker Con have been changed for privacy protection.

For safety reasons, 'Şebnem' in Chapter Two is a fake name and this person's identity has been obscured.

The names of refugees interviewed for Chapter Five have also been changed.

I did not visit every country I have written about in this book. In particular, interviews with homeworkers in Chapter Three were obtained via a series of Skype calls arranged with the help of Khalid Mahmood and Jalvat Ali at the Labour Education Foundation in Lahore, and Om Thapaliya from HomeNet Nepal, to whom I am very grateful.

PREFACE TO THE PAPERBACK EDITION

The fashion industry – which includes both the apparel and footwear sectors – generated $2.5 trillion in global revenues in 2019, making it one of the largest industries in the world.[1] But when the Covid-19 pandemic struck in 2020, it virtually collapsed. Lockdowns around the globe meant shoppers stayed at home, retailers shuttered stores and cancelled billions of dollars worth of orders, factories received official government decrees to shut down, closing either temporarily or permanently. Over the course of 2020 shoe production fell by almost 4 billion pairs.[2]

In the first spring lockdown, there were only a few reasons people in the UK were permitted to leave their home, one of which was for 'one form of exercise a day'. I took to walking in a neighbourhood loop, trying to find peace amid the nervous tension. Making these daily walks possible were a pair of navy and orange trainers which, when I looked, held a *Made in Indonesia* label.

As our global community grappled with Covid-19, these shoes became the opposite of disposable. They kept me moving even in a dramatically reduced physical orbit. In return I scraped off mud and replaced frayed laces, connecting with the shape of their soles and their stitches, each one sewn by another human – someone in Indonesia who I hoped hadn't just lost their job, or fallen sick in a crowded factory.

For workers who subsist on poverty wages at the best of times, the Covid-19 pandemic has spelt disaster. An in-depth study by the Asia Floor Wage Alliance into Covid conditions concluded that during the pandemic 'workers coped by engaging in their own mental and physical degradation' and that the pandemic saw the 'mining of workers' bodies' – descriptions I can't get out of my head.[3]

In my own reporting of pandemic conditions, I heard from one woman in Sri Lanka who lived on 'rice sprinkled with salt' for six weeks. Other families reported becoming so desperate that they considered killing their children.[4] Covid-19 quickly became a crisis borne by the people already exploited by the fashion industry – most of them women, many of them migrants, and the majority in the Global South.

Across production lines, tens of thousands of workers lost their jobs and thousands more were taken seriously ill as Covid-19 spread through cramped factories. Lockdowns and increasing authoritarianism also meant trade unions and activists in the Global South often could not travel, even locally, to advocate on behalf of workers. Where people dared to speak up about unsafe or unfair conditions, they were often met with redundancy or brutality – with labour violations reaching a seven-year high.[5] One of the most difficult stories I reported on during the pandemic was about soldiers shooting dead three people at a protest over unpaid wages outside a cowboy-boot factory in Myanmar. Six more people were sentenced to three years in prison by a military court.[6]

Super Winners

As the pandemic progressed, some fashion brands fell into bankruptcy and shut down. But others thrived as it became obvious that people had not stopped non-essential shopping, particularly online. The McKinsey consultancy firm has a list of fashion industry 'Super Winners' – the top twenty fashion corporations based on total annual profits. These include shoe brands Nike and adidas as well as H&M, Zara parent company Inditex, Burberry and Gucci parent company Kering.[7]

When the stock market plunged in March 2020, these brands weathered the storm. By October 2020, their share price was 11 per cent higher than pre-crisis levels. The world's billionaires also did extremely well, with their collective wealth rising to $10.2 trillion. Online shopping magnate, Jeff Bezos, was the richest person on the planet with a fortune of $189 billion.[8]

This accumulated wealth at the top of the fashion system is

inseparable from the hardship at the bottom of the chain. Capitalism is not built for equality, it creates intergalactic wealth for a tiny percentage of people, while billions of others are left in poverty. It is a system created so that when crisis strikes, those at the top are protected while workers take the biggest hit.

Built To Lose

The pandemic only intensified the crises set out in this book, further revealing the lie behind the promise that globalisation would make life better for all. When 50–80 per cent of everything a country exports is apparel, and suddenly people are buying fewer clothes and shoes, then the crisis is not just in one industry but becomes a national crisis. The Global South was encouraged by financial institutions to grow its garment and footwear sectors, on the basis that it remain a low-cost site of production, with low wages and suppressed trade unions. This is compounded by decades of brands minimising their tax contributions – reducing the ability of states in the Global South to spend on vital pandemic management like healthcare and unemployment benefits.

In an equitable system, a pandemic would not have caused this scale of death and chaos. The problem, however, is that we live under the dysfunctional system of capitalism with harm built into the system. None of this is a coincidence, rather what we are seeing with Covid-19 is the reality of millions of people being so badly exploited that they have no margin for error and no ability to save for emergencies.

In early 2021 I spoke with Khalid Mahmood at the Labour Education Foundation (who you'll meet in this book). He talked about the exacerbation of financial difficulties faced by garment and footwear workers in the industrial districts of Lahore, Pakistan. Lost wages meant that to try and make ends meet, workers took their children out of school, sold household items like mobile phones or washing machines and moved to smaller homes – while often forced to leave all their possessions behind to cover rent arrears. This crisis is replicated across the fashion industry, with 75 per cent of garment workers taking out loans during the pandemic.[9]

As with the 2008 financial crash, the informal sector was also hit extremely hard by the pandemic. In the informal sector, the signs that something was not right appeared as early as January 2020. Homeworkers in the Indian city of Tirupur – always sensitive to the slightest shift in domestic and global markets – found that both contracts and access to raw materials from China had begun to reduce. By March 2020, there was no work whatsoever. Once bustling streets fell silent.

At the same time, many of these informal workers became critical to mutual aid relief efforts. In Dharavi – a sprawling township embedded within the Indian city of Mumbai – it was the women of informal worker communities who distributed food rations, organised social distancing in queues, fed migrant workers who did not qualify for rations, and found and nursed families in crisis. Other homeworker networks grouped together to form producer companies and cooperatives who won contracts to make PPE such as masks and scrub caps.

* * *

When the weather turned cold, I switched to wearing my favourite black boots, boots that were *Made in China* before being shipped to a shop in North London. China made 2 billion fewer pairs of shoes during 2020, but is still the world's largest footwear producer.[10] These boots now carry me around my neighbourhood, emblems of footwear supply chains that are as global as the Covid-19 crisis. Reminders that this system needs to be rebuilt on a new set of foundations including workers' rights, equal access to free healthcare and environmental justice. Only then will we end the practice of brands pushing not only the economic pain but the social and personal cost of crises down to the hidden sections of their supply chains

November, 2021

What's Shoes Got to Do with It?

The ancient Greek philosopher and historian, Strabo, told the story of a beautiful courtesan named Rhodopis whose sandal was stolen by an eagle while she was bathing. The eagle dropped the sandal into the lap of the King of Egypt, who felt such admiration for its shape that he at once sent out emissaries to find its owner so that he could marry her.[1]

Storytellers in ancient China also told a tale of a beautiful young woman whose fortunes were transformed by a shoe. Recorded in the ninth century, the story of Ye Xian is said to have been old even then. Unlike Strabo's tale, it included a wicked stepmother and stepsister. Ye Xian had a magical benefactor in the form of a fish, and the slipper she lost was made of golden threads woven in a fish-scale pattern. At the end of the tale, Ye Xian marries a king, while her stepmother and stepsister are crushed to death by flying stones.

Folklorists from around the world – Native American, Javanese, Russian, Zulu and Persian to name but a few – have all told a tale of a lowly, but feisty, woman full of agency who was eventually helped by her shoes to marry high above her social rank.

When Charles Perrault published the story of *Cendrillon* in Paris in 1697, he sanitised the tale, excluding the bloodied feet, chopped-off toes and ghosts of earlier versions. From there it was a downwards slide towards Disney and the story of a girl who simpers, cowers and waits to be rescued, first by mice and then by a prince. Gone is the traditional folklore ability of the heroine to determine her own fate.[2]

From Cinderella, to the winged sandals worn by the Greek messenger-god Hermes, to the miraculous boots that took their wearer seven leagues with every step and Dorothy's ruby slippers in *The Wizard of Oz*, transformation through footwear is a timeless theme in shared culture. Where you find shoes, you often find magic.

But shoes are not magical. Each one has been made by human beings. No matter the tale, at their heart they are just pieces of leather, wood, metal, rubber, cotton and plastic.

Even the enchantment created by fabled storyteller Hans Christian Andersen, author of *The Red Shoes*, had at its heart his childhood memories of being a small boy in a one-room home filled almost entirely by a shoemaker's workbench. Little Hans slept each night beside his father, a man who rarely smiled but stitched and hammered shoes late into the night.[3]

Origins

Every single day in 2019, 66.6 million pairs of shoes were manufactured across the world. This adds up to a total of 24.3 billion pairs.*

Shoes have never been cheaper to buy, but their cost to the world has never been greater. Over-production, accompanied by over-consumption in rich countries, have collided to create a world that feels disposable, with innovation and progress funnelled into producing merchandise that can be piled high and sold cheap. Meanwhile the world's leading climate scientists say we have just eleven years to keep global heating beneath 1.5 degrees centigrade and avoid major catastrophe.[4]

Humans are the only species on the planet to routinely use shoes as protection from the cold and from dangerous ground.[5] Their invention has had a profound effect on humanity. Over hundreds of millions of years, the human body evolved from that of our primate forebears. We began to support all our weight on two feet rather

---

* https://www.worldfootwear.com/news/footwear-production-with-new-record-of-243-billion-pairs/5356.html [November 2020].

than four, and to walk and run in an upright position. Our spine changed shape, our pelvis broadened and our toes lost their ability to grip branches. This move to 'bipedal locomotion' is accepted as one of the most significant steps in human evolution. It was a transition that placed a lot of strain on our feet.

One of our long-lost ancestors eventually had the bright idea of wrapping a bit of bark around her feet in order to run faster after prey and away from predators; to avoid poisonous bites and stings; and to more easily cross desert or ice caps to find new hunting grounds.

Paleoanthropologist Erik Trinkaus believes humans started wearing shoes as early as 40,000 years ago. There is very little archaeological evidence from this time – a footprint that implies the use of moccasins, some stitched beading found around the feet of skeletons – so Dr Trinkaus took instead to examining toes. By inspecting the toes of ancient human remains, he found a gradual reduction in their sturdiness, a softening he believes is due to the spread of footwear.[6]

Made from plant fibres and materials prone to decay, very few prehistoric shoes have survived. The earliest examples include 10,000-year-old sandals woven from sagebrush bark and found in Oregon, and an 8,000 year-old sandal discovered in a cave in central Missouri. The Missouri sandal is made of dried woven leaves, it has a slightly pointed toe and ties on with a braided cord.

There is also a Copper Age moccasin-style shoe found in a preserving layer of sheep dung in an Armenian cave. This shoe was made 5,500 years ago using a single piece of cowhide folded up around the foot and sewn into shape. In today's terms it would be a size five, which might imply it belonged to a woman, or perhaps a small man or young person. Whomever they were, the people who wore these shoes have vanished, leaving behind an object both spectacularly ancient yet strangely commonplace and recognisable.

Invented at the dawn of human history, for thousands of years shoes remained objects that were crafted by people in small communities. By the time humans lived in the villages and small towns of recent history, shoes were still products of locally made, low-level commerce.

The definition of a shoe is pretty uncomplicated: a covering for a foot that doesn't reach above the ankle, made of sturdy material. Using a design that still holds true today, a shoemaker would firstly create a 'last', the wooden (or plastic) model of a foot around which a shoe is built. Next, a pattern would be traced onto material spread out on a workbench, most likely leather, with the template mapping out each piece needed to make a shoe. A clicking knife would then be used to cut out the material, with the clicker (a shoemaker's assistant hired to do the cutting) trying hard to minimise wastage.

The pieces would then be stitched together in a process called 'closing'. Traditionally a pointed tool called an awl was used to pierce through leather. Once the shoe had been stitched together, a closer's hammer was used to flatten seams and smooth out wrinkles. This process would create the top of the shoe, known as the 'upper'. The upper would then be ready to mould round the last so a sole could be attached. Once the sole had been attached, any rough edges would be shaved off and the finished shoe polished till it gleamed.[7]

Today the basic design of a shoe has hardly altered, though much of this process is mechanised, atomised and often automated. Clicking knives, for example, have been replaced by machines that use multiple bladed templates. But while the design may be recognisable, the scale of production is not. In fact, it is wildly out of control.

To understand how this has happened, we must ask an everyday object to tell us its stories. We must explore where these billions of shoes come from and what they reveal. In telling this story, the concept of globalisation is opened up to us, with all its complexities and controversies.

A map of the world

Picture a map of the world, rotate the globe and zoom in till you find Europe, zoom in a little further to the continent's most westerly point. Now you are in Lisbon, the capital city of Portugal. To the south-west is the suburb of Belém, the name taken from the Portuguese word for Bethlehem.

Belém is home to the Church of St Maria whose slim white pillars rise like the masts of tall ships. The church is decorated with carvings of coiled rope, sea monsters and elephants. Around door-frames stone faces peer out, chiselled portraits of an imagined Asia and Africa.

At the end of the church is an elaborate tomb, quite possibly empty of its intended occupant, as the man it was carved for died in Cochin, India in 1524. The tomb belongs to Vasco da Gama, a Portuguese navigator and contemporary of Christopher Columbus, who 'discovered' the sea road to India, mapping a trade route that brought huge wealth to Portugal for over a century.

This was not the first instance of international trade or travel. The Silk Road, for example, stretched across a continent, allowing trade between Europe and Asia, and bloating Italian city states with silks, spices and precious metals. But what the Portuguese did, with their maritime routes, was to pioneer trade that was truly global.

The shoreline in Belém is a fitting place to start discussing glo-balisation because Portugal's 'Age of Discovery' and the voyages of Vasco da Gama were undeniably conducted in the pursuit of wealth and conquest. Portuguese cannons and disregard for life account, as much as anything, for the riches that were accumulated.

Between the Church of St Maria and the River Tagus is the site of a former slave market. Though countries like Britain soon rushed to join the barbarism, the Transatlantic Slave Trade found its spark in fifteenth-century Portuguese colonialism. The sweep of European ships along the coasts of Africa began the biggest forced migration in human history, as an estimated 11 million people were taken from their homes and sold as slaves.[8] A white-and-red stone map, decor-ated with mermaids, depicts routes the Portuguese *caravels* took across the oceans. West to Brazil and Canada, south to the Cape of Good Hope and east as far as Japan. Each ship lugging cargoes of gems, spices, frightened animals and captured human beings. 'Globalisation' appeared as a buzzword in 1983 to describe one of the most rapid yet precarious social transformations in human history.[9] But with Vasco da Gama setting sail after a night of prayer in 1497, is globalisation a new phenomenon or the continuation of long-established processes of trade and travel?

Some theorists see the term 'globalisation' as lazy thinking for those who cannot be bothered to pick apart and analyse entirely separate financial and political changes.[10] I would argue, on the other hand, that globalisation is an overriding reality of our times.[11] In 1983, a new word was needed to describe how technology, from the internet modem to the oil refinery and the jet plane, had transformed the world along economic, political and cultural lines.[12] This change has dramatically reshaped production, consumption, the biosphere and even chances of long-term human survival. As a result, this book uses the word 'globalisation' as a useful term to signpost a process of rapid industrial conquest.

Gold from a sewer

Globalisation above all has been about supplies of people and raw materials. The industrial revolution moved British manufacturing from scattered rural workshops to concentrated urban areas like London and Manchester. These newly huge cities drew in vast quantities of people to feed privately owned factories. The land was cracked open to harvest coal, copper and iron ore. Foodstuffs to feed hungry urban populations, timber and brick for building materials and metals for machinery were all drawn into the melee.

Alexis de Tocqueville visited Manchester in 1835. He described black smoke covering the city, a dull half-light with no real sun, the 'thousand noises' of industry that never ceased and 'miserable dwellings' in rows of cellars where twelve to fifteen human beings crowded into 'damp, repulsive holes'.[13] To de Tocqueville, Manchester was a 'foul drain', but he also recognised that its people were producing great wealth: 'From this filthy sewer pure gold flows.'

This pattern of voracious factory cities took hold in North America, western Europe and Japan. When cities found they could not source what they needed from their immediate surroundings, ships, traders, armies and slavers set out to find more raw materials, more people to capture and kill and more lands to loot of their riches. Colonialism bloated the original factory cities while prescribing the name 'underdeveloped' to the rest of the world.

With the twentieth century came revolt. Liberation struggles were fought, Communist flags were raised, as were the flags of God. Bright young colonels and university graduates fought with bullets and books to drag their countries out from under the heel of an iron boot. Nations escaped colonialism but not the system of capitalism. Newly liberated countries in Asia, Latin America, eastern Europe and Africa saw migration to urban areas and piecemeal rises in education and skillsets. Blocs of people emerged: disciplined, hungry for work and used to low wages.

As the Cold War diminished and countries opened up, an intense new phase of accelerated integration began. Technology in the form of high-speed travel and telecommunications meant these blocs of people became obtainable resources for corporations nurtured in the original factory cities, but now looking to escape the taxes, wages and regulations of Europe and North America. Company executives flew to capital cities across Asia, Africa and Latin America to meet with politicians and business leaders who wanted to get rich quick.

Hundreds of millions of workers not only became available for hire but had to compete for the attention of corporations. Also available were rich new sources of rubber, oil, water, cattle and fresh air. More land to be cracked open in places that did not have stringent guards against exploitation.[14]

Like a hurricane?

The next question is whether this process was inevitable or political. Was the hunt for low-cost labour and resources out of control or a deliberate process? There are many economists who argue globalisation is inevitable, that it is a natural progression from local economies to national economies, followed by a global economy. This argument appears on both sides of the political spectrum, from Thatcherites stating 'There Is No Alternative', to Marxists drawing on the inevitable contradictions of capitalism.[15]

The inevitability argument was pushed hard in the 1990s by Tony Blair and Bill Clinton, who framed the power of the markets as some unstoppable force of nature, like a hurricane.[16] This book argues it is deeply problematic to see globalisation as inevitable and anonymous. Such an approach pushes for globalisation to be seen as a *fait accompli* that we must accept, while waiting meekly like Cinderella for things to improve. By seeing globalisation as apolitical and anonymous we lose not only our own agency but the ability to see agency in others, whether they be heads of state, corporate CEOs or global governing bodies like the International Monetary Fund (IMF) or the World Bank.[17]

In the chapters ahead you will find instead a different argument – globalisation is the result of deliberate action, or the absence of action, by political actors wielding political power.[18] We are on the edge of a cliff not because it is inevitable, but because it is ideological. We live in a world shaped by political decisions which tend to favour the interests of money, not people.[19]

Seeing globalisation as the result of political choices allows us to explore where power lies, not just in the shoe industry but in the world. Who has the power to decide to bail out banks, remove capital controls, create or rip up trade agreements, privatise resources, reconfigure factory production or smother environmental regulation?[20] This process also reveals who this system works for: who are 'the haves' and 'the have-nots', and who are 'the have-yachts'? Far from being an obscure, jargon-heavy topic, globalisation is a set of power relations with clear winners and losers – those with power make the decisions, those without power lose out.

Then there is the question of whether globalisation is the answer or the problem?[21] Proponents of globalisation promised that it heralded a global system of economic prosperity, democracy and harmony.[22] They promised that a rising tide would raise all boats, and that trickle-down economics was the answer, that consumers would get wonderful low-cost products to play with and that the poor would get jobs and stop being poor. Flick through any newspaper or news site and one might be forgiven for wondering: what the heck happened?

Before the term 'globalisation' was coined, the 1970s brought about a hurried new phase of this globalising world. It was an era based on a strict political ideology, an ideology that shapes the world we live in. At the centre of this ideology is the belief that control, regulation and economic direction must be handed over to the markets. By minimising the role of states, governments and the law, the market was allowed to rule almost unhindered.

As capitalism globalised, it became elevated to a near-mythical status. Held up by Augusto Pinochet in Chile, Margaret Thatcher in the UK and Ronald Reagan in the US as the one true saviour, *neoliberal* capitalism demanded sacrifices: deregulate capital flows across borders to make life easy for banks and businesses, shrink the role of the state in providing help for people's daily lives, reduce taxes for corporations and the already wealthy, aggressively drive the 'free market' into every corner of the world. Wealth creation was placed firmly in the global foreground and surrounded by phalanxes of financial institutions, biased trade agreements and corporate lawyers. The reality for many was the side-lining of democracy and the common good.

Globalisation has been hailed as a success in boardrooms and lecture halls, but this book exists because the shoes on our feet tell a different story. How can we celebrate globalisation without knowing what it means for the Chinese factory worker, the Bangladeshi tannery worker, the Brazilian environmentalist or the commodity-fixated teenagers caught up in this system? Globalisation is the story of transformation, but it has not been an equal process, nor one done beneficently. For many it is a story of how, as corporate influence spread and production levels rose, quality of life and standards fell.

In all the arguing over whether globalisation exists and whether it is inevitable or political, it is important not to lose sight of what is happening now. We must not lose the stories of the consequences.

Why now?

The story of globalisation did not end with the opening up of labour markets in Asia, Latin America, eastern Europe and Africa. Nor was it happily-ever-after for the people of the old factory cities. When the corporations jumped ship to make billions, they left behind mass unemployment and the loss of tax revenue. While profits soared, the gap between the rich and those left behind widened. In 2019, just twenty-six of the richest billionaires own as many assets as the 3.8 billion people who make up the poorest half of the planet's population.[23]

Inequality took root both in the old industrial centres and in the new factory landscapes. Politicians and business leaders experienced soaring incomes, while those they employed endured poverty wages. 'Sharply rising income and wealth inequalities thus characterised the new centres of capitalism as well as the old,' writes Professor Richard Wolff about the period following the 1970s. 'Globalisation distributed capitalism's deepening inequality throughout the world.' The trappings of inequality – personal debt, speculation, real-estate bubbles, corruption and bloated conspicuous consumption by the rich – have also spread.[24]

The result of globalisation – of the globalisation of capitalism – is that we live in a world characterised by corporate plunder of the natural world, heinous workers' rights abuses, climate breakdown and income inequality to the extent that a minibus-ful of people own more money than 50 per cent of the global population. Globalisation has not brought the promised economic benefits, nor has it ensured stability; instead it is a process driven by the needs of international corporations.[25]

This is not to say things have worked out for those at the top of society. Even the acquisition of private fire brigades, private islands and private bunkers can only provide a certain amount of insulation from impending climate breakdown. Nor can political turmoil be ignored.

In June 2016, the European Union was stunned by the UK voting for Brexit; months later the world was stunned by the election of Donald Trump. Both are mass votes that bear the shadow of globalisation. They placed discontent front and centre on a world stage, revealing the hopelessness brought about by austerity measures and the financial crash, and the factionalising and racism brought about by the fear of being left behind.

Trump has been explicit in his condemnation: 'We reject the ideology of globalism and we embrace the doctrine of patriotism,' he told the United Nations in September 2018. World leaders laughed openly at the speech and yet Trump is seemingly setting the world up for a turned-on-its-head moment where the US seeks protectionism, a retreat from the world stage and walls on its borders. China meanwhile, with its Belt and Road investment initiative and commitment to state-run industries and capital controls, seems to be championing multilateralism and globalisation.[26]

Why shoes?

The shoes on our feet are the propulsion and the consequence of globalisation. Among the first objects to undergo globalised production, shoes represent the interdependencies and injustices that shape our world. Thanks to technical transformations in communication and transport, and the global availability of low-waged workers, shoe manufacturing found itself scattered around the world as a pioneer of this process. Thus every shoe we own is a world within a world, the vast majority of them made from complex component parts on dangerous, low-waged production lines.

The fashion industry has been under a spotlight since the collapse of the Rana Plaza factory complex in 2013. In 90 seconds, the collapse of this building in Bangladesh killed an estimated 1,138 people. It was the biggest industrial homicide the industry had ever seen, but it was far from a unique event. The Ali Enterprises fire, the Tazreen factory fire, the Spectrum factory collapse and countless other horrific incidents are all bloody proof of an industry in crisis.

Despite having its own inventory of fatal fires and factory collapses, the shoe industry has managed to largely avoid this spotlight. As a result, industry experts interviewed for this book all stated that the shoe industry is far behind the rest of the fashion industry in terms of wages, conditions and corporate standards. Every nexus of shoemaking is in crisis. The job of modern-day shoe workers remains rife with noxious fumes, toxic chemicals and poverty wages. The impact of footwear upon the biosphere, upon animals and the living world remains unconscionable.

This book is an invitation to walk in your own shoes into the forgotten backwaters of globalisation. It includes visits to slaughterhouses, sweatshops, rubbish dumps and makeshift refugee centres. It holds interviews with people representing twenty-eight different countries.

Chapter One examines the heady world of consumption, exploring how the world divides between those with too much and those with not enough. We meet shoe obsessives and explore the allure of footwear. Chapter Two explores shoe factories across the globe from China to the Balkans, and we meet factory workers and factory bosses, and explain how we came to make 24,200,000,000 pairs of shoes per year.

Chapter Three follows the supply chain beneath the first tier of factories to meet a secret pillar of globalisation: homeworkers. Who are these hidden women and men, what are the consequences of market capitalism turning millions of homes into factories, and just how poisonous are our shoes?

The corporate ability to hide the reality of shoe production is explored in Chapter Four. How did branding begin, why do corporations want to link shoes with emotions, can we ever trust the labels in our shoes and what do counterfeit sneakers tell us about the world?

Chapter Five starts in a makeshift refugee camp and looks at the stories of people in battered, rain-soaked shoes. Why can money and products freely cross borders but people cannot? Who are the people making shoes in Turkish basements, and why have tens of millions of children been separated from their parents in China? Chapter Six is an exposé of leather production, of the industrial slaughter of billions of animals, of the tearing down of the rainforest and of Bangladeshi tanneries where the average life expectancy is fifty. From political violence to slavery and climate apocalypse, the leather industry punishes everything it touches.

Chapter Seven asks what happens next. Having been purchased, what happens when shoes – these complex, handmade and intensively resourced items – are discarded? Where do 24.2 billion pairs of shoes go once they are chucked out? From cobblers to second-hand warehouses and recycling laboratories, we count the cost of living in a disposable world.

Chapter Eight leaves behind the wastelands of the present and travels to the factories of the future. How have robots already changed the shoe industry and what does the rise of automation have in store? What are the consequences if millions of women lose their jobs to robots?

Chapter Nine questions why an object like a shoe can cause so much havoc. How have corporations got away with so much for so long, and where are the laws to protect people and planet? We explore how corporate programmes and greenwashing have blocked social progress. Finally, Chapter Ten looks at how things could be done differently. We've tried the globalisation of capitalism; is it now time for a new system of globalisation from below? What would the world look like if it was rearranged along more equal lines and what will it take for us to get there?

Something wondrous

Shoes meld with the body like no other piece of clothing, holding a person's shape long after they have stepped out of them. By the same token, nothing else that is worn tortures like a shoe with a bad fit. To be shoeless is to be rendered helpless, to be pitied as without hope, or feared as mad. Shoes protect, they carry us through life, and we might, if we are lucky, use them to signify something about our identity. But despite this assistive power, shoes have no agency of their own. Outside of fairy tales, shoes have no magical powers.

Billions of dollars are spent trying to make you believe shoes spring from puffs of pink smoke at the snap of a fairy godmother's fingers. Corporations prefer the illusion that there are no supply chains and that shoes can be made, sold, bought and discarded in their tens of billions without consequences. This is so dangerously far from the truth that much of the work of this book is necessarily an attempt to demystify shoes.

With each chapter that you read, you are invited to look at the shoes around you and picture the processes that created them. Never lose sight of these supply chains, firstly because if you can hold on to the fact that every single shoe in the world is the product of human hands, you can begin to counteract how the realities of its production are obscured. And secondly, because if you lose sight of this reality, you also lose sight of something wondrous. We are taught that kings, CEOs and celebrities have made our world, but they have not. If we forget that the source of all wealth and magic is ultimately the planet and human work, we forget that we already have everything we need to make things right, to create a society that is equitable, sustainable and which provides for all.[27]

CHAPTER 1

Lust for Kicks

Sneaker Con is an aircraft-hangar-sized convention that smells worse and worse as the day goes on. Now in London, the huge event has just been in Las Vegas and will soon be in Berlin, followed by New York. Thousands of 'sneakerheads' have paid £25 to get in and are browsing merchandise stalls piled high with sneakers, hoodies, T-shirts, rucksacks and more sneakers. The price tags on these shoes are not for the faint-hearted: £550, £600, £700. Fairground games offer the chance to win limited edition sneakers. People are queuing to take selfies with famous YouTubers. Cleaning product companies have set up shiny installations promising to protect sneakers against dirt and rain.

Sami is twelve years old, with Harry Potter glasses and a Supreme headband pulled over his hair. On the floor in front of him are a pair of giant Nike Air Uptempo trainers that have never been worn. They are so large, he could fit both his small feet into one trainer. The pile of banknotes he is clutching is almost too big for his hands. Sami has been counting and recounting his money and grinning since he sold a pair of trainers for £230 to two older, and much bigger, boys.

Keeping a close eye on Sami and repeatedly telling him to put his money away is Jade, a young woman in an oversized khaki jacket with long plaits piled on top of her head. Sami tells people that Jade is his nanny. She corrects him, explaining she is his tutor.

Sami and Jade are in the Trading Pit. Fifty people have created makeshift stalls by arranging piles of merchandise on the floor. It is a car boot sale run by teenage boys where all the goods are pristine and very expensive. T-shirts, hoodies and hats are wrapped in cellophane, limited-edition shoes balance on spotless shoeboxes, rucksacks still have their tags on. The Trading Pit is where sneaker-heads come to buy, sell and swap shoes, separate from the official stalls at the front of the convention. A basketball hoop has been set up on one wall and the hip-hop soundtrack is turned up loud.

Sami became a sneakerhead under the influence of his cousin in Saudi Arabia. Unsatisfied with Jeddah's too-small sneaker scene, Sami is relishing the possibilities in London. His purpose at Sneaker Con is to 'sell clothes and sneakers to buy other sneakers. To basically get money.'

When Sami is out of earshot – he does not seem to like her talking too much – Jade describes his family as 'super-rich', with Sami sent to London for boarding school. It was her idea for Sami to try selling some of his sneakers, rather than just buying more.

Next to Sami is Amir, an eighteen-year-old who has travelled from Leicester and is sitting cross-legged on the floor next to a single pair of shoes: 'Yeezy 350 V2s in semi-frozen yellow, in a size 9.5.' Nicknamed 'Yebras', these trainers have just come out and are so limited Amir had to win a raffle before he could buy them for £170. The highly sought-after adidas Yeezy sneakers first appeared in 2015, the result of a collaboration between the German sportswear brand and rapper Kanye West.

Amir is hoping to flip his Yeezys and get between £450–500. He tells people he's seen them sell online for £1,500. Amir rejects the idea that it's weird for a shoe to sell for £500. He is already planning how to spend his profit – on a pair of Virgil Abloh x Nike sneakers.

The crowd at Sneaker Con is approximately 95 per cent male. Of the women that are here, many are mothers of young boys. One exception is sixteen-year-old Khaira from Lewisham in South London. 'Me and my brothers, we go to Yeezy drops or shoe drops and we buy and resell. So we're here today to meet new people, sell our products.' Khaira and her brothers started trading shoes after their mother gave them starter money to buy their first pair of Yeezys at a drop – the moment a new design is released to the public.

'I sold my Human Races today,' Khaira says. 'I bought them for £195 and I sold them for £300, which is obviously profit.' To get her hands on the Human Race trainers, a collaboration between adidas and Pharrell Williams, Khaira went to Carnaby Street at 3 a.m. and waited in the rain for nine hours.

Does she ever think what she is doing might be a bit crazy? 'I enjoy it. It's fun.'

'We've got our Yeezy Oreos in that bag and the Yeezy Belugas in that bag. I bought this Sprayground bag today.' She proudly holds up a black rucksack with a cartoon shark mouth on it. On her feet are a pair of white-and-black Yeezy Zebras. She often finds herself the only girl in the queue at shoe drops. 'The scene is accepting, but at specific drops the boys take advantage, like they push you back in the line and stuff. But I made friends, and the boys help me out, so it's not that bad.'

Piled on a stall are baseball caps with the slogan *I Miss the Old Kanye*. For Khaira, the outlandishness and unpredictability of Kanye West, the celebrity behind the Yeezy brand she loves so much, is what makes him great.

Sami, Amir, Khaira and the crowds at Sneaker Con are all hunting hype – an elusive quality that determines the desirability and worth of sneakers. 'Depending on who makes them and who wears them is what makes it hype,' says twenty-one-year-old Chris from Manchester. Chris is a tall, thin young man who has accessorised his outfit with a cloth mask worn over the lower half of his face. Chris has come to buy and sell, and he lists three current hype brands: Yeezy, Bape and Supreme.

There is a general consensus at Sneaker Con that the pillars of hype are 1) famous people and 2) a limited run. Kanye West has mastered this art. His fame lets him advertise his sneaker designs around the world, while the trick of limited manufacturing runs, means fans stay ravenous.

The pair she wears on Sundays

Four hundred years ago in seventeenth-century Britain, a statistician named Gregory King attempted to estimate how many pairs of shoes were being consumed in Britain each year. The figure he came up with was 12 million pairs, at a cost of £1m. He estimated a further £50,000 was spent on buckles and shoestrings. According to King, there were 100,000 people in Britain who were entirely shoeless – the poorest of the poor. This left an average of two pairs a year being bought and worn by everybody else, though like today, the rich enjoyed an abundance of shoes not available to the vast majority of people.[1]

By 1953, footwear manufacture textbooks stated that young women in paid employment could be expected to own six pairs of shoes: 'the pair she goes to work in, the pair she wears on Sundays and for "dressy" occasions, a pair for dancing, holiday or beach sandals, winter boots, and her bedroom slippers. If she plays tennis, or some other sport, then a further pair may be required.'[2] Six or seven pairs to keep feet safe and allow for basic social expectations.

Twenty years into the twenty-first century, and the 'average woman in Britain' reportedly now owns twenty-four pairs, some of which she has never worn.[3] Such statistics are highly inconclusive (along with the very concept of an 'average woman'), but it is still the case that the majority of people in wealthier societies own far more shoes than they use. We might make 24.2 billion pairs of shoes, but they are not shared out equally between the world's 7.7 billion people. In the world of the rich and famous, shoe collections number into the many thousands, overshadowing Imelda Marcos's collection of 3,000 pairs, now housed in the Marikina Shoe Museum in the Philippines.

In 2016, Asia was the largest footwear-consuming continent – 60 per cent of the world's population consumed 53 per cent of the world's shoes. Both within Asia and across the world, China bought more shoes than any other country – nearly one in five of every pair made. The combined countries of the European Union make up the second biggest market after China. Europe is closely followed by the United States, with both places buying far more shoes than is proportionate to their population.[4]

Not all consumers are created equal. Over-production is being accompanied by seriously unjust distribution, where people trapped in poverty are not provided with what they need, and are systemically denied the economic capacity to buy shoes. The *World Footwear Yearbook* is an annual report analysing production and trade data within the footwear sector. Its maps of global shoe consumption show entire sections of Africa, Latin America and the Middle East as grey – indicating levels of consumption that barely register in comparison to the global scale.[5]

In highland areas of tropical Africa – for example, Cameroon, Rwanda and Burundi – people in rural communities face parasites like hookworm, and soil-borne diseases like podoconiosis, both of which enter the human body through the feet and cause debilitating illness and pain. Prevention of such conditions should be relatively simple: wear shoes. But farmers, villagers and children walking to school risk their health because they are too poor to buy shoes.[6] Meanwhile, the most expensive pair of shoes on record are a golden concoction of leather, silk and 238 diamonds, and carry a price tag of $17,000,000.[7]

Levels of over-production are staggering and unprecedented. Previous societies required people to be producers and soldiers, now the primary need is for people to consume.[8] Globalisation has propelled consumerism to previously unimaginable heights of choice and abundance for anyone with the money to indulge. In return, consumerism keeps globalisation functioning as a viable system billions of tonnes of objects are bought and the profits stack up and up. It is only through the production and sale of merchandise that capitalism is able to function, and it is only through globalised capitalism, with its hunt for low wages and even lower standards, that a life of over-consumption is available to so many.

Competition time

At Sneaker Con, fourteen-year-old Daniel is trying to sell a pair of green-and-purple Nike Air Jordans. What he particularly likes about shoes is their ability to make him stand out: 'You wanna look unique from other people, you wanna look better ... or not better, but you wanna show them that you're different.' No matter that in this gigantic hall, thousands of teenage boys are in indistinguishably similar outfits.

Daniel's friend Raymond is about a foot shorter than him but equally fanatical about shoes. For Raymond, shoes are linked with social status: 'If you walk on the road and you see someone with bad trainers, you can tell that person's not really a person to go to. But if you see someone with, like, vibrant trainers, you know they're a person who spends their money wisely.' Raymond is from Dagenham, one of the most deprived areas in London, but is given an allowance of £100 a month by his dad. He has spent the day swapping a pair of Nike 'Space Jams', then selling a pair of Prada trainers at a £250 loss because no one wanted to buy them. Raymond accepts that having no money doesn't make someone a bad person, but says that if he was wearing 'bad' shoes he would be negatively judged. 'You'd think – oh, he doesn't look after himself. If you saw me it'd have, like, an impact on *me* by the shoes I wear.' It is a value system Raymond says forms the basis of who he makes friends with, and who he avoids.

In the Trading Pit, this is echoed by seventeen-year-old Benji. 'If you want to look good, you need to wear good clothing and good shoes, it makes you stand out.' Benji has been trying all day to sell a pair of Pharrell Williams sneakers that did not live up to their hype and have become a 'brick' – an unpopular shoe that is hard to sell. Benji says he needs them gone. 'If you look good, you're more presentable, and in a way you're a better person.'

Navigating modern society means being bombarded with messages that tell us we are being judged on what we wear, eat and drive. Thousands of adverts link consumption to our social status and tell us to be insecure about what we have. This puts us in a cycle of perpetual competition. It is a process that starts young.

Two of the most excited people at Sneaker Con are twelve-year-old Hugh and thirteen-year-old Oliver who are actually jumping up and down because they have just met their favourite YouTuber. 'Blazendary and Urban Necessities are here!' Oliver says ecstatically. Behind them a line of boys wait to have their photo taken with an American YouTuber wearing a pair of trainers worth £14,000.

'It's so fun! It's just awesome, we just watch them all the time. And we love shoes! It's crazy! It's so crazy!' Hugh says.

What is it about trainers that they love so much? 'Dunno,' says Oliver. 'They're cool and you can, like, wear them, so it's good.' Hugh is also too excited to properly think of an answer: 'It's the fact of being here and seeing all these crazy shoes and it's so different and crazy. It's so crazy.'

Based at Boston College, Dr Juliet Schor is one of the world's leading experts on consumption. She says one reason people shop for consumption goods is because it is a highly visible way to prove you have money.

'You can say you have all this money sitting in the bank but how do you prove it? We have a system in which the proof of money in the bank, is partly the ability to spend it, to waste it,' Dr Schor explains. 'If we think about consumer goods that convey status, a key quality about them is their social visibility.' Sneakers, she says, are a great example of this because people wear them in public.

Dr Schor links modern-day over-consumption with the classic conspicuous consumption theories of Thorstein Veblen. Veblen argued that the wealthy leisure class used consumption as evidence of their wealth and power. It is a simple process: attach expensive items to your body, or the body of your wives and children, then parade around where people can see you.

Not much has changed, except that the constant presence of social media means people are more recorded and on display than ever before. One of the most depressing aspects of online sneaker culture is the trend for 'How Much Is Your Outfit?' – YouTube videos where people are asked to publicly admit the cost of each item they are wearing. The total is then added up and those who have spent the most are celebrated.[9]

As well as being a horrendous way of judging people, displays of status are often an illusion. Dr Schor highlights the phenomenon by which people use items like sneakers to gain status even when their overall financial or economic position is weak. Shoes attach to and move with the body, allowing people to appear with them in public and gain status even if their home life is far less affluent.

Filmmaker and photographer Lauren Greenfield has been documenting the subject of wealth for twenty-five years, exploring the lives of people who are wealthy, and those who aspire to be wealthy. She believes projecting wealth, whether people have it or not, has become more important than ever after twenty-five years of rising inequality and falling social mobility. 'In a way, fictitious social mobility, bling and presentation, has replaced real social mobility ... because it's all you can get,' Greenfield told NPR.[10]

On maps of the world, and on the streets, shoes reflect social inequality. On a basic level, they show who can afford expensive footwear and who cannot. Conspicuous consumption is a sign of wealth inequality, a sign that rather than being evenly distributed, there is a glut of money being hoarded by the rich at the expense of the poor. But shoes are also a means for social inequality to be reproduced. It has been argued by Pierre Bourdieu that consumption reproduces social inequality by giving wealthy people 'cultural capital'. The ability to acquire the 'right' tastes is something that can be leveraged into better access to jobs, capital, connections, promotions and so on.[11] As a classic status symbol, shoes are used to include or exclude people from favoured groups, and to maintain class boundaries.

For teenagers at Sneaker Con, consuming conspicuous trainers is, at its most positive, a desire to stand out and be noticed for something other than the negative assumptions often dumped on teenagers, particularly those from minority ethnic backgrounds. It rings as a cry for respect in a society that stereotypes and marginalises.

But what respect actually results from wearing a rucksack with an obscure cartoon graphic on it, or a pair of green-and-purple trainers? To the outside eyes of society, these are symbols that go unheeded, with the clothing and shoes worn at Sneaker Con looking interchangeable and unremarkable. Even within the subculture where these objects are highly prized, there is a replication of the values of the system that produced the items – a competitive stance that derives satisfaction from being better than other people and excluding those 'beneath' you.

The wall comes tumbling down

The word 'sneakerhead' does not get you anywhere near an accurate description of Scott Frederick. Sneakers have been Scott's obsession since the 1990s, but you won't find him standing in line for a pair of Yeezys or a Supreme T-shirt.

Instead, Scott will be poring over twenty-five-year-old JCPenney catalogues looking for photos of old-school trainers. Or he'll be carefully archiving the first ever shoe blogs like Charlie's Sneaker Page, a blog founded in 1995 by Charles L. Perrin, a man whose day job was working on the International Space Station.

Scott is a historian and connoisseur of sneaker culture. He owns a pair of shoes so rare, there's only one photograph of them online – on Scott's DeFY. New York website where he blogs about music, fashion and sneakers. The only way he's selling that pair is if a museum makes him an offer. These days, Scott is satisfied immersing himself in the ultra-obscure history of branding and marketing, but it was not always this way. At one point, Scott obsessively bought sneakers, building his collection to approximately 400 pairs. He doesn't know the exact figure, as he had stopped counting.

'It was funny. I mean, it wasn't funny at the time, but it's funny now,' he says. 'I was storing all these shoes in my closet, and downstairs in the garage. One day I put up these new shelves in the closet, one of them was on the beam and that's why I don't understand how it happened, but everything fell, just collapsed. The whole wall collapsed in my closet, and I had to sleep around it all.'

Surrounded by shoeboxes and rubble, Scott came to a realisation: 'Right there I'm like, oh my God, what am I doing with myself, like, what is wrong with me? It was literally a bed surrounded by hundreds of boxes. I'm like, this has gotten out of hand. About a year and a half after that, maybe two years, I purged everything. Everything. Every single shoe I owned.'

Having let go of his collection, Scott now describes himself as a 'sort of minimalist'. He owns fifty to sixty pairs of sneakers. 'I'm a minimalist collector, if that makes any sense,' he laughs. 'I really try to get down to the root of what I'm buying and why I'm buying it because otherwise it's out of hand, and I feel like before I was out of hand. It becomes too consuming. At the end of the day this is just product, people feel like they *need* to own these things, but if this company doesn't make these shoes it'll go out of business – so they'll be there! If you're not wearing them it's a waste.'

Scott didn't come from money. His first pair of Andre Agassi signature shoes were a special treat from his grandmother in 1990. As he got older and earned his own money, Scott headed for New York's flea markets where he could find pairs of the old-style sneakers he loved. When the internet arrived in his life in 1996, he discovered a burgeoning online sneaker community and got hooked. He describes connecting with people in the UK, France and Japan, people he has kept in touch with for years despite never meeting many of them. It has become, he says, almost like a family.

Global friendships formed through shoes provide a sense of why people consume objects like trainers. 'Goods are really central to social life,' says Dr Schor. She explains that while people create identity through consumables, they are a particularly key part of what makes meaning for people in their social lives.

A lot of consumption theories position shopping as a lonely act, something done as a result of unhappiness. Dr Schor cites the often-used cliché of the lonely suburban housewife making meaningless purchases to fill a void in her life. It is not a view of consumerism that Dr Schor accepts. Rather than seeing consumerism as a solitary activity, she argues it is overwhelmingly an innately social activity. Even suburban housewives consume in groups, remaining hyper-conscious of their peer group and their place in it. 'The primary forces that drive consumption,' Dr Schor says, 'are social forces, social dynamics, dynamics of inequality and social competition, and the role of goods in giving status.'

This is not to say that a consumer society is the path to happiness. Repeatedly searching shops and websites for fulfilment is a soulless task. The shifting sands of trends and new product lines mean any joy is destined to be fleeting.

Never enough

In 1953, the author of the *Textbook of Footwear Manufacture* lamented the influence of fashion in determining which shoes were bought. A designer, the textbook argued, could produce a perfectly good shoe using the finest materials and craft techniques, and yet nobody would buy it if it was not deemed fashionable.[12]

Of all the social factors that drive consumption, fashion is pervasive and dominant. Fashion is, by definition, about change. It is necessarily about something new coming along and making people tire of even their favourite things. Corporations have harnessed this power to stop shoes being about what we need, and to permeate perfectly good things with a sense of obsolescence.

This leads us to replace things not because they are broken or worn out, but because we want something more fashionable. In previous decades fashion was based around seasonal collections, with designers debuting new designs just a few times a year. This changed with the advent of fast fashion, a system that has overwhelmed traditional collection cycles and led instead to the ultra-fast production of trend-based, throwaway clothes. In the new world of 'pile them high and sell them cheap', some high street shops bring out new lines every single week, making it harder and harder to keep up.

Allowing people to keep up, however, was never the aim of the game. With the world already full of more consumer goods than we can possibly need, people must be compelled into wanting more. In the 1920s, car manufacturers faced a saturated market – everyone who could afford a car already owned one. Cars were sturdy and long-lasting so manufacturers preyed on the vanity of the wealthy car-owning public and convinced them that annual design changes meant a new car should be bought each year. The president of General Motors stated: 'The changes in the new model should be so novel and attractive as to create demand ... and a certain amount of dissatisfaction with past models as compared with the new one.'[13]

It was a strategy deliberately focused on shortening the lifespan of new cars. The process was outlined again by an industrial designer in the 1950s: 'We make good products, we induce people to buy them, and then next year we deliberately introduce something that will make those products old fashioned, out of date, obsolete. We do that for the soundest reason: to make money.'[14] The difference between today and the 1950s is that shopping cycles are no longer yearly. Never before has fashion moved so fast. This dependency on people going out to shop means many homes in wealthy societies are now overstuffed with resource-intensive objects.

Marc Hare is the product director for footwear at Lacoste and previously ran his own designer shoe label, Mr Hare. Why does he think people whose cupboards are already saturated, keep buying new shoes? In part, he says, it is because footwear unavoidably wears out, but people also buy way more shoes than they need because they just keep coming.

Marc points to sites like Hypebeast where new shoe releases appear every day, pushing people to consume. The story of how brands keep people shopping comes back to what Marc calls the simple story of fashion, and the creation of constant change: 'Unless you just totally switch off to it and just go, "No, I'm never going to get involved," then it's just easy and it's there.'

Escaping from the constant pressure to shop is not a simple task. Perhaps to truly escape would involve a drastic move. The Tsawa Gang Dolma Lhakang Monastery is 15,000 feet above sea level on a mountain top in Eastern Tibet. One of the most inhospitable places on earth, the ground is frozen solid for eight months of the year, no trees or crops can grow and even just drawing breath is difficult. Reaching the closest shop of any kind means travelling for three days across 1,200 miles of treacherous terrain. Everything that is needed, from building materials to medicine, must be transported back up the mountain.[15]

If all shopping trips required such dedication, we would undoubtedly take more care to stop and think about what we truly need. But for people not living at the roof of the world, there is a constant struggle. Consumer items have been disassociated from need and turned instead into an emotional rollercoaster of self-esteem, social standing and manipulated desire.

Shoes are a public item, visible to the people we meet, and visible to thousands more via instant uploads to social media. They create a tension not only with how we perceive ourselves, but with judgement from other people. Fashion theorist Joanne Eicher told decades of students: *If you don't think clothing is important, try to go to work without it.* The only way to prove you don't care about clothes, is through your choice of clothes.[16] The same is true with shoes. Any rebellion against social norms still necessitates the wearing of some kind of shoe, or the attempt to become conspicuously barefoot.

There remains a difference between criticising people for enjoying buying shoes, and criticising capitalism for constantly compelling people to consume.[17] If we do not recognise the compulsions that are at work, we leave the field open to multinational corporations whose *raison d'être* is to manipulate people's insecurities.

Over-consumption does not create a state of wellbeing. Instead, it is a mindset where consumers never rest but are kept in a constant state of both excitement and disaffection.[18] Sociologist Zygmunt Bauman wrote about consumption's need for people not to attach or commit long term to anything they buy. Rather than long-term love, consumerism is more a case of multiple brief encounters, with one eye peering over an object's shoulder to see what else is new and available.[19] In this way, there is an in-built temporariness in any consumer transaction: nothing is for life.

Traditionally, humans have had needs which they sought to satisfy. In today's consumer society, the relationship between need and satisfaction has been flipped. Need is now preceded by the promise that satisfaction can be found in the shops.[20] Even when shopping malls close for the day, the internet remains open for business. Every hour is now shopping hour, with people able to buy shoes from a Brooklyn store at midnight, from a factory in Shenzhen at 2 a.m. or from a Paris eBay account at 4 a.m. Globalisation has speeded up shopping to a 24/7 activity, no longer dependent on the location of shops or shoppers, and far beyond any natural need for the things we consume.

Dr Schor points out the exhaustion of trying to keep up with a process that takes up both money and time. Even among those with the resources to shop, fast fashion promotes dissatisfaction about what one already has, and anxiety about falling behind.[21] It is a mindset that directly opposes the counterbalance to constant consumerism: consciously questioning the rat race and fostering a sense of contentment and gratitude for what we do have.

More than just strolling

Shoes are not just about protecting the foot from the ground or helping the body move. Royal families in Ancient Egypt had a reserved style of sandal, as did priests and wealthy officials. Sandals from Tutankhamun's tomb have the insoles decorated with images of Egypt's enemies, allowing the Pharaoh to symbolically crush his rivals with each step.[22] Shoes are also used to symbolise the unholy and require removal before approaching sanctified places.[23]

Today, although there are no laws stating who can wear what shoe, people still find themselves governed by rules: what shoes must be worn for work, what shoes are acceptable for social functions. Many of these rules are outdated, with Julia Roberts going barefoot at the Cannes Film Festival in protest at the archaic rule that women must wear heels on the red carpet.

Brands work hard to create symbolic associations with their products, encouraging people to associate love, friendship, social status or power, with material objects. All the immaterial things an item communicates can be defined as 'Symbolic Value'. When objects become imbued with the right symbolic value, they become almost irresistible. Consider the power of red-soled Louboutins to symbolise sexual desirability, high-shined John Lobb brogues to symbolise power, adidas trainers to symbolise the creativity of US hip-hop, or Nike Airs to symbolise the street cool of British grime music.

Symbolic Value has knocked its dowdier but more down-to-earth cousin, Use Value, off the game board. Use Value is an object's ability to meet a human need, which surely should be the priority with something as practical as shoes. And yet our shoes remain weighted with symbolism. Marc Hare believes part of the transformative power of shoes comes from their physical effect, the way they alter the shape and movement of the body and force people to adjust how they move through the world: 'Physically, it changes your interface to the earth that you're walking on, so how can it not affect you?'

Then there is the effect of particular styles on the psyche: 'You put on a pair of smart shoes, you feel like a million dollars, you know you're going somewhere and you walk differently, you act differently,' Marc explains. 'You put on a fresh pair of sneakers and you bounce down the road in a completely different way. I challenge anyone to say shoes don't change them when they put them on.'

Shoes do provide a key connection between the body and physical space, they can be a tool which sets us free and amplifies what we are capable of.[24] Marc also places trainers, along with jeans, in a category of apparel status symbols that have developed and become cool not because of designers, catwalks or magazines, but because of working-class, rebellious or marginalised cultural spaces.

Elizabeth Semmelhack is a senior curator at the Bata Shoe Museum in Canada where she has worked for seventeen years. She says the extreme visibility of shoes has intensified with the diminishing popularity of other accessories. Hats, for example, were once worn every day as signs of both class and gender.[25] Elizabeth also believes shoes have gained a special place in culture because industrialisation has flooded the market with an unprecedented number of shoes in a myriad of styles and prices. This has allowed people to pick and choose, and to construct social identities through footwear.[26]

One does not have to be Sherlock Holmes to deduce the messages sent through shoes. Footwear can be used to signify a wearer's gender, sexuality, musical taste, cultural background or social interests. They are an especially good way to display status, to tell the world that you live a life that needs no traditional work. From Venetian noblewomen balancing on platformed *chopines* in the sixteenth century, to First Lady Melania Trump wearing stilettos to visit the devastation left by Hurricane Harvey. Impractical shoes send a deliberate message: the wearer does not labour nor endure public transport.

Head over heels

Sarah Jessica Parker, an actor almost synonymous with the expensive shoes Carrie obsessed over in *Sex and the City*, has written about shoes as 'mechanisms to elevate the style, stature, and status of women around the world.'[27] But is she right – do shoes elevate the status of women?

In a society where sexism, often accompanied by class and racism, prevents women from fulfilling their potential, women are expected to fetishise shoes. Karl Marx developed the idea of *commodity fetishism* from Portuguese anthropological writings about people believing religious icons, statues and totem poles held special powers. The objects themselves were just pieces of stone or wood, no matter how beautifully carved, yet were believed to have the power to bring wealth, cure illness or help win battles.

The same goes for shoes: strips of leather, a plastic sole and some glue. The power projected onto them comes from inside our heads, whipped up by advertising executives and marketeers who have replaced the priests and witch doctors of old.

There is no medical doubt that high-heeled shoes cause musculo-skeletal issues, breathing restrictions, a long list of foot ailments and even fertility problems. High heels drastically restrict movement and make women vulnerable. In the 9/11 Memorial Museum is a bloodied high heel worn by an office worker who had to run for her life.[28] Christian Louboutin is fond of saying he *hates* the very idea of comfort, yet high-heeled shoes still get marketed as a symbol of empowerment.[29]

Ask Elizabeth Semmelhack whether high heels are empowering, and she'll tell you: 'If in fact, the high heel really did signify power, then men would be as willing to wear them as women.'[30] The problem is that high heels are related to sexual power, which Elizabeth argues is not really a power in itself since it relies on other people to find you attractive. 'Erotic currency requires constant negotiation,' Elizabeth explains. 'I would argue the person who is attempting to be sexy holds less power in that exchange than the person who says, *Oh yes, you are sexy*.' Sexual power is so subjective that if no one agrees with you that you're sexy, you've got no capital. And in an ageist society, sexual power also has a sexist age limit, hardly a deal that women should settle for.

There was a time when men in power were extremely willing to wear high heels. Elizabeth's research shows high heels were originally men's shoes – an essential part of military and equestrian attire in Persia and the Ottoman Empire, because they kept feet in stirrups.[31] High heels arrived in Europe from the Near East in the sixteenth century and became a craze among aristocratic men.

The work of court painters like Anthony van Dyck shows men, including King Charles I, in what would now be considered extremely feminine shoes complete with high heels and pom-poms. In the French court, Louis XIV became famous for wearing bright-red high heels. He decreed that only people in his favour could wear red heels, turning them into a true accessory of power.

Then came an abrupt about-turn. The ideas of the eighteenth-century Enlightenment firmly split the sexes into two camps: strong rational men and fragile irrational women. Fashion, and in particular the high heel, was turned into a signifier of emotional impracticality. Fashion theorist J. C. Flügel termed this 'The Great Male Renunciation'. Having popularised high heels and outlandish fashion, men then shed jewellery, bright colours and high heels in favour of a dark austere look.[32]

Despite the fact that women only took up heels as part of a trend for adopting elements of men's dress, they were now stuck with them. This is perhaps the biggest ideological backlash in fashion and footwear. An authoritarian assault that left women trapped between the idea that women are irrational and foolish for wearing heels, and the social pressure to keep wearing them to maintain their desirability and social standing. The French Revolution popularised the idea of equality and led to the rejection of aristocratic practices like wearing high heels. Aside from notable exceptions – for example drag queens impersonating women, and short-statured men wishing to be taller – heels have been strictly for women ever since, with the perceived link between women, heels and irrationality also remaining fixed in place. Shoes feature heavily in films and pop songs, gift shops are clogged with novelty shoe-shaped items, women's T-shirts bear slogans like *Will Work for Shoes!* and greetings cards aimed at women feature shoes on a seemingly mandatory basis. Shoes have been mythologised and women taught that they relentlessly desire them. Isn't it time to stop and think about whether this is true?

Many people simply have either a peaceful or grudging co-existence with shoes. Fashion writer Colin McDowell writes that for every shoe fanatic, 'there are millions of people who see shoes as nothing more permanent or important than an item of clothing designed to last for two or three years at the most and then to be forgotten.'[33] Yet this is not a socially acceptable state of mind for women.

There exists a relentless media onslaught of messages saying women not only love shoes, but are obsessed by them, addicted to them and slavishly devoted to them. 'The female as genetically hard-wired shoe-fetishist has become a stock character of advertising, magazines, and self-help books, and of the new gender-specific cultural genres such as chick-lit and chick-films,' writes feminist academic Dr Debbie Ging. She argues that in the burgeoning feminist era of the 1960s and 70s, this reduction of women to a stereotype would have been seen as insulting; now it is not only accepted, but shoes are seen as part of the liberation of women.[34]

So do high heels deliver anything more than an illusion of power? Marketing rhetoric argues high heels are weapons for women in the struggle for equality, Dr Ging on the other hand argues shoes have been weaponised against women, perpetuating a myth of women as irrational, greedy, narcissistic and trivial. Women who want to use shoes as weapons, she concludes, should follow in the footsteps of Muntadhar al-Zaidi, not Victoria Beckham.[35]

Muntadhar al-Zaidi being the broadcast journalist who spent years reporting the war and occupation of Iraq before throwing his shoes at George W. Bush during a 2008 press conference. After serving time in prison al-Zaidi wrote: 'Do you know how many broken homes that shoe which I threw had entered? How many times it had trodden over the blood of innocent victims? ... When I threw the shoe in the face of the criminal, George Bush, I wanted to express my rejection of his lies, his occupation of my country, my rejection of his killing my people.'[36]

Al-Zaidi's protest sparked numerous copy-cat protests around the world, boxes of old shoes being dumped at the US Embassy in London, and a giant bronze shoe statue being made in Tikrit, Iraq.

You can watch me walk if you want to

For some, the appeal of shoes goes very deep indeed. As a time-honoured fetish object, shoes, along with feet, can create an intense erotic pleasure. 'I defy any lover of painting to love a picture as much as a fetishist loves a shoe,' wrote French surrealist Georges Bataille.[37]

In the 1980s and 90s Dian Hanson edited the fetish magazine *Leg Show*, and received thousands of letters from fetish fans. One of her favourite correspondents wrote many letters which included offering up his skin so she could have it made into shoes. 'I am an ordinary man,' he wrote. 'Ordinary height. Ordinary looks. Women never look at me. I'm invisible. But women love shoes. If I were a pair of shoes, women would want me. I fantasize about being a pair of shoes.'[38]

This is at the extreme end of shoe fetishes, with this man only able to see his body as desirable or sexual if it is transformed into what is, to him, a sexualised object. It is not possible to generalise about why fetishes develop, but shoes have secured a particularly potent place in fetishism.

While society generally treats fetishes as comedic or grotesque, fetishes that are consensual, legal and do not lead to isolation, can be a pleasurable part of human sexuality. Although not many psychotherapists today are pure-Freudian practitioners, it was Sigmund Freud who devised the foundations for ways of thinking about sexual fetishes. In 1927, Freud wrote that shoes are fetish objects because of 'the circumstance that the inquisitive boy peered at [his mother's] genitals from below'.[39] For Freud, shoes symbolise the moment a boy realises his mother has no penis. This, he said, creates a fear of castration, which most men get over, but which sees some men appoint shoes as a substitute for the penis.

Sexual attraction to shoes can be triggered by the thought that a foot has been in the shoe, a foot belonging to a sexualised female (or male) body that can be overcome. Contrary to urban myth, Marilyn Monroe did not need to wear heels of differing heights to walk so seductively. But nearly sixty years after her death, there remains the obvious fascination with how heels cause buttocks and breasts to jut out, and leg muscles to become taught, simulating and suggesting sex. The corny line, 'Is that a ladder in your tights or a stairway to heaven?' indicates the fantasy of a direct line from shoes to desired genitalia.

For other shoe fetishists, there can also be seductive power in the fact that their fetish is a hidden secret that no one else knows about. Or the attraction may come from the fact that an object, unlike a human, requires no seduction or effort – a shoe can simply be taken out of a cupboard.

A specific attraction to high heels is known as *altocalciphilia*. There are no generalisations to be made here either. Attraction to heels can spring from a desire to submit to them, an excitement at the imprint of a spiked stiletto and the requirement to kiss and thank the shoe that caused the pain. Or it can come from the imagined idea of heels advertising sexual availability. Or from a desire to dominate, to be attracted to the sight of a woman in heels because she is 'lame prey' – the more sinister sense that she feels pain and is unable to run away.

Monkey trap

To describe consumerism, political theorist Benjamin Barber used the analogy of a monkey and a small metal box with a nut inside. The monkey can reach into the box with its hand open and flat, but once it has grasped the nut it can't pull its hand out because its clenched fist is too big. All it would have to do to escape is to drop the nut and remove its hand. Clever hunters, Barber wrote, discovered they can secure their monkey prey for hours or even days later because the monkey, driven by desire, would not release the nut, even until death. He then asks the question: is the monkey free, or not?[40]

A society with its hand stuck in the trap poses a grave threat both to its individual members and to the planet. It has been argued that to be a good consumer, one must firstly be in love with the idea of choice, then secondly with the consuming itself.[41] This addictive love of choice leads consumers to be vociferously against anything they feel reduces it.

Strong regulations, for example, could protect us from consuming chemically contaminated shoes, but instead regulation is framed as something to oppose because it limits choice. Consumers can end up as cheerleaders for corporations and the free market, never pausing to consider what they lose in this relentless pursuit of newness. Think for example of the crusade against EU regulation in the UK, or the furore over the provision of free healthcare in the US.

In her book *The Overspent American*, Dr Schor noted that the rise of middle-class 'over-spending' was accompanied by these same people being less willing to support public spending on things like education, social services, public safety, recreation and culture. One result of consumer society is the poor and the near poor being left without public services or a social safety net. The result, Dr Schor wrote, has been a substantial increase in poverty, the deterioration of poor neighbourhoods and rising levels of crime and drug use. People with money might try to spend their way around such problems, but that does not provide a solution for social ills.[42]

Consumerism and privatisation lead people to withdraw from the public sphere into gated communities where private resources turn public goods like rubbish collection, policing and schooling into private commodities. This destroys the very point of public services which aim to keep all of society clean, secure and educated and which do not work as pockets of isolation.[43] It is the difference, Barber believed, in asking 'what I want' and 'what we need'. The first question is answered by the market, the second by the community.

They gave us shoes, and took the paths[44]

Helen lives in a rented three-bedroom house on the outskirts of London. She shares the house with her husband Luke, and his collection of trainers. The shoes have filled up the loft and the spare room. When they started invading her bedroom, Helen told Luke she needed some space.

The couple booked a table at Sneaker Con, and their stall is piled with trainers. Luke is nowhere to be seen. 'We're here to sell off a private collection of Nike Air Jordans,' Helen explains. 'It's really slow. It's all boys here, and they want sizes 8 and 9, but these are 10s and 11s.'

A potential customer approaches the stall and picks up a pair of Nike Air Jordans, turning them over in his hands and examining the soles. He asks how much they cost. '£250,' Helen says. 'Someone else is selling them for £350, so we've been told it's a very good price.' The man nods, puts down the shoes and walks on to the next stall.

The rows of trainers, on the table and in boxes on the floor, cost tens of thousands of pounds. The loss of this money has become a source of tension. 'That's why he had to stop,' Helen says. 'Some of the releases, they're quick-strike releases – we'd be on a night out and we'd have to pull over on the motorway to follow a Twitter link, to get a released pair of trainers.'

She says Luke has spent a lot of time investing in 'one-off' train-ers which are now being re-released and are no longer unique. 'He's like *It's my mortgage money*. But we need to sell them first.'

Luke walks up to the table shrugging his shoulders and frowning. 'It's dead for Jordans,' he says. 'No one is buying Jordans.'

The unwanted trainers are a certified global product. Designed in the Americas, made in South-east Asia and purchased in Europe. For Helen and Luke, they have come at the cost of a home to live in. Scale this up to 24.2 billion pairs of shoes and they represent something more: the threat not just to one home, but to the whole world. The true cost of production on this scale is, as we shall see, terrifying.

CHAPTER 2

Factory Gates

Six days a week Şebnem wakes up alone. She ties her hair into a ponytail and pulls on leggings and a jumper. She leaves the house at 6.25 a.m. to make sure she is there when the factory bus pulls up at 6.30. Missing it means walking three kilometres, or paying for a taxi. A line of buses drives through the quiet streets, carrying hundreds of sleepy workers to factories on the outskirts of town.

Şebnem climbs the stairs to her workstation. Her shift begins at 7.00 but she has no idea what time the work will finish. She cleans the new batch of boots in front of her with a detergent. Drips of the chemical make her skin burn. Her eyes sting and her mouth fills with a bad taste.

A few winters ago, the factory owner put the heating on for just half an hour, then ordered the windows covered over to conserve heat. The only breeze comes from the two doors of the factory. Over the course of the morning, the dim room fills with fumes from the glues and dyes. Occasionally, an inspector comes to the factory and Şebnem is given a mask to wear. But with no ventilation, the mask is suffocating.

'You must be stupid if you can't see the truth,' she thinks as the inspectors walk round the factory taking photos. They check everything and write notes, but nothing ever changes.

Lunch arrives as a twenty-minute break. There is no staff canteen or common room, so Şebnem sits at her workstation and eats the food she has brought from home. After fifteen years the state of her scarred hands still upsets her. She wants to wash them, but it takes nearly ten minutes to reach the toilets and then she'd have to wait in line for the basins and to fill her water bottle. By then the break would be almost over.

After lunch, Şebnem must polish the boots. She pulls each one up over her arm so her hand is inside it, then rubs the boots till they gleam. As she does so, her arm turns black. In her pocket is a bar of soap she's brought from home to wash off the polish at the end of the day, which should be 2.30 p.m., the time Şebnem thought she signed up for. But her contract has no hours on it. Rumours swirl around the factory that they might all be part-time employees. Some workers don't know if they are legally employed at all.

Not knowing when she will go home has become normal. The worst months are in summer when the factory makes winter boots and shoes. The demand to meet orders grows even more intense, the factory becomes swelteringly hot and Şebnem is forced to do unpaid overtime until 5 p.m. The managers shout and swear at her to work harder, so she tries to switch her brain off. Don't react, she tells herself. Imagine you are somewhere else.

She'd started at the factory thinking she'd soon be moving to a new town, or even country, with her new husband. A lot more people had worked at the factory back then, and there had been talk of starting a union. Now she dreams of having a radio to make the day go faster.

Şebnem also dreams of spending her Saturdays going for a walk or spending time with her family, but she had a friend who refused to work one Saturday and was fired. He was a good man who always helped people who had too much work. She also wishes she could have a few consecutive days of holiday time, but instead of her allocated twenty-one days, one year Şebnem had just five days off, picked for her by her manager when the factory had less work.

No matter the hours, Şebnem's pay cheque stays the same. Sometimes she is told she's being paid for her hours, sometimes for the number of shoes the factory has produced, sometimes that her pay is docked because certain quotas have not been reached. No matter how much overtime she has done, each month Şebnem receives €197.

Sometimes she is told to stick price tags on the merchandise. The

boots she has polished will be sold in western Europe for €200 –
more than she has earned working six days a week for a month.

There are Italians in the factory keeping an eye on their orders.
Şebnem likes them more than the local managers because the Italians
do not shout at the workers. They have fancy phones and laptops
and tell Şebnem that in Italy they wouldn't do her job for less than
€1,600–2,000 a month.

A complicated leather shoe order gets stopped and must be re-
done because the Italians say the colour of the dye is wrong. *Why do
you come here?* she wants to ask them. Is it the quality of our work,
or is it that we are cheap? They never ask us if we can manage all
this work.

When the bus drops her off, Şebnem has a few hours with her
eleven-year-old son, a sweet boy with a wide grin. She asks him
about homework; he always says he has none. The boy's father,
Şebnem's ex-husband, left the country to start a new life. If Şebnem
can save some money, she will send her son to visit him for the
summer.

When it is time for him to go to bed, she walks him to his pa-
ternal grandparents' house. The boy sleeps there because Şebnem
wants him supervised in the mornings when she is working and
because he is too afraid to wake up on his own. Şebnem lives in her
parents' home. Everyone in the family still works. Her parents cover
the utility bills and do not charge her rent. Şebnem's salary goes on
food for the family and towards her son's clothes, shoes, school trips
and education. He would love to own a laptop with an Apple logo.
She wants him to go to a foreign-language teacher, but the classes
and travel to the school are too expensive.

Once, before she got married, she would have argued with the
factory for more money. Now she thinks of her mother coughing
through the night, her breathing harsh after years of factory work,
and believes nothing will ever change.

'The Italians are rich,' she tells her friends. 'The factory owner is
rich – but what does our company give us? Nothing. Not even a free
pair of shoes. They destroy the ones that have a scratch, or if they
are extra, they throw them away. If they had a scratch, I would still
wear them but they throw them away.'

Painstakingly made

Rampant consumerism shrouds our sense that human beings make all of the objects we buy. Rather than magically appearing out of thin air, every pair of shoes on the planet has been painstakingly made by people, the overwhelming majority of whom are women who have mostly been paid far less than they need to survive.

Globalisation has spread low standards and an expectation that factory orders will be fulfilled within weeks – a pressure borne by workers on the factory floor. As a result, women like Şebnem, bearing the brunt of this racialised and gendered labour system, are to be found in shoemaking towns everywhere in the world.

While she is a real person, with her unpaid overtime, miniscule wages and dangerous working conditions, Şebnem also represents shoe factory workers across the world. As a working-class woman struggling to support a family, and as someone with little education and few options in the labour market, she represents the people holding up the economic system we live in. Şebnem represents the Global South.

Dividing the world into Global South and Global North is about far more than geography. A relatively recent term, 'Global South' loosely refers to what was once labelled 'the third world' or 'undeveloped countries'. But it is also a term interlinked with globalisation and its problems. The Global South, explains anthropologist Thomas Hylland Eriksen, has come to represent countries that are 'subject to the forces of global neoliberalism', rather than the countries that impose it upon others.[1]

Put simply, if a country benefits from the globalised neoliberal capitalist economy it is Global North but if it suffers under this system it is Global South. But there is an additional element to the term because distinguishing between victims and benefactors of global capitalism cannot be restricted by national borders.[2] India has its billionaires and powerful elites, while Britain has its food banks and destitute homeless. 'Global South' therefore is more a concept than a set of lines on a map.

It is not a coincidence, rather it is a purposeful business strategy that shoes are primarily made in the Global South. A country with low wages and labour costs, low environmental standards and scant ability to enforce health and safety standards is a fertile place for corporate profit. Countries like this are actively sought by shoe brands wanting cheap factories. As a bloc, Asia accounts for 83.3 per cent of the world's shoe production.[3] Thailand recently knocked Italy, the last European country, out of the top ten of producer nations. This leaves Brazil and Mexico as the only non-Asian countries in the top ten.[4]

Since the 1990s Asia has seen some of the worst human rights abuses in the shoe industry. Indonesian shoe manufacturer PT Panarub Industry went into partnership with adidas in the late 1980s, producing among other models, the adidas Predator X football boot, which has been widely promoted at World Cup tournaments around the globe.[5]

In 2012, 2,000 mostly women workers went on strike at PT Panarub Dwikarya Benoa, part of PT Panarub Industry, to demand trade union rights as well as better pay and conditions.[6] The manufacturer had a history of treating workers poorly, with forced overtime, low wages and menstruating women required to undergo humiliating physical examinations before obtaining their legally granted two days of paid leave.[7] PT Panarub Dwikarya Benoa's response to the 2012 strike was to sack 1,300 people. Six years later, with 327 sacked workers still denied severance pay, campaign group the Clean Clothes Campaign filed a complaint against adidas with the German National Contact Point of the Organisation for Economic Co-operation and Development (OECD). The ongoing suit, which was not rejected by the OECD, accused adidas of breaching OECD Guidelines for Multinational Enterprises, as well as the UN Guiding Principles on Business and Human Rights.[8]

'In the last five years adidas has insufficiently used its leverage over one of its main shoe suppliers, Panarub, to provide workers with severance payments,' stated Mirjam van Heugten at the Clean Clothes Campaign. 'Workers have been evicted from their homes or had their children drop out of school because they could not pay the school fees anymore.'[9]

adidas, it was argued, had long known about workers' rights violations at PT Panarub Dwikarya Benoa, including the issues that led to the strike. It was also argued that adidas has enough leverage with PT Panarub Industry to secure severance pay for the 327 sacked women. In response to the criticism, adidas said they 'have stepped outside the normal boundaries of what would be expected of any buyer to help resolve this case' and stopped contracting to PT Panarub Dwikarya Benoa, though they continue to do business with PT Panarub Industry.[10] At the time of writing, it was not known when the OECD suit would be resolved.

In October 2016, the International Labour Organization (ILO) Committee on Freedom of Association concluded in an interim report that there was no justification for sacking the PT Panarub Dwikarya Benoa workers and that their fundamental right to freedom of association had been violated. After years of campaigning, in February 2019, the local workers' union accepted a settlement on behalf of their members, and as a result a month later the ILO closed the case.

In Vietnam, excessive overtime, incomplete employment contracts and the denial of independent worker representation continue to blight the garment and shoe industry.[11] While in Cambodia, factory workers continue to suffer from a mass fainting epidemic. In 2017, hundreds of workers across factories supplying garments or shoes to Nike, Puma, Asics and VF Corporation were hospitalised having endured ten-hour days, six days a week, in 37-degree heat. Unlike Vietnam, where factories must not be hotter than 32 degrees, Cambodia has no upper limit, although employers must provide for workers in 'very high' conditions and some brands set their own codes of conduct.[12]

As the epidemic continued through 2018, different studies reached different conclusions about why the mass fainting occurs.[13] It has been argued that the nutritional status of female factory workers is to blame, with workers too poor to buy sufficient amounts of food. The physical taxation of the factory environment has also been highlighted with its extreme temperatures, lack of water and excessive overtime.

Other studies have considered the psychological toll of factory work as a reason for the mass fainting – with stress and anxiety compounded by extreme fear caused by seeing other workers collapse.

Cultural beliefs, that factories are 'spiritually haunted' by victims of the Khmer Rouge regime or dead workers, have also been flagged as a possible cause. Finally, it has been suggested that mass fainting is a form of social protest against terrible working conditions, a way of circumventing the brutal lack of trade union and civil society rights in Cambodia.[14]

'Conditions and brand policies are very far behind the garment industry,' says Dominique Muller, policy director at British NGO Labour Behind the Label. Compared to the garment industry, shoes have been ignored both in terms of monitoring and the media spotlight. This is partly because there has not been a disaster in the shoe industry equivalent to the Rana Plaza garment factory collapse which killed 1,138 people. It is also, Dominique says, because supply chains in the shoe industry are longer and harder to monitor. From the moment they are ordered, component parts for shoes are made then assembled in multiple countries. As a result, Dominique says shoe brands are ten years behind the garment industry, with many corporations actively resisting reporting on their supply chains.

Power house

One country in Asia is the undisputed leader in its field. After six years of continuous decline, factories in China accounted for 64.7 per cent of global shoe production in 2018.[15] No other country comes close to matching the output of Chinese factories.

Concerns have been raised about conditions in China's shoe factories, including reports of hyper-intense work, low wages, dangerous conditions and no freedom of association to allow people to form trade unions or workers' organisations. Ivanka Trump came under fire in 2017 for using the Ganzhou Huajian International Shoe City Co. as a supplier. In 2017 the NGO China Labor Watch investigated claims that the Chinese factory inflicted gruelling overtime, low wages and violent threats upon staff members. Workers reported one man being assaulted by an angry manager who hit him with a high-heeled shoe, causing his head to bleed.[16] The Huajian Group denied all the allegations and said they operated in accordance with the law. The Ivanka Trump brand expressed concern about the reports and the company noted its code of conduct that prohibited physical abuse and child labour.

The *Washington Post* reported that shipping data suggested Ivanka Trump products had been made in more than two dozen factories across China between 2010 and 2017.[17] The Ivanka Trump fashion brand shut down in 2018.

In the spring of 2015 and 2016, Hong Kong-based NGO SACOM (Students and Scholars Against Corporate Misbehavior) sent undercover teams into Chinese factories supplying major fashion brands. One of these factories was Nanhai Nanbao Shoes Factory Ltd in Guangdong Province. They reported on bad conditions in the shoe factory and stated that in some instances conditions there were notably worse than in garment factories.

Both garment and shoe factories are subjected to demanding deadlines set by brands, but in shoe factories the hours can be even more intense. One worker at Nanbao in the packaging department told SACOM that overtime shifts sometimes ended at 3 a.m.: 'The packaging department always asks us to work overtime, especially when the factory is rushing for an order ... The salary is about 4,000 RMB [about £470]. Long working hours, low wages and exhausting work.'[18]

The investigation found that gruelling hours are made doubly intense by productivity targets based on how many seconds managers say each procedure should take. To make it even more stressful, workers are judged and paid as teams, so anyone not working fast enough faces censure from co-workers as well as managers.

'Workers in Nanbao told us they have to run to the toilet when they have to pee because they don't want to impact others,' says Pin-Yu Chen, project officer at SACOM. 'When the production line starts, it won't stop. If you go to the toilet the shoes will pile up in front of you and then your co-workers in the next stop will have to wait for you.' SACOM also reported that being absent from work, even due to sickness in some cases, results in workers being fined.

Another reason shoe factories can be worse than garment factories is constant exposure to toxic chemicals. In some factories, glues and cleaning chemicals are often used with inadequate gloves and masks, or even without gloves and masks, resulting in toxic chemical exposure. One of the better-paid jobs at Nanbao was processing the sheets of rubber adhesive used to stick shoes together. This process produces clouds of toxic dust which workers can inhale if wearing inadequate masks. A number of workers at Nanbao reported to the SACOM investigation that their noses bled easily, causing them to spend extra money on medicine.[19] It is not known how Nanbao responded to SACOM's findings, and what changes, if any, have been made since the investigation.

China's shoe industry is also marked by fatal fires and building collapses. In 2015, fifty-six people were hard at work in the Jieyu Shoe Factory in Wenling when it collapsed on top of them, crushing to death at least twelve shoe workers.[20] The year before, sixteen shoe workers were killed in the same town in Eastern China when fire consumed the Taizhou Dadong shoe factory.[21]

A Kumanovo tale

According to the *World Footwear Yearbook 2017*, Europe accounts for 13.8 per cent of global shoe exports,[22] but conditions in European factories can also be extremely poor. In eastern Europe shoe workers are paid 25–35 per cent of an estimated minimum living wage, often leaving people in a worse position than in China because low wages in eastern Europe are not matched by low living costs.[23] Research found it would take a shoe worker earning an average salary in Albania or Romania an entire hour of work just to afford a pint of milk. This is compared with just 4 minutes' work for someone earning the UK minimum wage.[24] There are tens of thousands of footwear factories in the world, containing millions of workers who make 24.2 billion pairs of shoes each year. A few hundred of these factories are located in the Former Yugoslavian Republic of Macedonia, where local trade unions estimate there are 3,331 people employed in leather and leather-related production, compared with 34,819 people employed in textiles and clothing factories.[25]

North Macedonia is a green, fertile country of 2.1 million people, 80 per cent Orthodox Christian and 20 per cent Muslim. Many Albanian and Roma people also live in this landlocked pocket of south-east Europe, a country that managed to avoid erupting into the terrible wars that devastated much of the Balkans after the break-up of Yugoslavia.

Having assumed many names and incarnations, the six countries of Yugoslavia became the Socialist Federal Republic of Yugoslavia in 1964, led by General Tito. The newly formed collective became an important player on the world stage, refusing to align with either the USSR or US, and turning itself into an economic force until Tito's death in 1980.

Yugoslavia had worked to build up manufacturing across the republic. With its history of textile production, Macedonia became a thriving centre for garment and footwear factories, where many leading brands such as Wrangler were made. In socialist times, the majority of these factories were run as Socially Owned Enterprises.[26]

In the north-eastern town of Kumanovo stood Čik, a socially owned shoe factory which employed 3,600 workers in its heyday.[27] Take a visit to Kumanovo today and the Čik site is still there, but in very different form. The factory site entrance is adorned with trees and pretty lawns. The fountains are now empty but the buildings are colourful and there is a large sign for Italian company Formentini on one of the buildings at the front. But walk further along and down the steps into the main complex and the place has a very different feel. It is a big industrial site. Streets of two-storey buildings with peeling paint and dangling wires. Through grimy windows that have not yet been boarded-up, rows of workers can be seen at machines. Each workshop has the name of a different company. Shoeboxes printed with the name and logo of an international sports brand are stacked in a window. A refuse area holds skips full of cardboard and mounds of empty metal glue canisters.

The factory

Walking into one of the buildings on the morning of 19 April 2018, the smell of glue is immediate and strong. Concrete stairs wind up two flights. An industrial lift is set into the side of the staircase, exposing mechanical chains and pulleys. At the top of the stairs, the metal safety barrier has come off its top hinge and is blocked open, revealing a drop down the stairwell onto concrete two floors below.*

Through a set of double doors is a shoe factory staffed by workers in matching red T-shirts. All but a few are women. They are bent over workstations around a green conveyor belt. The workers take pieces of shoes out of green baskets attached to the conveyor belt. Completing their task, they return the pieces to the basket as it moves on to the next station. The conveyor belt moves slowly but never stops. Everyone must work in tandem.

In a corner office is the founder and boss of the De Marco Dooel factory and label. Lidija Milanovska is dressed in slim-cut black trousers and black high heels, her black shirt is open at the neck to reveal a silver necklace. She has long dark nails and short chestnut hair. On a shelf is a miniature bucket of shoe-shaped lollipops. Her computer screen shows CCTV of the factory floor.

At the behest of Angel Dimitrov, president of the Organization of Employers of Macedonia, Lidija has kindly agreed to open her factory up to a German TV crew making a critical documentary about leather supply chains. I have secured an invitation from the TV crew to join them.

Lidija has been in the shoe business for twenty-three years, working her way from factory worker to factory owner, to become president of the Kumanovo shoemakers' association. She has no illusions about her factory, which she named after her son. She describes it as 'in the middle' in terms of Macedonian standards. There are, Lidija says, both better and worse factories, and she is striving to improve conditions and salaries for the fifty-six workers she says she employs.** The factory makes 300 shoe uppers a day. For complicated models, output drops to 200, but simple models like sandals can be churned out at a rate of 400 uppers per day.

In their rows, the workers sew, snip, glue and solder, repeating

---

* As the visit to De Marco factory took place in April 2018, I emailed Lidija Milanovska to ask if anything had changed since. She emailed on 2 December 2019 to say the metal barrier was removed by workers from a different factory to allow a machine to be lowered.

** Email from Lidija Milanovska, 2 December 2019: '. . . the number of current workers is thirty and that number is decreasing daily.'

their task hundreds of times a day. The sewing machines whir and stop, whir and stop. A woman positions a machine above a bolt of leather, then lowers it to cut out templates. In a cupboard-sized room, a woman in a mask screen-prints logos onto tiny ovals of silver leather ready for appliquéing. Fumes sting my eyes and nose. The windows are open but I cannot see any other ventilation system.

Large metal containers of glue are stacked next to shelves of thread. Each container is printed with a flammable warning sign in bright red. A woman has a burning candle next to an open pot of glue a few metres away. She is using the flame to singe the edges of shoe templates. At another workstation, a coffee pot balances on a small gas stove. Lidija later told me that the workers had undergone safety training and were aware that there should never be glue on the desk while using candles or flames. Nevertheless, as there was just one way into the factory, I worried that if a fire started, the only way out for workers at the back of the long rectangular room would be to jump out of the first-floor window.*

That day the factory was assembling boxes full of shoe uppers in grey, navy and soft gold. These are shoes for little children. One of the brands being produced that day is Rainstep, a line of outdoor kids' shoes sold by the Italian Naturino brand. Naturino is owned by Falc SpA, who describe themselves as 'a leading Italian company in the children's footwear market'.[28] Falc SpA also own the Falcotto baby shoe brand, which is also being made at De Marco.

The Rainstep shoes retail online for around €80–90 per pair. Lidija pays the workers at De Marco €200–350 a month, depending on their role in the factory.** On this salary she says a household of two people could have a decent life, but accepts that if there was just one breadwinner it would be really hard. She says she ensures women have access to the top jobs instead of reserving them for men, as happens in other factories.

---

* Email from Lidija Milanovska, 2 December 2019: 'An additional fire exit is under construction, they are metal stairs which will be laid out according to the plan of the building.'

** Email from Lidija Milanovska, 2 December 2019: 'The monthly wage is increased from €250 to €400.'

Shoe factories here face a problem replicated across the region – not many people want this job anymore. In Kumanovo, many of the older workers were trained by Čik, but have retired or are nearing retirement. Anyone with options is avoiding the shoe and garment industry.

In the town, a vocational secondary school prepares people to work in factories. Lidija says factory owners are collectively encouraging young people to enrol in the school by offering to pay them for the 30 per cent of the course that is an on-site training module. With a wry smile she explains that this strategy has led to a 100 per cent increase – there are now six students instead of three. But all is not lost. When students graduate with other non-vocational qualifications, Lidija says they will eventually come knocking on the factory door after they find there are few other job options.

One of the reasons people do not want to work in shoe factories is that this is seasonal work. People are hired from September to February, then again from March to August. February and August are the two points in the calendar when next season's shoes are already made and brands have not placed new orders. Lidija says the gaps – ten days paid and the rest unpaid – last from twenty days up to a month. Workers are let go when there is no money coming in.

She talks animatedly about how the industry could improve and pay workers more. She suggests taxes could be cut or social healthcare benefits slashed so workers get the money straight into their wage packets. But asking the customers for more money is difficult. 'We don't even ask for a higher price,' she says. 'We know what they are willing to pay.' There is a rigid fear in Kumanovo of losing what little market share they have. The factories face two threats: 'The first threat is here in Macedonia, that [customers] will move next door. The second threat is that they will move to factories in Tunisia, India or Albania.'

Yet the customers greatly influence how much workers are paid. Lidija explains that brands pay the factory on a piece basis, calculated according to the estimated time for making each item. She explains that productivity, however, can be a problem due to staff shortages and insufficiently skilled staff, causing a fall in revenue. The most the factories feel they can do is avoid the Italian and Macedonian middlemen who peel off their own share of these precious cents.

Nor is there a chance of all the factories in Kumanovo clubbing together to ask for a better deal. 'Even in the [shoemakers'] association there are bigger factories who have worked with the same brands for years and don't tell what they are paid,' Lidija says. She explains that it is even tougher for smaller factories reliant on just two or three customers. Lidija says: 'We do not stir the water.'

The landlord

But what of basic health and safety at De Marco Dooel? The lack of effective ventilation. The lack of a lunch space which meant workers eat at workstations covered in pots of glue. The two toilets between fifty-sixty people, with missing seats and a broken window.* The horror of what would happen if there was a fire.

Lidija Milanovska acknowledges these problems but says it is a rented factory. She says that she had been told that a fire exit and a special room for a canteen would be provided, but they had not materialised when we visited.** Lidija says she is saving up to build her own facility where standards will be better. She wants somewhere workers will be happier, not least because better productivity means more money.

A white van in the factory car park provides a clue as to who now owns Čik. The side of the van advertises a restaurant in the capital Skopje. A burly, tattooed man in the car park does not like photography or filming in the factory complex, and says he will call 'Gino', which is also the name on the side of the restaurant van.

Mr Gino Guazzini comes from Tuscany in Italy. The restaurant website shows a small photo of a balding, silver-haired man, clean shaven in a red and white shirt.[29] He is also pictured on Twitter posing with the Italian ambassador to Macedonia at the opening

---

* Email from Lidija Milanovska, 2 December 2019: 'There are still two toilets, refurbished, but the number of current workers is thirty and that number is decreasing daily.'

** Email from Lidija Milanovska, 2 December 2019: Since our visit, workers are now allowed to use the canteen in a neighbouring building.

of a new machinery plant.[30] When contacted, Mr Guazzini says he owns 50 per cent of a company called Regia which now owns the Čik complex.

He also stated the building housing De Marco Dooel had been renovated in 2006 to meet legal standards in Macedonia, but that it should only house twenty-five workers. He described factory inspections as the job of state inspectors, not landlords.

As a conclusion Mr Guazzini stated: 'You know the egoism of those who have power, and how the market works. E.g., we sell shoes to English companies, and if we ask for 10p more, they answer that we would remain without work and they would go buy from others that would accept to work at their prices. So there is a degree of absurdity that on the one hand, you journalists conduct investigations because the conditions of work in these so-called third-world countries are not good, there's not enough investment, and the wages are low – but on the other end the very same English impose starvation prices on us.'

When contacted by email, Milan Petkovski, president of the Macedonian Occupational Safety and Health Association, said that according to Macedonian legislation, responsibility for the occupational health and safety of a factory's employees lies with the employer who must identify and mitigate all risks that could potentially damage the health of employees.

What happened to North Macedonia's socially owned factories is a source of controversy and pain for many people who work, or worked, in the industry. Factories that had once been the pride of Yugoslavian manufacturing, exporting to the world and winning contracts for well-known brands, were suddenly declared unprofitable or bankrupt, and sold off for cheap to wealthy Macedonians or foreign investors.

Makes one hundred pairs to my one

In 1878, Northamptonshire, to the north of London, was called 'the land of shoemakers', its streets haunted by grimy-faced men in leather aprons.[31] For centuries, shoemakers in Britain had shod the feet of their local community by working out of small home workshops where they were aided by their wives, children and apprentices. Though never likely to be rich, shoemakers enjoyed a good status in communities where their skills provided a vital service. Shoemakers also had high levels of literacy and enjoyed an unusual degree of autonomy because they could set their own hours and pace of work.*

Shoemaking was also an occupation with low set-up costs; 'only the kit and half a crown' were needed, or so the legend goes.[32] The accelerated economic and technological development of the industrial revolution changed this forever.

By the 1840s, shoemakers in Northampton could still be found working from home, but many were now in the employ of large manufacturers who amassed warehouses full of ready-to-wear shoes. These shoes were sent to big cities like London, or shipped overseas to countries that had been invaded and colonised by Britain. It was also the end of the majority of people wearing shoes that had been individually made for them; they were now mass-produced for all but the very few.

The arrival of machines in Northampton was preceded by whispers, rumours and fear. Vast improvements in transport and steam power had begun to turn shoe production into a capital-intensive business. The spectres of mass unemployment or toiling on smoky production lines led to the establishment of groups like the Northampton Boot and Shoe-makers Mutual Protection Society, founded in April 1858.

Posters appeared across Northampton a year later stating that the introduction of sewing machines could be delayed no longer as they were being used across England. The first machines to arrive in Northampton were for sewing on shoe uppers. It is said these machines were accepted because they were installed into homes to

---

* Shoemakers are not to be confused with cobblers, who repair rather than make shoes. Cobblers have traditionally held a lower place in society, and for reasons unknown hold the following dubious honour: the historic collective noun for a group of them is 'a drunkship of cobblers'. Who knows why cobblers were singled out as being drunkards, but it seems to have been accepted that they would have enjoyed many pints of medieval ale at the end of the working week. (C. Rhodes, *An Unkindness of Ravens: A Book of Collective Nouns.* Michael O'Mara, 2014)

supplement a job traditionally done by women. By 1864, there were 1,500 of these machines in Northampton alone.[33]

Change did not stop there. Bigger, heavier machines arrived: machines unsuitable for home use as they required large amounts of money and space. Machines that turned shoemaking from a low-capital, independent profession to an industry controlled by capitalists with big sums of money to invest.

The first factory-owners went out of their way to protest that they were not running a factory: 'the system we propose is not "the factory system",' stated Isaac, Campbell and Co. 'It is a carefully considered system of constant, orderly, regulated work, without any of the bad features which have made the factory system distasteful to you.'[34] Despite the protestations, this was the irrevocable end of artisan workshop life. By 1861, for example, the Turner Brothers factory in Northampton was producing 100,000 pairs a week on steam-powered machines. No family unit could come close to competing with this scale of production. It was either the factory or the workhouse.

Boots on the ground

It is impossible to properly understand how humanity came to make 24.2 billion pairs of shoes a year without understanding what inspired super-fast production. Rather than an obsession with beauty or consumer demand, technological change was often propelled by the darkest and most lethal aspects of human nature. The history of shoe production is inseparable from the history of war.

Northampton's early prosperity was a result of civil war. The unpopularity of King Charles I, caused by tax hikes, wars, religious prejudices and his disregard for Parliament, sparked the brutal bloodshed of the English Civil War. Parliamentarian Oliver Cromwell led the fight against the King's royalist forces. Records show Cromwell not only occupied Northampton but handed out military contracts for the shoes and boots needed to fight the Royalists. In 1642, thirteen Northampton shoemakers were given a contract for 600 pairs of boots and 4,000 pairs of shoes for troops being sent to brutally crush a rebellion in Ireland.[35]

When the Napoleonic Wars began at the start of the nineteenth century, huge numbers of boots and shoes were required to supply the armed forces, causing the Navy Office to repeatedly order thousands of pairs of boots and shoes from Northamptonshire.[36]

But it would be the vast industrial conflict of the First World War which would propel the British shoe industry to truly mass production. By the start of the twentieth century, British industry was in trouble. Across the Atlantic, settlers were plundering the territories of the 'American Wild West', using its great wealth and space to set up factories.[37] Britain began to feel the pressure of an 'American Invasion', huge quantities of shoe imports ranging from cheap shoes for the poor, to high fashion for the rich. Imports, coupled with mass strikes between 1890 and 1905, meant bleak prospects for British shoemaking.

The First World War's rocketing demand for kit transformed the fortunes of British industry. In the course of the war, British companies made roughly 70 million pairs of boots and shoes to equip not only the British army but also soldiers from Russia, France and other allied countries. Money was poured into designing boots that could handle route marches, heavy equipment, hot or freezing conditions, plus 'rot, rust, bacteria and leeches, despatch-riding on motorcycles and even tunnelling through the limestone rocks of Gibraltar.'[38]

Fresh from making specialist shoes for Ernest Shackleton's Antarctic Expedition in 1914, the Crockett & Jones factory in Northampton doubled its output by making army boots. Records show over 70 per cent of all boots worn by troops, 50 million pairs, were made in Northamptonshire. With able-bodied men expected to enlist in the army, shoe factory jobs opened up for women.[39]

Because footwear is a fundamental military necessity,[40] when the Second World War broke out, Britain's shoemakers once again produced tens of millions of pairs of shoes and boots, including half a million pairs sent to the USSR during the German invasion.

Traditional leather boots proved completely unsuitable, however, for swamps and jungles, leading to American jungle boots becoming highly prized by soldiers fighting in waterlogged terrain.[41] When the film producer Richard Goodwin, who served in the SAS in the Malaysian jungle from 1952–4, contracted dysentery and was airlifted to hospital, he was advised: 'The last thing my sergeant said to me was *never let them get your boots,* he meant I was to keep my boots with me so that I could get up and leave when I felt better, or run away if the hospital got bombed. Since then I've always kept my shoes to hand.'[42]

As well as being tools of efficient warfare, shoes have also come to symbolise the despicable horror of conflict: 43,525 pairs of shoes were found after Russia's Red Army liberated the Auschwitz Concentration Camp in January 1945. Of the 1.3 million people deported to Auschwitz, it is estimated that 230,000 of them were children and young people under eighteen. In the centre of the North Macedonian capital Skopje is a bronze statue outside the Holocaust Memorial Centre. Two children sit beside an empty chair, with a row of empty shoes in front of them. The little boy is cuddling one of the shoes.

In Hungary, *Shoes on the Danube Bank,* sixty pairs of iron 1940s shoes set into the concrete, is a powerful memorial to Hungarian Jews shot by fascist militia. Many of the victims were forced to remove their shoes before being killed and thrown into the river because footwear was a valuable commodity during wartime. The power of such sculptures arises from the sense of unease at seeing an empty pair of shoes in a public place – whose shoes were they, and what must have happened to leave them imprinted with a human body, and yet empty?[43]

Just Do It, or else

The next step in understanding how humans gained the capacity and desire to manufacture tens of billions of pairs of shoes in a single year, is the big factory shift of the late twentieth century. In the twenty years between 1970 to 1990 there was a dramatic change in where shoes were made, the amount people were paid to make them and the conditions they were made in.

In 1996, the International Labour Organization (ILO) noted several key things: the past twenty-five years had seen a dramatic change in where shoes and clothes were being made; Europe and North America had suffered big job losses while Asia and other parts of the Global South experienced big job gains; and while the global shift had created more jobs, it had shifted the industry from the formal sector into the informal sector with negative consequences for wages and conditions.[44]

The report found that from 1970 to 1990, the number of workers in textiles, clothing and footwear (TCF) increased by 597 per cent in Malaysia, 416 per cent in Bangladesh, 385 per cent in Sri Lanka and 334 per cent in Indonesia. During the same twenty-year period, countries in the Global North haemorrhaged jobs. Germany lost 58 per cent of its TCF workers, while the UK lost 55 per cent, France lost 49 per cent and the US 31 per cent. Factory clocks stopped ticking as production headed south.

As the wage gap widened between higher- and lower-income countries, brands rushed to take advantage. They could now pay $1.70 an hour in Mexico or $3.80 an hour in Taiwan, instead of paying $18.40 an hour for a German worker, or $13.40 an hour for a French worker.[45] This drop in wages meant shoes could be piled high and sold cheap. They were not, however, remotely affordable for the people making them. A Chinese worker toiling fifty hours a week would have had to spend half her monthly wage to buy a pair of Nikes.[46]

Globalisation also meant the overwhelming majority of companies stopped being shoe manufacturers. They subcontracted the job of running factories and concentrated on selling dreams instead. Production came to be defined by tiers. Tier One factories are manufacturers who contract directly with brands and retailers; they may have worked with brands like adidas or Clarks for many years and have strong relations with the brand. They are often owned by an individual or company from a different country; 85 per cent of Cambodian garment factories, for example, are controlled by Chinese, Taiwanese, Singaporean and Malaysian investors.[47]

Tier One factories routinely subcontract work to Tier Two factories – smaller production units that may do the assembly work the Tier One factory was hired to do, or provide a specialised element of production, for example embroidery or dyeing. Tier Three takes the form of even smaller workshops or factories who receive subcontracted work from the first two tiers. Within the

TCF industry, however, different brands can, and do, define the tier system differently.[48]

To shift all this suddenly available cheap product, shoes had to become far more than just foot coverings. Brands now concentrated on creating an obsession to match the technology, creating an artificial demand for new fashions, while disowning stories of workers' rights abuses.

Advertising, celebrity endorsements and popular culture helped create a symbolic value for shoes that was detached from their material value. As factories closed down, people in the voraciously consuming countries of the Global North lost their links with production; they no longer had friends or family working to make shoes. The objects in shop windows began to become mysterious.

They also became elevated by more and more obscene sponsorship deals. The $20m Michael Jordan earned in sponsorship in 1992 was calculated to be more than the total wages of all the women in South-east Asia who stitched Nike Air Jordans.[49] It was also reportedly almost double the annual wages of the entire workforce of Nike contractors in Vietnam.[50]

Nike was founded in 1964 by Phil Knight and Bill Bowerman, who both invested $500 to start a business importing Japanese running shoes. Sales reached almost $2m by the early 1970s, when the company began to design and subcontract its own lines.[51] By 2002 Nike was manufacturing in over 700 factories in 51 countries using 500,000 workers, and 59 per cent of its $9.5b revenue was from footwear.[52]

But these profits came at a terrible human cost. A 1997 internal inspection report for Nike by Ernst & Young found workers at a factory near Ho Chi Minh City in Vietnam were exposed to carcinogens that were between 6 and 177 times higher than local legal limits. Seventy-seven per cent of employees were found to have respiratory problems, and workers were forced to work 65-hour weeks for $10.[53]

As child labour and appalling working conditions were exposed in sweatshops, Nike became the poster child for the anti-globalisation movement. Phil Knight eventually admitted in 1998: 'The Nike product has become synonymous with slave wages, forced overtime, and arbitrary abuse',[54] before laying out the changes Nike had made and said it would continue to make. He retired in 2016 and has a fortune of $34.9b.[55] For their part, Nike say they are 'committed to responsible employment practices and we expect the same of our suppliers'. They say they require suppliers to 'pay their employees at least the local minimum wage or prevailing wage (whichever is higher)', and 'including additional payments for overtime or benefits'.[56] Nike has pledged to remove labour and environmental abuses and has tried to position itself as a leader in sustainable supply chain management, though the company continues to fall foul of some outside assessments and investigations.[57]

In her shoes

The International Labour Organization (ILO) has calculated that at least 60 million people are formally employed by the global garment industry. Of these 60 million people, approximately 80 per cent are women. Typically, these women are aged between eighteen and thirty-five and have often migrated from rural areas to seek employment.[58] Within Asia, the ILO estimates that the TCF industry formally employs 43 million people and once again, the overwhelming majority of them are women. In Cambodia, Laos, Myanmar, Thailand and Vietnam, at least 75 per cent of TCF workers are women.[59]

When it comes to footwear specifically, worldwide estimates vary between 4.2 million workers according to the United Nations Industrial Development Organization (UNIDO), and 7.1 million according to industry sources. UNIDO estimates 46 per cent of shoe workers are women, but advises caution.[60]* The difficulty in ascertaining what percentage of shoe workers are women is due to the limited number of producer countries who record data on women's employment at an industry level. What we do know, however, is that the shoe industry simply would not exist without the systemic exploitation of women.

---

* This figure, for example, does not include data from Bangladesh, Pakistan, Vietnam or Cambodia. In addition, according to the ILO, the global leather industry employs anywhere between 1.1 to 6 million workers.

The TCF industry has created millions of jobs which have given women the possibility of work outside the home. But it remains a double-edged sword. The reality of factory work in the shoe system is that it is insecure, low paid and exploitative. Wages in the shoe industry remain low and are particularly bad for women. While women continue to do the majority of the jobs in this industry, research has found gender pay gaps as large as 66.5 per cent in Pakistan, 36.3 per cent in India and 30.3 per cent in Sri Lanka.[61]

Sexism and social discrimination against women mean they are over-represented in industries that entail poor wages and conditions, like the TCF sector. This same sexism means there is less of a drive to improve wages and conditions, a factor compounded by the repression of civil society and TCF trade union groups who would ordinarily provide a route for overcoming gender- and class-based social norms. If TCF workers are being silenced, then women are being silenced.

As for who holds the cards in the shoe industry, Dominique Muller says it is the brands who have the power. 'You could say it is a colonial attitude, the big corporations are global and they can shift to wherever they want, and impose their own conditions for going into a country,' Dominique says, listing tax breaks, hampering of unions and minimum wage exemptions that shoe brands have been handed. 'This move into Africa is part of the same thing – it's their move into their next frontier.'[62]

Ethiopian dream

Fashion's hunt for 'the next big thing' does not just mean discovering the next colour trend, street style muse or fresh designer, it also means relentlessly pursuing the next pool of exploitable labour. This hunt has brought mass shoe production to Africa. As a continent, Africa currently produces a small fraction of global shoe production, just 3.6 per cent.[63] But Chinese corporations in particular are working hard to increase this market share by opening factories. This strategy is part of China's 'One Belt, One Road' initiative, an ambitious campaign which China hopes will boost trade and economic growth while spreading Chinese influence.

The scale of this investment means the biggest shoe exporter in Ethiopia in 2017, with exports of $19.3m, was the Chinese company the Huajian Group (the same firm that also previously made Ivanka Trump shoes in China).[64] This work was celebrated in a Chinese government film *Amazing China*, with Huajian portrayed as benevolently exporting economic success to Ethiopia.

But when the Associated Press news agency visited Huajian, they found some Ethiopian workers telling a very different story, with many expressing serious disquiet at their working life, including very low wages and poor health and safety. Angesom Gebre Yohannes is a senior figure at the Industrial Federation of Ethiopian Textile, Leather and Garment Worker Trade Unions. He has watched the industry undergo great change as foreign investment pours into the sector.

With Ethiopia's population now over 100 million, Angesom says the shoe sector is good for Ethiopia. It brings employment, trade for Ethiopia's large livestock and leather industry, and foreign currency from exports. But it is a fledgling sector with huge challenges ahead, not least the battle for the right to have trade unions in factories so that wages and conditions can be improved.

'The [foreign] investors are not willing to have a union, especially some of the Chinese investors are not willing,' Angesom says. 'Initially, when they were investing they agreed to respect the labour laws of the country, but when we are trying to unionise in the factory they are not willing.'

The mission to secure decent wages is hindered by the fact that there is no consistent minimum wage in Ethiopia, though some public sector institutions and enterprises have set their own minimum wages.[65] Factory owners are left to set their own standards, and unsurprisingly these standards are at rock bottom. In a 2019 report, the NYU Stern Center for Business and Human Rights described how the Ethiopian government's 'eagerness to attract foreign investment led it to promote the lowest base wage in any garment-producing country – now set at the equivalent of $26 a month.'[66] Angesom says a typical salary in the shoe sector ranges from $50 to $100 a month, better than for garment workers but still very low. 'How can you have a good life on $50 a month?' he asks.

Workers at the Huajian factory have also been subjected to what some perceive as humiliating practices. In 2017, journalist Zhang Zizhu described the following scene inside the Huajian factory:

'Eyes Right! Eyes Front!' The team leader calls out the command in Chinese and the workers follow, slapping the sides of their pants while turning their heads. 'March! One, two, one . . . one, two, one . . . One! Two! Three! Four!'

The workers were being made to march on the spot twice a day underneath a slogan reading: '100 per cent understanding, 100 per cent cooperation, 100 per cent obedience, 100 per cent execution.' Workers were also sometimes made to sing the factory song in Chinese.[67]

Angesom confirmed this practice takes place at the Huajian factory and emphasised it is not normal for Ethiopia. One factory manager told Zizhu: 'The assembly and the singing of the factory song are different forms of corporate cultural education that is meant to make the workers like and love the company. This is to implant the right spirit and culture in the workers.'[68]

The Ethiopian government has made textiles and shoes an industrial priority, offering huge incentives and tax breaks to foreign investors. Ethiopia also has duty-free access to the United States as a result of the African Growth and Opportunity Act (AGOA). But the main attraction of Ethiopia is its low-waged workforce.

Factories now encircle the world as a web of production. As this web spreads it draws tens of millions of people into workshops and industrial parks, integrating them into a world economy on the basis that they remain a source of cheap labour. This web, and this exploitation, are visible in every stitch that holds our footwear together, in every sole that is securely glued to its upper and in every shoe we buy that comes pre-laced.

This is the work of human hands, hands that crack and bleed from needle pricks and harsh chemicals, hands that sew and stick and scrub, and hands that, at the end of the working week, carry home a pittance wage.

What country is printed on the label of your shoes? Were they pieced together in China or in Vietnam? Or perhaps in Bulgaria or Mexico? If you are lucky you will see the name of a country, printed in small inked letters. Along with the country there should also be the name of a town, and of a factory, and the name of a person who made your shoes. But these vital details have been quietly erased as something we are not allowed to know.

CHAPTER 3

Living on a Shoestring

With a large empty bag slung over his shoulder, Muhammad Iqbal sets out on the half-hour walk to the factory. When he arrives, he is handed piles of shoe parts. He fills the bag and sets off again for home. Waiting for Muhammad Iqbal are his wife, Ishra, and their two daughters aged seventeen and fifteen. He empties out the bag and they sit down together to begin their work.

The family is paid 16.6 rupees for every pair of 'gents' uppers' they stitch together. The orders come in sets and they get 200 rupees for a completed dozen. If they work from 8 a.m. until late at night, they can stitch four dozen pairs and earn 800 rupees per day, just under $8.

The stitched uppers Muhammad carries back to the factory are sent to a production line to be attached to soles. Muhammad has been making shoes since he was a child, but has not always worked at home with his family. Nine years ago he worked in a factory in Faisalabad, the second-largest city in the Punjab in the north-west of Pakistan, a highly polluted place known for poor labour conditions, including child and bonded labour.

Muhammad's wife, Ishra, sits beside him, her red *salwar khameez* chequered with dark-gold squares. Muhammad shifts in his seat and uncrosses his arms. Under his blue jacket, one of his white shirt sleeves ends without a hand.

Muhammad was not a bonded labourer in Faisalabad, just a man fed up with being paid too little to support his family. He told the shoe factory owner his wages were too low and he was leaving to work elsewhere. He said the factory owner told him he was not allowed to leave. A fight started with other men joining in. The fight culminated in the factory owner cutting off Muhammad's hand.

He draws up his shirt sleeve. His right arm ends in a smooth stump. Muhammad went to the police, and the case rumbled on for eight months before being dropped because the factory owner was rich and politically influential. Without justice or compensation, Muhammad, Ishra and their two daughters moved to Lahore.

Ending in tiers

In moving from factory worker to homeworker, Muhammad entered an even lower strata in the global economy. Across the globe, people have traditionally worked in their homes to weave carpets, sew clothes, make rope, shell nuts and weave craft goods to sell.

Today, homeworkers are an essential feature of the economy, producing goods for both local and global markets. As supply chains get ever longer and manufacturing is compartmentalised and spread across the world, people even assemble electronic goods in their homes.[1]

Yet despite numbering in the hundreds of millions, homeworkers are invisible, casual and lacking even the meagre protection of being in a formal factory workforce. Despite often working for the biggest brands in the world, their work is temporary and unprotected, their wages and workflow fluctuate dramatically.

Tiered supply chains do not end at Tier Three factories. At any stage, any factory can subcontract work out to homeworkers. Homeworkers have no contract with a factory and do not receive anything beyond their piecework wage. This allows factories to shrug off as much of the burden and risk of manufacturing as they can, pushing it instead onto people working at home who shoulder both manufacturing costs like space and electricity, and also the downtimes when orders run out and there is no work to do.

Homework is the world beneath the first, second and third tier of subcontracting. A world of supply chains that descends far below any kind of regulation or factory inspection system. A world that goes ignored.

Nagina, Yasmin and Razia

In Pakistan, it is estimated that 80 per cent of the total working population are in the informal sector of the economy and lack any kind of recognition, regulation or protection by the state. This informal sector includes day labourers on building sites, people working in small factories, street sellers hawking food, cigarettes and newspapers, as well as workshop apprentices and waste pickers. It also includes home-based workers, where roles range from sewing garments and making glass bangles to embroidering, carpet weaving and stitching footballs.

Estimates of the number of homeworkers in Pakistan vary wildly: UN Women concluded that no large-scale national survey exists to provide accurate data on the extent of home-based work.[2] All studies agree, however, that there are millions of workers in this category in Pakistan. Across South Asia, the ILO estimate there are 50 million home-based workers, 80 per cent of whom are women.[3]

Nagina works in her home making embroidered uppers for women's shoes. She lives in the impoverished industrial neighbourhood of Badami Bagh in Lahore, and an agent for a factory near to her home delivers the work to her and collects it once she has finished. One of the shoe designs she is working on involves pasting on tiny beads with an electric glue gun that the factory gave her. This is work that requires her to spend her own money on electricity both to power the glue gun and for the lights which Nagina needs because the intricate work makes her eyes hurt.

Even as it damages her sight, the work of sewing uppers and sticking on beads is crucial for the survival of Nagina and her four children. She was once married to a man she describes as work-shy. When they were married he did not work, now they are divorced he offers her no support.

Nagina's two eldest sons are grown up and are working, her two daughters are still in school. One of the biggest problems she faces is that work from the factory is not regular. Nagina describes how work can suddenly dry up for whole weeks at a time, leaving her struggling to pay her rent and expensive utility bills, and adjusting the rest of her family's life to whatever money remains.

Wearing a dark-red *salwar khameez* with a headscarf over long hair, Yasmin is also a homeworker. Her work involves sewing designs onto the uppers of women's shoes. For this work she earns a maximum of 4 rupees for each pair (about 4 US cents), with each design taking 5–10 minutes to complete.

Like Nagina, the work Yasmin does brings in a vital income. Yasmin is married and has two children, but she is her husband's second wife. She stayed living with her parents until they died, and now Yasmin and her two children, a son aged twelve and a daughter aged eight, live with Yasmin's unmarried younger sister who works at home sewing garments.

Working from home allows these women to look after their children and on occasion to have their children help them with sewing or gluing. They do not want to go and work in the formal setting of a factory, seeing it as a workplace full of men that would not be appropriate for them, and which would stop them from caring properly for their children. Instead they shoulder a double burden of household chores, cooking and childcare as well as very long hours of piecework.

With a royal-blue headscarf and a direct gaze, Razia Nisar is a home-based shoe worker and an advocate of rights for homeworkers. She is adamant homeworkers are worse off than factory workers: 'There is no time limit while working in our homes. Factory workers normally have to work for six to eight hours but there is no limit here. Sometimes we work late into the night, as late as 12 a.m. some days and this is all without a holiday.

'Factory owners provide all the basic needs to their workers but in our case we can't even take a break from the work,' Razia Nisar continues. 'If we do, they'll cut our daily wages. This is not the case with factory workers, their salary is fixed and has to be paid even if they perform poorly.'

She has no illusions about why factory owners outsource to people working in their homes: 'Factory owners try to save their expenses by putting an extra workload on us because in this way, they can save on their electricity consumption. Moreover, they don't have to pay us social security and medical allowances.'

Homework traps people in dire poverty. The minimum wage for so-called 'unskilled workers' in Pakistan is currently 15,000 rupees per month (approximately $142).[4] Many home-based workers end up earning as little as 20–25 per cent of the minimum wage. A monthly salary of 3,000–4,000 rupees per month ($28–38) is a starvation wage that leaves nothing for savings or to cover medical emergencies. Even basic needs like food, rent and utility bills cannot be covered. Homeworkers often end up asking for loans from relatives or friends, then struggle to repay the debt.

A lack of savings and exclusion from any kind of regulated system means homeworkers have no benefits or pension: 'We have seen a lot of old women who are not able to do the work they used to do,' says Khalid Mahmood, director of the Labour Education Foundation, an NGO founded to organise for workers' rights. 'There is no protection for these women from the government, there is no pension of course because they are not registered workers. They are just surviving and dependent on their children or their husband or whatever dependence system is there in the family.' If elderly women have no family support system, they are reduced to begging on the street.

When global crisis knocks

Homeworkers might be hidden from sight, but their presence is right there in the price tag of consumer goods. The ultra-exploitation of homeworkers is central to a strategy that creates corporate profit by squeezing labour rather than increasing the price of goods.[5] It is a key reason why items like shoes, which take so much work to assemble, have cheap price tags.

While homework might appear traditional and even nice in some way, it is far from being an outmoded form of production. The modern economy is not a choice between either factory work or homework, rather homeworkers and factories are co-dependent. Wherever manufacturing is taking place and factory owners are being squeezed to produce goods at extremely low prices, you will find homeworkers from India to England, Guatemala to Tunisia, manufacturing increases, so too does homeworking.[6] Export-led growth in many countries is linked to the expansion of home-based production because there is often no other way for factory owners to meet the cost-cutting demands of multinational corporations.

Homeworkers make a huge contribution, not only to their own families, but to the local, national and global economy, yet they are swept about on the seas of international markets. In the global recession, homeworkers were among the first to lose their work and income.[7]

In 2009, a year after the 2008 global financial crash, the Inclusive Cities Project carried out research in ten Global South cities to discover how the informal economy, including homeworkers, had been affected by the crash. They found that homeworkers who had been producing goods for global value chains (exports for multinational corporations) experienced a sharp decline in their work orders. Those working for the domestic market fared a little better, though were still impacted by increased competition for their jobs and by the global drop in people's purchasing power.[8]

A year later, in 2010, Inclusive Cities again found the informal sector lagging behind the formal sector in terms of recovery. Persistent unemployment and underemployment in the formal economy had driven many people into the already crowded informal economy. Orders and sales remained low while inflation and living costs had risen. This resulted in homeworkers cutting down on food for themselves and their families, and taking their children out of school.[9]

A woman's work is never, ever done

Like factory work, homework is gendered exploitation. Across the world, the majority of homeworkers are women: 70 per cent in Brazil, 88 per cent in Ghana and 75 per cent in Pakistan.[10] In Pakistan, it is estimated 65 per cent of all working women are home-based workers, compared with just 4 per cent of working men.[11]

Different trades, however, have different numbers. Shoemaking is a relatively better-paid form of homework, so significant numbers of men are found in this trade. But women in the shoe sector, like Nagina and Yasmin, still get stuck with the least profitable roles in home shoe production, receiving embroidery or beading piecework from factory agents if and when it is available.

Gender also intersects with poverty and urban deprivation. As the poorest people in society, city-dwelling homeworkers often live in overcrowded slums where public services and infrastructure are patchy at best. Not only must women like Nagina, Yasmin and Razia do piecework, housework and childcare but an impoverished, over-crowded home-workspace entails constantly moving things around and doing extra cleaning and washing.

Simply by being within the four walls of a home, the upkeep of workspaces generally falls on women. Lack of adequate sanitation and waste management, and infrequent or non-existent rubbish col-lection, add to a woman's burden.[12] Every moment spent carrying water or hauling away rubbish is time lost at paid work. Poor-quality housing also carries an extra risk of merchandise being spoiled by leaks, mould, dirt or floods.

A study of twelve slum projects in India found women particu-larly benefit from improvements to water supply, flood prevention and street lighting. The provision of public spaces where they can safely work – communal courtyards with in-built tables and chairs, along with playgrounds where children can be supervised – greatly helps homeworkers.[13] But more usually, urban homeworkers face the constant threat of upheaval and eviction.[14] Slum-clearance pro-grammes that destroy homes are a double burden on this community because they eliminate livelihoods as well as houses.[15]

Home-based shoe workers must travel to and from factories and markets to collect and deliver orders and raw materials. They can take a rickshaw or a public bus, or they can walk. One study found transport made up a third of expenditure for homeworkers. There is also the question of whether the available public transport is a safe environment for women who routinely face street harassment and abuse.

Home sweet home?

Perveen and Muhammad work together in their home in Lahore. Muhammad walks fifteen minutes to a nearby factory, collects sacks full of women's uppers and brings them home to Badami Bagh. They work for twelve hours a day, from 8.00 in the morning until 8.00 in the evening. They work hard because the work is not regular – Muhammad says several days a week can pass with no work at all. They survive on what they have and are always trying to find more work.

The uppers they work on need both stitching and gluing. The materials Perveen and Muhammad use are given to them by the factory and stored in their house. This means they are required to store large quantities of industrial glue in their home. In a safe workplace such storage should be governed by strict health and safety rules, and overseen by risk assessments, inspectors and on-site monitors. Workers should be protected by fire exits, sprinkler systems, fire monitors and evacuation procedures. None of this exists in individual homes in Badami Bagh.

Muhammad describes a day when he was working at home and did not notice his small children playing with the kitchen fire. A store of glue in the house ignited and caused a serious fire that badly damaged his home and left him with burns to his feet from saving the lives of his children.

Since then, he says, he knows the glue he works with is a fire hazard, so it is kept away from any place where there is a fire. He says people in the Badami Bagh shoemaking community know the glue is dangerous, but that accident prevention is based on people telling each other about the hazards. Muhammad says he still hears of fires in people's homes. But, he says simply, they all have to work, so they take the risk.

The dangers of flammable solvents and glues in the shoe industry should not be underestimated. In 2002, forty-four workers were burned to death in a shoe factory in Agra, India after there was an apparent electrical short-circuit in a drum storage room.[16]

When market capitalism invades people's homes there are consequences beyond just wage exploitation. This is a system in pursuit of not simply cheap labour costs, but ways to circumvent the accumulative cost of basic standards. It is not just any homes that are being invaded, rather it is Global South homes that have been turned into dangerous workplaces. The hunt for cheap production has led transnational corporations into the poorest areas of the Global South and encouraged the scattering of work into households.[17]

This system has negatively impacted global attempts to regulate dangerous work. In addition to building rent and utility bills being passed on to individual labourers, homeworkers are also expected to shoulder more sinister costs. Homes are not supposed to be workplaces; in an ideal world they should be clean, safe spaces where food is cooked, and where families and individuals can relax. Factories on the other hand are very loud and full of fumes, they are pressurised environments crowded with people and dangerous machinery. People can't live well in factories, and should not have factories in their homes.

Tamil Nadu in Southern India is a hub for leather shoe exports. When investigating conditions for homeworkers one NGO, Homeworkers Worldwide, found women working in tiny apartments where both ventilation and seating arrangements were far worse than in factories. The women were experiencing the debilitating effects of working crouched over for long hours, they had back and joint strain due to long hours stitching tough leather, eye damage from continuous detailed work and skin problems from exposure to chemicals.

Many of the women had worked in factories until they married. None of them had pensions, health insurance or security after years of work. Some were paid as little as 9p to hand-sew the leather uppers of shoes which then sold for over £40.[18]

In home workshops, space is cramped and crowded. The light is dim and the air grows thick with dust and fumes. Squinting workers pull their shirts, or headscarves, over their noses to try to stop coughing. There are no proper workstations so people sit hunched over, often on the floor. The strain on backs, shoulders and hands grows with every hour spent in an unhealthy posture.

These occupational hazards lead to bills for healthcare. Treatment for lung ailments, back pain and poor eyesight is expensive and unhealthy homes can affect entire families. If there is no way to pay for medical help, the productivity of each homeworker is reduced, causing household income to drop even further.[19] It is an exploitation compounded by neoliberal drives like the Structural Adjustment

Programmes (SAPs) imposed by the IMF. SAPs allow countries in need of assistance to be given large loans; the preconditions attached to the loans, however, tend to focus on the liberalisation of national economies. They typically push for the privatisation of healthcare and the reduction of spending on education and public health, all of which negatively impact the citizens of an already struggling country.[20]

Breath of life

Some 700 miles to the east of Lahore is a small house in Kathmandu, the capital of Nepal. Krishna Bahadur Nepali sits at a workstation covered in pieces of leather, shoe soles, tools and pots of glue. Further along the narrow rectangular room is a large loom where Krishna's wife is weaving a carpet. They sit together side by side, each engaged in their own form of homework.

Krishna Bahadur has been making shoes since he was eleven or twelve. He was taught the trade by his father as a traditional family occupation going back to his grandfather, great-grandfather and great-great-grandfather. As a child Krishna would make shoes before and after school before eventually dropping out to help his impoverished family full time. He now has grown-up children of his own.

He holds up a child's laced shoe in dark polished leather. The orders for school shoes come from a wholesaler at a nearby market; for one pair of shoes he is paid 100 rupees, the equivalent of $1. Unlike the homeworkers in Pakistan, this is reliable work and Krishna Bahadur is always busy.

Working hunched for long hours over so many years has left Krishna Bahadur with bad back pain. He has been to the doctor for treatment that cost 500 rupees and now has physiotherapy exercises that he is supposed to do, as he is unable to take any time off work.

As well as back pain, Krishna also experiences problems caused by the paint-can-sized pot of glue on the table next to him. 'This is very much toxic,' he says, holding up the glue he bought from the market. Closer examination reveals the only safety instruction printed on the label is a warning to keep it out of the reach of children.

Krishna Bahadur says using the glue makes him sleepy and 'affects his senses'. He does not use any special protection on his hands or his eyes when he uses the glue to assemble shoes. He does open a window though – a square window through which the noise of a crowing cockerel can be heard.

Just what is the glue being used to make shoes? Dr Pia Markkanen has visited dozens of home-based shoe workshops in Thailand, Indonesia and the Philippines as part of her work as a chemical engineer and research professor at the University of Massachusetts Lowell. She is haunted by the first home workshop she visited in Thailand, a two-storey apartment with no fire exits that she describes as being a crowded sea of workers. On the second floor she found children and babies in among sewing machines, gluing stations and pattern-making stations, the air thick with an overpowering chemical smell.

'I found so little about safety on the glue labels. There were instructions about how to get the most effective bonding, but nothing about the active ingredients, nothing about safety measures,' Dr Markkanen continues. 'These chemicals, whether they are glues, primers, or cleaning products for polishing the shoes, when you inhale them they are very hazardous to your health, to the respiratory system, the individual organs, reproductive systems – you name it, these are neurotoxins.'

Working day in, day out with a neurotoxin is no joke. These poisonous substances act on the nervous system and can cause a multitude of serious problems from headaches to loss of memory and cognitive functions, depression and chronic fatigue.[21] Solvents, substances that can dissolve or disperse other substances, also have a heavy presence in the shoe industry. Organic solvents are based on carbon and are used in products like paints, varnishes, glues and cleaning agents.[22] Despite the word 'organic' they are not friendly, but can cause numerous conditions including being a reproductive hazard. In shoe production, organic solvents are found in glues, primers and shoe cleaners. Many organic solvents are recognised as neurotoxins,[23] *and* carcinogens – substances or environmental factors that can lead to cancer, either quickly or after prolonged exposure.[24]

Such chemicals have three main ways to enter the human body: the most common method is inhalation, the second is skin absorption and the third is ingestion. People making shoes at home are particularly susceptible to all three.

Homeworkers work quickly and generally do not take rest or lunch breaks away from their workstations. 'What I saw is that they work as much as they could and they eat their lunch, their dinner and their breakfast while they were working,' Dr Markkanen explains. 'Maybe they had a stick to spread the glue but sometimes they used their bare hands and then they'd eat.'

In offices around the world, eating lunch at workstations is rightly discouraged in order to prevent stress, but for people working surrounded by poisonous chemicals it can be life-threatening. Dr Markkanen describes people interspersing making shoes with eating snacks or bowls of rice, and smoking cigarettes. This risks ingested chemical exposure which, she says, goes straight to the stomach, the digestive system, the liver and systemically through the body, targeting organs.

Don't inhale

In the 1970s the term *shoemaker's polyneuropathy* was coined to describe the extremely adverse effect of long-term solvent exposure. The most famous person to contract shoemaker's polyneuropathy was the co-founder of Nike, Bill Bowerman, who poisoned himself by working in a small fume-filled workshop while obsessively working on new trainer designs.[25] Award-winning author Joan Brady became ill when her neighbour, a shoe factory in Devon, England, flooded her house with extraordinarily high levels of chemical fumes.[26] While the shoemaker denied any damage caused by their solvents, Brady was ultimately awarded £115,000 in an out-of-court settlement.

Away from the spotlight, the shoe industry is awash with chemicals and the air is left thick with pollution. The proven link between shoemaking chemicals and cancers, has led to the development of water-based adhesives as an alternative to solvent-based ones. Independent designers have also worked on modular shoes whose assembly requires no glue at all. There remains a bias, however, towards stronger solvent-based glues. By their nature, homeworking environments remain the least regulated parts of supply chains; no inspections or rules apply when the supply chain drops out of sight.

Three of the chemicals found in glues and solvents that have been found to be major health hazards are methyl ethyl ketone (MEK or butanone), benzene and toluene. Methyl ethyl ketone is used in industry as a solvent and is found in paints, varnishes and glues. It is toxic by all routes of exposure, and can be absorbed into the body following inhalation, ingestion or prolonged skin exposure. It can cause headaches, dizziness, tiredness, slurred speech, low temperature, fitting and comas, heart problems and high levels of blood sugar.[27]

Benzene is used in the manufacture of plastics, dyes and solvents.[28] Short-term air exposure may cause irritation to the eyes, nose and throat, as well as breathing difficulties. Occupational exposure to benzene has been linked to illnesses including a decrease in white blood cells, leukaemia and damage to DNA, and the International Agency for Research on Cancer (IARC) has classified benzene as carcinogenic to humans.[29] Because of these dangers, the British government states that benzene levels are under stringent control in the UK and 'exposures to benzene at work, in water and air are reduced to the lowest practical level to minimise possible risks to health.'[30]

Last, but not least, toluene is used in the manufacture of glue, paint, dye and plastics. It has a sweet, pungent smell and its vapours can cause drowsiness, dizziness, headaches, sickness and memory problems. Large amounts can cause permanent damage to the nervous system, and can induce comas, heart problems and even death.[31] If you need a reason to quit smoking: outside of industrial environments, methyl ethyl ketone, benzene and toluene are all found in cigarette smoke.[32]

Dr Markkanen points the finger at the powerful petrochemical industry hard-selling dangerous products that people do not fully understand. 'You push these hazardous chemicals at the doors of local producers and they don't have the power to question, *Are these glues really helpful to my children, to my family? Am I going to be harmed by them?*' Dr Markkanen says. 'They are not asking that question, they are asking where is my next pay cheque coming from? How do I earn bread for my family?

'When you can make the argument that something is hazardous for consumers, then people wake up, especially when they are hazardous for little children,' she concludes. 'But there is still this invisibility to workers, workers who are still exposed to this bad stuff on a day-to-day basis.'

Dandy

These dangerous chemicals do not remain secured in shoe supply chains. Homework means the casualisation of industry and industrial materials, resulting in the proliferation of toxic substances throughout society. Glues and solvents meant for assembling shoes, sticking down carpets or repairing tyres are not locked away in factories each night, rather they are readily available in shops and marketplaces. Where industry has spread through societies that already lack regulation, there are often no restrictions on the sale of harmful chemicals – with devastating consequences.

In the junkyards, rubbish dumps and alleyways of Kathmandu Valley are thousands of homeless children. They deal with abandonment, extreme hunger and cold, violence and sexual exploitation. Finding little chance of escaping the physical and emotional turmoil of their lives, many of these children are caught in a vicious glue-sniffing epidemic.

Bishnu Prasad Paudel has worked with street children at the Child Workers in Nepal Concerned Centre for over eight years. He says the reasons children give for inhaling glue all involve some form of pain. They inhale to escape from hunger, from loneliness, from fear, from fights, and to bond with their social group.

In Nepal, glue can be found being sold in tiny street shops alongside parcels of *paan* chewing herb. 'Normally they sell *paan*, but beside that they sell glue for the street kids since that is the more profitable option because they can sell more,' Bishnu explains. A toothpaste tube-sized packet of glue costs 65–70 Nepali rupees, but street children often get charged a higher rate of 100–150 rupees because shopkeepers know they are addicts.

This problem is replicated across the region. Shahed Ibne Obaed works at a night shelter and drop-in centre for street children in Bangladesh.[33] He regularly encounters street children addicted to shoe glue or 'Dandy' as it is nicknamed in Bangladesh. Dandy is readily available from local grocery shops and is far cheaper than other drugs like alcohol, marijuana or heroin, so cheap that child beggars sleeping on the streets can afford it. Shahed says the shops never refuse to sell the glue, which children then pour into a polythene bag so they can inhale the fumes.

Research carried out by Shahed's centre found glue being used by girls as well as boys. This is a substance abuse problem linked with child sex work, with girls as young as ten enduring sex work to buy glue. 'These are children living on the streets, they are ten, eleven, twelve, and fourteen years old,' Shahed says. 'These are not adults.'

The brand of glue on Krishna Bahadur Nepali's workstation, the one that gives him headaches, is called Dendrite. It comes in brightly coloured yellow packaging and is one of the glues used by street children. Dendrite appeals to child addicts because it contains the sweet-smelling solvent toluene. This is an extremely dangerous addiction. Low levels of toluene inhalation can cause people to seem drunk. A large amount inhaled over a short time can cause unconsciousness or even death. The long-term effects can include muscle wasting, and permanent damage to body and brain.[34]

The Dendrite brand is owned by Calcutta-based company Chandras' Chemical Enterprises (Pvt.) Ltd who manufacture adhesives, primers and putties. As well as being exported across Asia (though not to Pakistan), Dendrite products are sold in Dubai, Bahrain and Qatar. Amit Dasgupta, vice president of export and technical sales, explains that a new expansion is planned for Turkey and North Africa.

When asked about street children sniffing Dendrite glue, he said that all necessary precautions are taken. He argues that chemical levels never exceed permissible limits, and containers display 'very prominent stickers' to warn people of the dangers. It is, he says, a problem of education.

'There is so many things in the world, you know, knives and scissors are made for cutting fruits and for use in your household.

But with knives and scissors, people murder also. Knives are used for murdering people, but you cannot stop the production of knives. Then you will have other problems.' Some varieties of Dendrite are sold as toluene-free, but tubes of the glue bought easily in India were not toluene-free, nor did their packaging have any warnings about the contents.

Academics from the Bankura Sammilani Medical College in India published a paper describing solvent abuse as a growing problem and a 'curse' on children in Asian countries.[35] They warn of the easy availability and cheapness of solvents and say government measures are needed to regulate glue sales among children and teenagers. The paper points to cases where chemical corporations have bowed to public pressure – in South Africa, a glue company removed a particularly toxic chemical from a glue that paralysed numerous street children; and in the Philippines a company altered the smell of its glue to make it unpleasantly bitter and unappealing to children.[36]

The distance between us

The interconnectedness promised by globalisation is contradicted by the isolation of homeworkers who sit alone and atomised in their homes. They are part of transnational supply chains but profits depend upon homeworkers never accessing this interconnectedness. The globalised corporate search for cheap production relies on low-cost workers remaining detached from each other so that they cannot collectively raise their wages and better their conditions. But could homeworkers circumvent this trap?

Home-based workers lack rights in part because they are not properly recognised as workers. A major obstacle is the absence of a clear employment relationship.[37] Shoe supply chains snake out across the world, leaving the question of who ultimately employs homeworkers. In the case of Nagina in Lahore, is her employer the agent who acts for the factory, the factory itself, the contractor who engaged the factory, the supplier who engaged the contractor or the retailer who will sell the finished goods?[38]

'It's not the immediate contractor,' says Dr Martha Chen, lecturer in public policy at the Harvard Kennedy School and co-founder of WIEGO (Women in Informal Employment: Globalizing and Organizing). 'Often the contractors are from the same communities and have very slim margins themselves. There should be joint liability up the chain to the lead firm.'

The problem, Dr Chen says, is that multinational corporations often do not know, and do not want to know, what is happening at the dark end of their supply chain. The challenge therefore is to bring homeworkers into focus and ensure they are visible as workers rather than remaining an invisible part of the chain that relates to the factory, but not to brands or retailers. WIEGO is pushing for national and regionally agreed piecework rates for homeworkers, to give workers a standard to collectively bargain over.

Another problem is the distinct absence of laws covering homework. Over twenty years has passed since 1996 when the ILO adopted the Home Work Convention, known as C177. The convention aimed to promote and protect the rights of people working at home to create products for an employer. C177 states homeworkers should be treated like salaried workers in the formal economy. They should be fairly paid, receive social benefits like maternity leave, have safe workplaces and the right to collectively organise themselves. In twenty years, only ten countries have signed up to C177: Albania, Argentina, Belgium, Bosnia and Herzegovina, Bulgaria, Finland, Ireland, North Macedonia, Netherlands and Tajikistan.

This leaves the overwhelming majority of the world's homeworkers without any recognition of their rights. In Pakistan, for example, homeworkers are not covered by Pakistan's labour laws, though two provinces – Sindh and Punjab – have both passed policies to recognise the rights of homeworkers and to give them social protection, and in 2018 the Sindh Assembly passed the Sindh Home-Based Workers Act.[39]

To ban or not to ban?

A combination of shocking exposés, and the corporate desire for supply chains that can be presented as squeaky clean, means there are often calls to simply ban homework.

Dr Martha Chen is adamant a ban would be 'a terrible, terrible mistake'. She points to the Pakistani football industry as an example of a counterproductive ban. Recent statistics have Pakistan accounting for 80 per cent of the world's match-grade footballs. This craft, based on stitching together millions of small leather hexagons and pentagons, was valued at nearly $50m each year for Pakistan's economy.[40]

In the past, much of this stitching was done by women in their homes. When child labour was found – the result of children sometimes working with their mothers to make footballs – production was moved into workshops and factories. This ignored the social barriers in Pakistan which prevent women from working in male-dominated public spaces like factories.

'The problem is, in Pakistan, some women are not allowed to work outside the home,' explains Dr Chen. 'The move had very contradictory outcomes; not only were the children no longer working on footballs, but the mothers couldn't work in the sector either.'

Child labour exists because families are extremely poor, so children work to help meet quotas. Banning what could be a woman's only socially acceptable means for making money in order to try and eradicate child labour is entirely counterproductive. Only improved pay and conditions for homeworkers will stop children working.

While Dr Chen sees homework as 'the dark underbelly of the global system', she also sees it as something that enables women to earn money if gender norms are so stacked against them that they cannot work outside the home. 'Don't ban homework,' Dr Chen says. 'See it as an essential component of the global production system and one that allows women to work from their home if they have to. Some have to because of cultural or gender norms, or some have to because at certain times in their lives they are juggling all the things that women have to juggle.'

More understanding is also needed of women's desire to protect their children. A lack of after-school facilities means mothers would often rather their children stayed home with them, than get into trouble out in the streets.

Bundle of sticks

Instead of banning homeworkers, an alternative is the creation of collective organisations and unions that push for decent pay and conditions. Back at the Labour Education Foundation in Lahore, project coordinator Jalvat Ali lists some of the obstacles she has faced while organising homeworkers over the past twelve years, the main one being gendered social norms that see women prevented from leaving their homes by husbands, fathers or brothers. Women also find themselves restricted to their homes by the duty of bringing up their children. 'Even for a training workshop they say – what we will do with our children?' Jalvat says.

For Jalvat, this restriction on movement is a key reason why homeworkers in Pakistan are predominantly women. The requirement to stay in the home, and being tied to the home by children, means women often end up having to work there too. Once they are isolated the expectation is they will accept being paid whatever is offered.

In a factory setting it is much easier for a trade union to organise people. Work is done in shifts, so organisers can find large groups of people together and educate and recruit them. Once a critical mass has been reached a union can sit down to negotiate pay and conditions with the factory employer. Homeworkers on the other hand may be completely unaware of their rights; they may also be unwilling to join a union because they think doing so will mean losing their work.[41]

Jalvat says under such conditions it has been hard to get women homeworkers to trust outsiders, or to entertain the idea that things could change. The sheer volume of work shouldered by women homeworkers also often leaves scant time for labour organising. But recently, Jalvat says, there has been a shift, with women stepping forward: 'Home-based workers do not organise themselves but when we intervene and tell them their rights and how to get benefits from the middlemen and how to enhance their wages, they do,' she explains. 'There are many women who are with us, who are leaders now, and who are our source in communities to mobilise other workers. Initially we just have to activate them.'

'A worker who is not in a union is like a single stick. She can easily be broken or bent to the will of her employer.' So said Mary Macarthur in 1907, as she organised women homeworkers in the chain-making industry. A trade union on the other hand, Mary said, is like a bundle of sticks – workers are bound together and are strong because of it. Today, organising homeworkers is achievable and two recent examples, one from Indonesia and one from Bulgaria, show some of the possibilities.

As the fourth biggest producer of shoes in the world, in 2017, Indonesia produced 886 million pairs of shoes, 4.1 per cent of the global total.[42] Exporting shoes is a vital part of Indonesia's economy, and accounts for over half a million jobs. Nike has used Indonesian factories since 1988, and Bata has been producing there as far back as 1940.[43]

German shoe brand Ara owns a subsidiary factory in Indonesia. On its website Ara states: *Ara shoes are created by a production process requiring intensive hand-crafting and up to 130 individual operations.* In 2017, the German research association Südwind-Institut interviewed thirty-seven Indonesian homeworkers who received work from the PT Ara Shoes Indonesia factory, a facility that retires workers once they reach the age of fifty.

The PT Ara homeworkers told Südwind-Institut staff that their job was to sew uppers onto shoe soles; they received two bags containing ten pairs of shoes and had two days to sew them. They were paid per piece regardless of the hours they worked or the complexity of the shoe, be it sandal or boot. A third of the homeworkers said their children had to help them sew shoes. If shoes did not meet the factory's standards, workers were fined.

Contrary to Ara's calculations, wages were catastrophically low. The average monthly wage was €27.74 – a quarter of the local minimum wage. The homeworkers told Südwind they were ready to collectively push Ara for better wages. Südwind returned to Germany and took their findings to Ara's headquarters. Ara responded by raising the wages of the homeworkers, providing new bags with which to transport their shoes and opened a depot closer to the homes so the workers didn't have to travel quite so far. These steps were welcomed both as an improvement and a sign that taking action works. However, Südwind are quick to point out that the wages are still low and a number of 'the underlying problems have not been completely solved.'[44]

WIEGO also list the case of the Home-Based Workers' Association in Bulgaria which formed in 2002. The association discovered shoemaking was being outsourced to 150 workers in a number of villages surrounding the town of Petrich in the southwest of Bulgaria. They also discovered workers in the villages were being paid less than workers in Petrich – BGN 0.60 to stitch a pair of shoes in Petrich, compared with BGN 0.40 in the villages. After four months of building trust with the villagers, the association finally convinced them it was time to ask for a pay rise.

The village women gathered together and told the agent that unless they were paid the same as the women in Petrich they would stop working. The agent, who was just a distributor, rebuffed their request, believing that they would be back and begging for work before too long. With the backing of the association, and workers in Petrich, the village women stopped working.

Raw materials were being delivered to the villages twice a week but as production stopped, the agent's employer started panicking. Stitching shoes is a skilled job and shoe workers are not easily replaced at short notice. Losing 1,000 pairs of shoes per day, and facing the threat of paying substantial damages for unfulfilled contracts, the employer gave in after two weeks. Women from eight villages gained the same wages as those in Petrich.[45]

The hidden truth

The informal sector is the hidden truth of globalisation: as companies encounter increasingly unstable markets, they rely upon flexible and decentralised working arrangements to cut their costs and pass on the pain of fluctuating demand to the most vulnerable communities.

Globalisation is a process of interdependence and intermingling, but not in a joyous or mutually beneficial sense. As supply chains get longer and more complex, manufacturing is compartmentalised, subcontracted and spread across the world. As multinational corporations pursue this relentless desire for rock-bottom costs, Global South homes are targeted as manufacturing sites.

Isolated, and with corporations taking advantage of unfair gender relations, fighting back is a gargantuan task for homeworkers. The use of these ultra-exploited workers keeps consumer goods at very low prices; it is a strategy that creates corporate profit by squeezing labour rather than increasing the price of goods.

Because homes are not equipped for working, this maelstrom of economic and gender exploitation is globalisation borne by the backs, eyes, fingers, skin and lungs of the poorest people in the world. This pain is why items like shoes continue to be so cheap. And yet we see none of this process – it is kept almost entirely hidden by the web of mythology that makes up branding and labels. A web that pretends that everything is fine and dandy.

CHAPTER 4

Branded

On 9 July 1769, butcher's assistant Daniel Spencer set his tankard down on the bar and left the Kings Head pub in Holborn to walk home through darkened streets. With ale in his veins and thoughts of bed on his mind, Spencer was caught unawares when a man knocked hard into his shoulder. Turning, Spencer found himself surrounded by six figures. A blow knocked him to his knees and he was soon pinned down on the cold cobblestones.

Spencer's attackers proceeded to rob him of his hat, the six halfpennies in his pocket and his shoes complete with metal shoe buckles. As they ran off, they threw Spencer an old pair of slippers and an old hat, laughing at him and calling out that exchange was not robbery.

Struggling to his now bare feet, Daniel Spencer followed the attackers and saw them go into a nearby alehouse. He called the Constable of the Night and reported the crime. The constable, whose official occupation was that of shoemaker, began his detective work and eventually found Daniel Spencer's shoes in a Holborn shop called Elson's.

The shopkeeper identified John Stafford as the person who had come in to sell the stolen goods. John Stafford was arrested and charged with violent theft on the King's highway. Despite producing character references, Stafford was unable to come up with a convincing defence to gain either freedom or clemency. He was found guilty and sentenced to death.[1]

During the trial Daniel Spencer swore he recognised his stolen shoes by the two rows of nails round their heels. Had he bought from a different shoemaker, there might have been a specific mark he could have pointed to.

This is what happened to shoemaker Edward Pitman who, in a separate case, did a double-take while walking past a pawnshop in the London parish of St Ann's. Hanging in the window were several pairs of shoes he was sure were his. When Pitman asked who had pawned them, he was told it was Charles Potter, a man who had worked as Pitman's assistant for five years before being fired on suspicion of thieving. The case went to court, with Pitman cross-examined as to how he knew the shoes were his. He replied that they bore his mark.

Q: What is your mark?
Pitman: There was the letter P.
Q: Does not the letter P. stand for his name, and a hundred names besides yours?
Pitman: It may, but I knew my man's work, and from among other shoes pick'd them out, and they answered to the pawn-broker's book, as brought by him.

Charles Potter was also found guilty and sentenced to seven years' transportation to Australia, a brutal punishment that many did not survive.[2]

Similarly, Anne Pugh was found guilty of stealing a pair of women's shoes by hiding them in a basket of fruit. Shoemaker William Clement told the court: 'Here is my mark on the inside of the upper leather; they are my property.' The shoes were worth 2 shillings. Anne Pugh's punishment was to be stripped to the waist and publicly whipped.[3]

Stamped

London in the 1760s was a brutal and diseased place, a city at the heart of an empire, stuffed with alehouses, tenement workshops, docks, mud roads and squalid housing. Human waste was carted away by night-soil men, and water had to be hand-drawn from communal pumps. Yet this flea-bitten hell hole is noted as the place and the moment where the modern world was born.[4] For the shoe industry it marked the birth of branding.

These prosecutions are cases of the poor robbing the poor, and a mark in a shoe or a stamp on the sole that only one shoemaker can decipher could hardly be called branding. But away from the slums were the squares, parks and mansions of the West End. Life on the other side of the divide involved dances, dinners, drawing rooms – seeing and being seen. This was a moment of population growth, technological advancement and an expanding upper and middle class. Bespoke shoes were still commissioned for wealthy feet, but extravagant, fashionable, ready-to-wear shoes were available for a lower price from warehouses or expensive shoe shops.[5]

For the makers of these shoes, there was a new problem. Once upon a time, village or small-town life meant people lived within a stone's throw of their local shoemaker. If they loved (or hated) the shoes they'd bought, they knew precisely where to go. The same shoemaker might make every pair a person would ever wear. Now the market was vastly bigger, with shoes made on the other side of the city, the country or even in unimaginably exotic places like Paris. How could shoemakers help customers trace them once they had sent their products out into the world?

'From the 1760s, thereabouts, is when shoemakers started putting labels in shoes, little paper labels that they would stick inside on the lining on the insole,' says Rebecca Shawcross, senior shoe curator at the Northampton Museum and Art Gallery. 'They're all individual and they basically say who the maker was, and where they were based. With this new increased market opening up an audience for ready-made, it was like advertising themselves.'

This information, along with pictorial trade cards, allowed customers to repeat buy from the same makers. It allowed craftspeople to show off and be acknowledged for their skills. It was also a way of taking responsibility, Rebecca says, for shoemakers who were proud of their work, or who wanted people to know where to complain.

Most of these little paper labels have been found on women's shoes and all on shoes made for wealthy people. Rebecca attributes this to the fact that fancy women's shoes have been more commonly kept and collected. The shoes of the poor are rarely found and, when discovered, are so worn and repaired that no labels – if there ever were any – could possibly survive.

Emotional ties

'From the beginning, we've tried to create an emotional tie with the consumer,' stated Nike founder Phil Knight in 1992. 'Why do people get married – or do anything? Because of emotional ties. That's what builds long-term relationships with the consumer, and that's what our campaigns are about.'[6]

In the modern world, labels have come a long way from hand-written slips of paper pasted onto shoe linings. Advertising and branding are a multibillion-dollar business. Far from the workshops of the 1760s, the American Marketing Association defines a brand as 'a customer experience represented by a collection of images and ideas'. Often, it refers to a symbol such as a name, logo, slogan and design scheme.[7] In 2018, $628.63b was spent on advertising around the globe. By 2020, it is predicted that 50 per cent of all adverts will be on digital platforms.[8]

The power of branding today is such that it can convince people to pay a premium for a product that is functionally identical to a cheaper one.[9] Branding is to a large extent the creation of mythology around otherwise identical goods, mythologies that lead people to feel not only a sense of loyalty, but a sense of self when they encounter certain brands. It is a system that means Nike Inc. has annual revenues of $36.4b.[10]

Dr Juliet Schor says there is no single reason why people consume branded goods. Some brands, she says, have simply cornered the market in terms of superior design. These designs create a status value for products which people are willing to pay more for, over and above the original cost of the design. Dr Schor calls this an 'additional status premium'.

But what about products which are functionally identical and have no major design differentiation, from shirts, to shoes, to bottles of water? When people pay a premium for this kind of product, branding has created a belief in status, that something is different.

'They don't understand their purchase as a status, they don't think,

"Oh, I'm a status consumer, I need to take the brand",' explains Dr Schor. 'They have a sense that the branded good is superior. That superiority, depending on what it is, takes different forms. They might think it's longer lasting, or it tastes better, or it looks better, etc. The brands are able to create a perception of product superiority.'

Other people buy branded products because they feel they have to. 'For some people it's because they don't want to be caught dead in a generic because a generic is a stigmatised product,' says Dr Schor. 'Sneakers are a great example where the failure to have a good logo in certain circles is really stigmatising because the logo has been set as the minimum acceptable level of sneaker. So then people who can afford it will pay for the logo.'

Dr Schor defines this as 'defensive branded consumption', where people feel compelled to defend themselves against the social stigma of owning unbranded products. As we saw at Sneaker Con, this stigmatisation, and the linking of brands with self-esteem, is happening at a younger and younger age, with small children, in particular boys, now aware of which trainer brand they want to wear and which feels stigmatising.[11]

Labels create a hierarchy of the most fashionable shoemakers, allowing people to show off their wealth and taste. But like in the 1700s, with the exception of sportswear, shoe labels are often inside shoes and invisible when a shoe is being worn. This has led to brands copying sportswear and plastering their shoes with logos or using tell-tale signs like recognisable prints or colour schemes.

Social desire for logos and branding, as much as for the objects themselves, has led some consumption theorists to hope the shift towards craving images and social meaning, instead of material products, might produce an economy with less production, or even a weightless economy partly based in the virtual world.[12] It is a line of thinking Dr Schor dismisses. Signs and symbols, corporate logos on shoes, change rapidly under fast fashion. A shoe that is 'hyped' and worth hundreds of pounds at Sneaker Con one day can become a 'brick' the next. In the age of social media more and more brands pop up every day, all producing yet more consumer products. Basing value on symbolism, rather than usability, means it lingers for a brief moment and then needs replacing, which creates an increase in production and further stress on both people and the planet.[13]

Rebecca Shawcross also sees shoe branding as a social experience, linked with the desire to belong to a group. 'It's wanting to be part of something, feeling you identify, not so much with the brand as with the group that wears that brand, like punks and Dr. Martens,' she says, arguing that in one sense the type of footwear doesn't matter as much as the fact that people wear it and identify as part of a group.

Logomania previously peaked in the 1980s and 1990s when everything from underwear to sweatshirts and shoes became drenched in overt logos. It was a trend to match the money-mad conspicuous consumption fever of a period that defined people's worth by their bank balance. Logomania took a hit with the financial crisis in 2008, when it was no longer considered tasteful to display cash in such a gauche manner, a sentiment that gave rise to the 'stealth wealth' trend.

Fast forward from the 1980s to the 2020s, and logos are back in a big way. In a world where life is documented and shared on social media, logos are the perfect advertising tool. Big logos turn white T-shirts and boating shoes into company adverts, and turn selfies into billboards.[14]

Social media has also intensified the relationship between celebrity and shoes. The sneakerheads at Sneaker Con knew exactly what hype was made of, describing its creation as depending upon 'famous people and a limited run'. The current celebrity God in trainers is Kanye West, who leveraged his music industry reputation and design skills to create Yeezys with adidas.

Similar celebrity collaborations include Puma appointing Rihanna as its creative director, Roger Federer's ten-year sponsorship deal with Nike followed by a deal with Uniqlo and Taylor Swift becoming a brand ambassador for Keds. Despite retiring from basketball in 2003, Michael Jordan recently earned $100m from Nike in just twelve months, bringing his personal fortune to $1.3b.[15] In 2015, $3b worth of Jordans were sold in the US. Nike wants this figure to hit $4.5b globally by 2020.[16]

One investigation into sponsorship levels found that in 2017, adidas paid €11m more to Lionel Messi than to Zinédine Zidane fifteen years earlier. €11m would have allowed adidas to pay decent wages to more than 44,170 Indonesian workers or 52,600 Vietnamese workers in garment factories for one year.[17]

The power of celebrity endorsement is largely the promise of transference, that a celebrity's wealth, achievements or attractiveness will somehow be transferred by wearing the trainers they have been shown promoting. It is a promise of a connection to a person or lifestyle, where no possibility of a real connection likely exists.

When Nike announced a sponsorship deal with NFL player Colin Kaepernick, it was aiming at capturing both his sporting skill and rebelliousness. Kaepernick had become world famous in 2016 for getting down on one knee during the pre-match US national anthem. 'I am not going to stand up to show pride in a flag for a country that oppresses black people and people of colour,' Kaepernick said in a statement. Kaepernick's endorsement by Nike led to online protests by Trump supporters and, overwhelmingly, angry white men who filmed themselves burning or binning Nikes.

But for Nike, association with Kaepernick was a clever business move, the acquisition of his bravery and radicalism without any need to confront their own violation of people of colour across the Global South. It is a reminder that to succeed, radical critiques must go beyond branding, into the heart of the system itself.

Legit Check

In the middle of Sneaker Con is a long queue to a table. At the table sits a serious-looking young man wearing glasses and a black hoody. Around his neck is a red ID lanyard. Throughout the day hundreds of people will stand anxiously in line to seek his opinion. The ruling this oracle will give is whether their shoes are real or counterfeit. This is the Legit Check station. Fakes are outlawed from Sneaker Con and anyone found touting them gets kicked out. People wanting to sell or trade sneakers have a far easier time if they have been verified and tagged.

In the queue is seventeen-year-old Martin from London. He has floppy hair, glasses and a white hoody. In his hands are a pair of tattered trainers with holes in the soles. He spent £200 on these 'Yeezys', buying them from a website that he acknowledges was not particularly reputable. Martin is with his friend Stewart. The boys are both at college. Stewart washes dishes in a restaurant to earn money to spend on clothes and shoes.

When Martin reaches the front of the queue it is no surprise when his consultation lasts less than 30 seconds. 'He said they were obviously fake.' Martin shrugs but doesn't seem downhearted. 'People thought they were real when I bought them so I'm fine with that. I'm not gonna wear them anymore now.' He says he will keep the grubby shoes on display at home. Stewart agrees not to tell anyone they were fakes.

Fake branded shoes have become a big issue in the sneaker world. Deliberate scarcity of cult-status brands creates a market for counterfeits, as the vast majority of fans miss out on buying the real thing, but do not want to pay $1,500 for a flipped pair. Instead they turn to black-market sellers who advertise 'replicas' on sites like Instagram and the Repsneakers page on Reddit. In forums, sneaker fans discuss their purchases, comfort each other over worries about being 'called out' for wearing fakes and make recommendations about which dealers are the best.

The symbolic power of branding can grow so strong that it becomes detached from the object it is supposed to be promoting. This is partly what has happened in the world of counterfeit shoes, where people are so fixated on owning or associating with a brand that the question of whether a shoe is genuine is less important.

China is the heartland of replica shoes, the city of Wenzhou even has a shop called Yeezy which only sells counterfeits.[18] In the east of China, the city of Putian has been a sneaker manufacturing hub since the 1980s, and it is now home to many online counterfeit dealers. One dealer, who caters to the English-speaking market, told the *LA Times* that on a slow day he sells 20 to 30 pairs of replica sneakers online; the day after a new release, this jumps to 120 pairs.[19]

Online fakes range from the terrible to the almost imperceptible. The ability to create convincing replica shoes comes from skilled shoemakers who have worked in factories for years, moles who sell designs and materials to counterfeiters, factory workers who throw shoes over the factory wall and even official factories which switch to producing replicas by night.[20]

Floggers

Because shoes are such a visual, social product, sneaker culture is closely linked with sites like YouTube where vloggers review shoes, plug businesses and build hype for forthcoming releases. But YouTube has also become a hub for the promotion of fakes.

It is a situation that exasperates old-school fans like Scott Frederick who explains how wannabe vloggers create YouTube channels and begin reviewing sneakers that have just released in stores. Sometimes the vlogger will realise that, being new to the scene, reviewing shoes that have already been released will not bring the type of attention they seek.

'From there they will either seek out, or be sought out by, manufacturers of fake shoes – these guys will try to solicit all the time,' Scott says. 'They then get a steady supply of fake shoes or "early release" pairs and they review them, give everyone an on-foot view and gain a lot of followers.'

In return for the shoes, the YouTubers plug the sites who have been supplying them – unknowingly, or knowingly, sending hundreds of trusting viewers direct to counterfeiters. 'If there was some disclosure that these may or may not be authentic it wouldn't be as shady,' Scott continues. 'But so many people think what they are buying from the promoted sites is real, and that's really not fair.'

Having been in the sneaker scene for so many years, Scott finds it 'kind of mind-blowing' that so many people get scammed. 'I would be able to pick out someone that's shady within a matter of seconds and stay away from them,' he says. 'I guess for newer buyers it's much more difficult.'

It is difficult, agrees James Needham, who worked as director of authentication at the ToeBox website. At his stand at Sneaker Con he holds up a pair of Yeezy 350 V2 Beluga 2.0s bought for £400: 'These are the most faked shoe around at the minute, the fakes have almost gone 1-to-1, but there's some things that they just can't replicate.'

Needham explains how he spots a fake: 'I check the material they use on the shoe, as often the fake factories can't get hold of the same material. Another thing to check on this model is the insole, and how well defined the print is. You can also check the stitching that attaches the sole to the upper shoe. I also check how the heel-tab lines up with the writing on the side of the shoe, and the stitching around the heel collar as the fake factories use less stitches and material.'

This particular pair of Yeezys turns out to be real, leading to a big sigh of relief from the customer and his mum, but there are thousands upon thousands of fakes out in the world. The power of the brand is so strong that even an imitation of it brings social status and the willingness to risk anything from wasting money to criminal charges. The collective compulsion to chase imitation shoes reveals not just a desire to dodge exorbitant prices, but the driving power of wanting to belong.

It also shows the social value of the shoe is in its branding, its logo and design. Both these elements, it turns out, are detachable from the 'real' thing. In buying fakes, people are not getting an authentic shoe, but if everyone thinks it is real, they get the authentic experience of receiving praise and status. It begs the question: what, if anything, is the difference between real and fake?

Countering counterfeits

Interpol statistics for goods seized at EU borders in 2015 show 'sports shoes' are the leading counterfeit item when measured by caseload; by unit volume, cigarettes were the most seized item.[21] Interpol have also discovered an increasing volume of labels and packaging being smuggled into the EU, which are then used to brand fake products, from cigarettes and batteries to shoes. Interpol state that gangs from China make shoes on the Italian mainland or smuggle them in from Asia through the port of Naples. Brand logos are often added only once the shoes have reached the point of sale, to avoid scrutiny from authorities.[22]

Scamming someone by selling them an expensive but low-quality item they believe to be real, is clearly not a good thing to do, but is knowingly buying counterfeit shoes really that bad? Should we feel sympathy if a billion-dollar company is denied profit and intellectual property rights, especially if it can be argued that the people wearing fakes still act as billboards for the brand?

While it may be hard to summon up sympathy for brands, there are hidden costs to fakes. Minimal quality control in the world of counterfeit goods poses an immediate threat to consumer welfare. The risk is obvious with regard to counterfeit medicines, but long-term injury risks also apply to uncertified sports shoes or high heels.

And just who are you handing your data over to? The City of London Police highlight the case of 'Emily', a woman whose identity was stolen after she bought phoney bridesmaid shoes online. Having shared her name, address and credit card details to buy the shoes, she ended up with four different counterfeit shoe websites being run under her name.

The total lack of regulation around counterfeit goods also spells disaster for the environment. There are no rules governing the use of toxic dyes or chemicals with fake goods, nor are there any rules surrounding the disposal of toxic factory run-off.[23] When hauls of fakes are found they are often incinerated or publicly crushed by police forces, leading to an extra layer of waste.

If that wasn't bad enough, the International Labour Organization has linked counterfeit goods to workshops where there is little respect for labour laws. Practices highlighted include the confiscation of immigrant workers' identity papers and housing illegal workers in hazardous and unhealthy dormitories.[24] There is already scant protection for people producing goods like shoes and handbags – when workers end up in a criminal framework, they become even more vulnerable to threats and violence.

Opposite ends of the village

Wollaston is a village of beautiful stone cottages, ancient trees and narrow roads leading to misty distant hills. There is no litter, it has its own museum and the Parish Council has put up dozens of green history plaques.

One of these green plaques reads: *Walkers Factory – Wollaston's First Shoe Factory. Built in 1883 by Mr Pratt Walker. Produced high quality boots and shoes till 1934.* Walkers Factory became an armaments plant during World War II and was eventually converted into flats in 2005.

Like much of Northamptonshire, Wollaston has a long history of shoe manufacture. In the 1960s, seven shoe factories and a rubber vulcanising plant dominated the village. The Wollaston Heritage Society describes how these factories brought in life and industry with busloads of workers arriving every morning from surrounding parishes.[25] Such was the demand for depositing wages that the village had five banks and a post office. Seven pubs also offered workers the chance to relieve themselves of their hard-earned salaries. But when the factories closed, most of these services blinked out, leaving Wollaston tucked in sleepy hills. What remains of this vibrant trade is two shoe factories at opposite ends of the village.

Dr Klaus Maertens (also sometimes spelt Märtens) worked as an army doctor in Nazi Germany during the second World War. Legend has it that after injuring his foot on a skiing holiday he found his army boots so uncomfortable that he worked to develop a new design with a thick air-cushioned sole. After the war Maertens headed for Munich to try and sell his invention. He went into business with a friend, Dr Herbert Funck, who had a Luxembourg passport so could circumvent the post-war ban on German citizens trading with the US army. The pair bought up rubber from abandoned Luftwaffe airfields and started producing shoe soles.[26]

As the business grew and became more successful, it caught the eye of British shoemaking company R. Griggs & Co. This Wollaston family business specialised in work boots and had supplied the British army during the war. Bill Griggs contacted Dr Maertens and bought the exclusive licence to produce his air-cushioned soles.[27]

Griggs anglicised the name Maertens, came up with a logo, the product name AirWair and the slogan 'With Bouncing Soles'. But in order to produce the new eight-holed boot, R. Griggs & Co. needed help. Griggs made shoes using a process called cementing, which involves using an adhesive to attach the upper to the sole. Air-cushioned soles, however, had to be welted on – a more specialist and labour-intensive process.

Enter the second factory. At the other end of Wollaston is a factory called NPS Shoes. The Northamptonshire Productive Society (NPS) was founded in 1881 by five Wollaston shoemakers who got tired of a gang master parcelling out work to them. They decided to band together and apply for contracts as a collective. They were so successful that they went on to build and expand their own factory.

NPS Shoes are experts in a technique called Goodyear welting which involves stitching the component parts of the upper, and the insole, onto a specially made welt – a ribbon of leather that runs around the edge of the upper. The shoe or boot is then stitched again to attach it to its sole. It was because of this expertise that Griggs turned to NPS Shoes in 1959.

'Griggs made the top part, they closed the upper and brought it to us where we welted it and we affixed the sole,' explains Christian Castle at NPS Shoes. '[Griggs] granted us a sub-licence to make on their behalf. So we made for AirWair for about thirty-five years, from about 1960 to the mid-1990s. It was always under the brand Solovair – "Sole Of Air", so it always said, "Dr. Martens – Made By Solovair".'

The Dr. Martens brand went on to become world famous; millions of boots were made using top-quality factories across Northamptonshire. The brand became synonymous with 'British-ness', beloved by celebrities and skinheads, popstars, punks and even the Pope. Sales peaked at nearly 10 million pairs in 1998.[28]

But love for brands can be fickle. Dr. Martens was selling 60 per cent of its products in the US[29] where trainers were becoming increasingly popular and where Timberland boots battled for atten-tion. In 2001, R. Griggs & Co. had losses of £20m. Despite Max Griggs and his son Stephen being on the *Sunday Times* Rich List, the company kept losing money.[30] Facing a similar outlook in 2002, Griggs announced it was moving its manufacturing to China.

The announcement was met with shock and anger. 'The workers have been given a kick in the teeth – with a Doc Marten,' declared local trade unionist John Tully.[31] Despite a prolonged outcry, six months later, on Friday, 28 March 2003, a thousand British Dr. Martens workers clocked off for the last time.[32] It was a devastat-ing moment for the British shoe industry. 'Apart from our members losing their jobs, it affects the local communities and it affects the suppliers, the leather producers, the component producers,' said John Tully at the time of the closure. 'This is really going to have a knock-on effect throughout the county.'

But the power of the brand was strong. A Coca-Cola executive once said: 'If Coca-Cola were to lose all of its production-related assets in a disaster, the company would survive. By contrast, if all consumers were to have a sudden lapse of memory and forget everything related to Coca-Cola, the company would go out of business.'[33] This was true for Dr. Martens; its value was not in its factories but in its brand. The brand survived and in 2013, R. Griggs & Co. was bought for £300m by Permira Funds, an investment management firm. At the end of 2019, it was reported that Permira Funds planned to sell the brand for £1b.[34]

At the other end of the village, NPS Shoes were in crisis. By 2006, all they had was a factory which had now lost its biggest customer. NPS Shoes had no brand identity or shop of their own, and orders had all but dried up. The factory had remained a workers' cooperative since 1881; you only had to work there for a week to become an equal shareholder. At a downhearted meeting, the workers reluctantly voted to close themselves down and sell their building to a property developer.

Then came a counteroffer from local businessman Ivor Tilley who believed there was still a market for British-made boots and shoes. Tilley guaranteed six months' more work if the cooperative would sell him the company. The sale went through and Tilley recruited his son-in-law Christian Castle as managing director. Castle replaced handwritten ledgers with computers and set to work turning 'Solovair' into a brand. Where 90 per cent of NPS Shoes output used to be for other brands, now 60 per cent of what they make is Solovair. The most popular line is its speciality: an eight-holed air-cushioned boot.

This former mainstay of British shoe manufacturing has split in two, as if the right boot and the left boot walked off in separate directions. The Dr. Martens boot kept the classic branding and promise of 'Britishness' (which was actually Germanness in disguise) and marched off to China and Vietnam. Despite neither the boots nor the component parts being made in Britain (though the brand has reopened a token factory in Wollaston to produce about 1 per cent of global output),[35] the brand brings in £348.6m in retail, wholesale and online sales.[36]

The left boot meanwhile stayed in Wollaston, where it is made from British or European component parts in the original factory, with the original tools. But without the symbolic value of a famous logo and branding, NPS Shoes assets are valued at less than £1m according to Companies House.[37]

Visitors to Wollaston can compare the two boots for quality as both companies have factory shops. Dr. Martens is housed in the old village smithy, Solovair in the old NPS leather store. They can decide for themselves if one has more substance and is going to last longer. They can decide what a logo counts for, and whether anyone except shareholders benefits from symbolic value. They can decide for themselves which, if any, is the 'real' boot.

A fifteen-minute drive from Wollaston is the market town of Wellingborough, another prime site for shoe manufacture until the pressures of the global economy devastated local industry. Wellingborough now has the second highest proportion of deprived households and the lowest weekly wages in Northamptonshire. Old shoe factories are easy to spot: some have been converted into housing and some, like the old Rudlens factory, a beautiful red-brick giant, sit empty, fallen into decay as the domain of pigeons and empty beer cans.

In between a Polish grocery and a council-run 'Library Plus' is a branch of Shoe Zone. A strong synthetic smell rises from the racks of shoes, including dozens of black eight-holed boots priced £14.99 in the sale. At the lowest rung of the boot ladder, these imports weigh very little and would not last long as a work boot or as protection from rain or snow. There is nothing to indicate where they were made. The manager says it's usually Turkey or China but advises checking with head office. An ignoble outcome for the eight-holed boot, once a jewel of British manufacturing.

Lux?

When corporations discarded factories in favour of subcontracting, they were freed from manufacturing costs and able to follow exploited labour and materials around the world. They could deny responsibility for human rights abuses in their supply chains and concentrate on the real money spinners: design and branding.

A catchy description for branding is the 'emotional aftertaste' that results from an experience with a company or product.[38] The purpose of branding is to form a positive aftertaste and positive associations in people's minds which then can be harnessed to make money.[39] One thing that can spoil the aftertaste of a brand is news of exploited factory workers, environmental destruction or sexually harassed models. Branding's other job therefore is to obscure supply chains.

In the global marketplace, labels have come to mean everything and yet they mean nothing. The label on the outside of a shoe might be used to construct an identity for a consumer, but what does the label inside say about the person who made the shoe for them? What does it say about the factory or the wages that were paid? Whether the shoe contains carcinogenic materials, whether the glue that stuck the shoe together is toxic and if the leather process involved chopping down part of a rainforest? Shoe labels often say less than clothes – telling customers absolutely nothing except the name of the brand and the shoe size. By law, manufacturers and retailers in the UK are required to state what material forms 80 per cent of a shoe's upper, its lining and its outer sole. This can either be in English or in pictorial form.[40] The European Union has attempted to introduce mandatory country-of-origin labelling for non-food products, but currently 'made-in' labelling is voluntary. Instead of answers, the blankness of labels and the veneer of branding work to hide ugly truths.

Just because something is expensive does not mean it has been ethically made. No matter how much a shoe costs, it has to be made somewhere. Despite being labelled as a luxury or designer product, higher prices for consumers do not guarantee better conditions for workers or communities. What an exorbitant price tag does reflect is a larger surplus value – profit. This surplus could ensure decent wages for factory workers, the people who create the value with their labour. But what happens instead is that two stages of production, distribution and branding, take approximately 60 per cent of the final price of a shoe.[41]

A report by Italian academics, titled *The Real Cost of Our Shoes*, outlines an upward spiral of money that makes the rich richer, and the powerful even more powerful. The richer a brand, the more capital it has to spend on marketing campaigns. The more this marketing increases its selling power, the more money the brand makes and the more it can exercise power over its suppliers. This creates a huge 'imbalance in bargaining power' in shoe supply chains.[42]

In the shoe industry, this power is commercial. A small number of luxury brands have access to the luxury market, and they hold the key to a dollar-green sea of wealthy shoppers who have developed a penchant for certain logos. On the other hand, there are a huge number of supplier factories competing to supply luxury goods. The brands set prices and conditions by playing the suppliers off against each other. In the process they further increase their profits.[43]

Suppliers are often cowed into not discussing their exploitation, for fear of losing customers or because of clauses written into their contracts. The Italian academics concluded that this has created a field ripe for abuse. A supplier might speak out once their relationship with a luxury brand has ended, or in some cases because they have gone bankrupt as a result of the behaviour of a luxury brand.

Yet expensive brands are not seen as being as notorious for bad practices as high street brands. This is for two reasons. Firstly because expensive brands have successfully cultivated an air of respectability through their branding. Secondly, NGO investigations tend to concentrate on discounted retailers, because they are more ubiquitous. This means expensive brands have not been subject to the same level of scrutiny as high street brands, but scratch the surface and for many luxury companies the issues might well be the same.

Made in _____?

The Outward Processing Trade Scheme (OPT) is a specially designed blip in European Union legislation that allows manufacturers to export raw materials or semi-processed goods to non-EU countries and then re-import them when they have been worked on.[44] For shoes this means leather is cut in Italy, then exported by Italian manufacturers to eastern European countries like Albania, Bulgaria, Georgia, Moldova, Romania, Serbia and Ukraine.[45] Once the shoes have been assembled, they return, duty free, to Italy where they receive a 'Made In Italy' label and an expensive price tag. Sometimes the final stage in Italy can be as slight as polishing or being put in a box.

The biggest shoe factory in the east of North Macedonia is called Bargala. Visitors to the factory shop can peruse the dozens of British and European shoe brands made at the factory. Along the rows of shoes is a striking anomaly: many of the shoes are labelled 'Made In Italy'. The boxes say 'Made In Italy' and the imprints on the soles say 'Made In Italy'. Yet Bargala is hundreds of miles to the east of Italy, not even in the European Union.

The OPT system was developed by the European Union in the 1970s and was instigated by the governments of Germany and Italy who wanted to outsource labour-intensive garment and shoe production to low-cost satellites while safeguarding their own industries. Today German and Italian companies remain the biggest recipients of garments and shoes from eastern Europe.[46]

'"Made In Italy" just means finished in Italy,' says Lidija Milanovska, owner of the De Marco Dooel factory. 'We only stitch uppers here because if they are put together in Italy they can be called "Made In Italy".' Lidija says sometimes shoes from her factory go back and forth between different Balkan countries before finally being shipped to Italy. 'Shoppers in western Europe want a product that says "Made In Italy",' she concludes. 'For "Made In Macedonia" they would expect a lower price.'

This is a system based upon the idea that there is something inferior about the Balkans when compared to Italy. A preference for 'Italian' products is based on little more than prejudice from a bygone age and a deluded belief in 'Western superiority'. The continuation of the OPT system and the 'Made In Italy' façade, denies credit to the countries and people who actually make these shoes. It is a trap that keeps wages low and leaves countries like Macedonia less able to elevate their own brands or national status.

Every supply chain has an imbalance of power, with brands able to dictate costs and conditions to suppliers. But with the OPT, there is an even greater dependency on the part of the supplier because all they are supplying is factory labour. If they were doing other stages of production, like shoe design or sourcing materials, there would be areas where factories could make more money, but labour is a single, low-cost service that buyers constantly try to stamp down even further.[47] As a result of the OPT, workers in east and south-east Europe endure poverty wages and poor working conditions.

Eastern European and Baltic countries are kept in the yoke of the OPT by a promise that things will change after 'development'. Many of the countries, like Romania and Bulgaria, are already in the European Union and part of the EU customs-free system, so could be afforded an upgraded trading system, or one that enforces decent pay and working conditions.

Bettina Musiolek is a tall woman with a loud, infectious laugh. She grew up surrounded by the work of her mother, acclaimed East German fashion designer Hanna Musiolek. She now works in Dresden with the Clean Clothes Campaign. As a long-term campaigner for garment worker rights, she specialises in conditions in eastern Europe. 'The wages are just horrible, it is poverty wages, and it is basically nothing,' Bettina explains, 'It is far below a living wage, it is far below even a subsistence minimum for a family – it is far below everything.'

Exploitation in eastern Europe's garment and footwear industry is once again deeply gendered, with the overwhelming majority of workers being women who are driven into a cycle of loans and debt as they struggle to pay for basics. 'Families are constantly rescheduling loans because of the poverty wages,' Bettina continues. 'For schoolbooks, school uniforms, refrigerators, for everything they have to take out a loan. They can only get these loans if they are employed, which makes them additionally dependent on the employment despite the terrible conditions.'

Musiolek recounts one story of a HR manager in a factory in Serbia who stood in front of a production line holding a box of shoes that had not passed quality control. Taking the shoes out of the box, she threw them one by one at the workers while yelling insults. 'They are really treated like slaves,' Musiolek says. 'Not even like robots, but like slaves.'

Bettina says a game-changer in OPT factories would be stronger labour rights and trade union organisations led by women who care about organising women and know how to do it. The trade unions that should be actively organising in shoe factories are often feeble, male dominated and too close to employers. 'That is the most important problem,' Bettina says. 'In these countries you have a sort of nineteenth-century capitalism, with an extremely employer-friendly environment, and workers organisations that are extremely weak.'

Four corners of the globe

Shoes, and their component parts, come from all four corners of the globe, travelling along supply chains that stretch thousands of miles. The processes and truths of this production chain are hidden behind labels which have come to mean everything, and yet mean nothing. In order to understand why the world works as it does, we must look beyond branding to see what labels really mean, and what they allow corporations to get away with.

Some crises become so big that they can no longer be hidden. In the midst of a terrible refugee crisis, with millions of people displaced by war, environmental destruction and poverty, shoes lead us into the heart of migration. We turn now to one of the greatest injustices of the modern world, that our globalised society encourages flows of capital but prevents flows of desperate people.[48]

CHAPTER 5

A Mile in Refugee Shoes

On the side of a road in Calais are two black shoes. One is a trainer and the other a leather ankle boot, both are wet through and barely fit to be worn. They have been placed neatly together, their laces tied. On the curb next to the shoes sits a young Eritrean man. 'Very wet,' he says pointing to the shoes. 'Very cold.'

A group of seventy young Eritreans, all men except for one woman, have formed an orderly queue beside the white van of a refugee charity. The young man had finally reached the front of the queue and traded his odd shoes for a new pair of walking boots.

The Eritreans have made a temporary home in a patch of scrubland next to a roundabout. Despite the icy rain they have had their shelters raided by the French police who have confiscated their tents and sleeping bags. The walking boots and winter coats that are being handed out are intended to be worn 24/7 so even if a raid happens, the refugees won't freeze to death in the night.

Clare Moseley stands at the white van watching the line grow. She founded Care4Calais in September 2015 after witnessing conditions in French refugee camps. The people Clare met had walked across Europe in sandals or mangled trainers. Others walked with no shoes at all, just multiple pairs of layered socks. Many refugees refused her offers of walking boots at first, arguing that they were too heavy and made their feet feel squashed up and tied together. There was also widespread denial that Europe could possibly get colder than September.

Winters in Calais come with a bitter chill, wind and grey skies rule the flat, unforgiving landscape. For Clare, these winters mark the passage of time: 'That first winter I did not ever want to do this again. By the second winter I couldn't believe we were still here. By the third it had sunk in. I stopped thinking what I had thought before: we won't be here next winter as everyone will find out about this and fix it.'

That morning, preparation for the planned boot distribution started early. In the warehouse, crates of donated boots were sorted by size and checked for holes. Women's boots are often a better fit for the slight refugees arriving in Calais. On one pair, the name 'Emma' was hastily crossed out.

In the queue for the van is twenty-four-year-old Samuel; he has been in Calais for eight months and was in Paris for two months before that. Having left Eritrea, he travelled up through Sudan and Libya before crossing the Mediterranean to Italy where he lived for two months. He arrived at the van wearing wet trainers with a hole in them. It is his dream to reach Britain.

At their most basic, shoes act as a barrier between the human body and the earth. Like the rickety boats that carry people across the Mediterranean, shoes carry refugees along desert roads in Libya and through the snow on sub-zero Italian mountainsides. Like the boats they are often not fit for purpose, they sprout holes and fill up with water. Even when people reach Calais, they continue to walk for miles each day, to find food, water and shelter, to escape from police, to find lorries to hide in for an attempt at a Channel crossing.

Step by step

In her memoirs, the Russian writer Teffi recalls being one of the million Russians who fled the Bolshevik Revolution. Sailing away from Odessa on a steamship requisitioned by refugees, Teffi is ordered to scrub the deck. She did so wearing a pair of completely inappropriate silver shoes because she needed to save her practical footwear for life on whichever shore the ship might reach.[1]

One question we must repeatedly ask of shoes is what stories they tell about where they've come from? This is a question that must also be asked of the people who wear them. In the midst of the highest ever levels of international migration, now is a key time to scrutinise the global movement of people and its causes.

Not everyone who moves country is a refugee. The definition of an international migrant is a person living in a country other than her or his country of birth. In 2017 the number of international migrants worldwide stood at 258 million, a number that has rocketed from 173 million in 2000.[2]

In terms of which regions international migrants come from, 106 million were born in Asia, followed by 61 million who were born in Europe, 38 million were born in Latin America and the Caribbean and 36 million in Africa. Country-specific statistics show that India has sent forth the largest number of international migrants (17 million), followed by Mexico (13 million). As for where they are ending up, migration occurs primarily between countries that are located within the same world region,[3] so over 60 per cent of all international migrants reside in Asia (80 million), followed by Europe (78 million) and then North America (58 million).

While such figures may seem high, they represent only a tiny proportion of the global population. Humans have been described as a migrating animal species, with *Homo sapiens* emerging in Africa approximately 200,000 years ago, then migrating to Europe some 60–70,000 years ago once the ice retreated enough, and arriving in Australia 50,000 years ago via a now-vanished land bridge. Since then, humans have moved around all the time.[4]

In terms of the shoe industry, migration has been instrumental to creating some of the world's most famous brands. Jimmy Choo was born and educated in Malaysia before moving to London to study shoemaking. Manolo Blahnik was born on a banana plantation in the Canary Islands and lived in several European countries before settling in Bath in the south-west of England. Having made his first pair of shoes aged nine, in 1914 Salvatore Ferragamo set sail for America aged sixteen.[5] He made a name for himself in Hollywood by making shoes for movie stars, before returning home to his native Italy in 1927.

Similarly, the melting pot of migration means Linda Bennett, founder of L.K.Bennett, is of English-Icelandic descent; Patrick Cox has both English and Canadian parentage; and Charlotte Dellal, creator of the British Charlotte Olympia brand, was born in Cape Town to a British-Iraqi father and a Brazilian mother. But while migration produces global success stories, it is far from an equal process.

Sole searching

Brinco is Spanish for 'jump'. The Brinco trainer is a shoe designed by Argentinian artist Judi Werthein in 2005 to help immigrants cross the Mexican–American border. Built into the shoes are a compass, a torch, pockets to hide money and some painkillers to help with injuries. The shoe also has a removable sole printed with a map of the most popular illegal crossing routes from Tijuana into San Diego.

Having been commissioned to make something that reflected the border crossing, Werthein was drawn to the fact that anyone attempting the crossing relies heavily on their feet. Walking through the desert for eight hours risks injury and pain from uneven ground as well as tarantulas and snakes. Accordingly, Werthein made the Brinco into a sturdy boot-style trainer.

The shoes are decorated with an Aztec eagle on the heel, and the American eagle on the toe to represent the pursuit of the 'American dream'. As part of the project the trainers were distributed free of charge in Mexico to people attempting to make an illegal crossing, while at the same time they were sold in an expensive San Diego boutique as a one-of-a-kind *objet d'art*, to make a further point about the inequality between economies.[6]

'Everyone is in favour of free movement, as long as it is for themselves,' says Guy Taylor from campaign group Global Justice Now. Migration for work, gap-years, study programmes or retirement has become something many people in the Global North expect to be allowed, but the same principles are not expected to apply to everyone, particularly people from the Global South.

What is frequently ignored in debates is that movement is often driven by people being pushed out of homes which have become unbearable to live in, with migration a traditional human answer to social stress.[7] 'A lot of migration isn't so much about choice, rather it has been forced on people by conflict, climate change, resource exploitation, or poverty,' Guy continues. 'If we created a world where people were happy to stay where they were, we would see migration fall.'

Take Eritrea, for example, which the *Wall Street Journal* has called 'one of the world's fastest-emptying nations.'[8] A quarter of a million Eritreans live in refugee camps and cities in neighbouring Ethiopia and Sudan, tens of thousands more have undertaken the dangerous journey to Europe. Asylum seekers commonly list conscription into Eritrea's national service programme as their reason for fleeing. The requirement for people to serve eighteen months in military or civilian service was extended indefinitely in 2002, meaning adults can get stuck serving the state into their fifties.[9]

An inquiry by the UN stated that Eritrean national service is 'an institution where slavery-like practices are routine' and 'arbitrary detention, torture, sexual torture, forced labour' take place. Escape is often only possible via desertion followed by fleeing the country. Outside of national service there are few employment opportunities, and the country's mining industry has faced accusations of forced labour.[10]

Guy argues that while recognising people's right to move and seek a better life, we should also enshrine people's right *not* to move. The right not to move means tackling climate breakdown, conflict and the unequal distribution of wealth and food.

This is not to say that movement is in any way easy for the majority of the world. In 2017, Chinese artist, dissident and former refugee Ai Weiwei made *Human Flow*, a film about the refugee crisis. Stunning in its global reach, the film encompasses twenty-three countries and forty refugee camps. *Human Flow* points out that when the Berlin Wall fell in 1989 there were eleven countries with physical walls and barriers designed to keep people in or out of countries. That figure has now increased to at least seventy-seven.[11] These physical barriers, along with carefully drawn border lines on maps, are all designed to control, and keep out, people.

Inspired by the chappal

What these borders and lines do not keep out, however, is goods or capital. SATRA Technology specialise in providing intelligence on the technical aspects of footwear supply chains. SATRA say typically footwear may be made from over forty separate components and almost as many different materials. Material to make the upper, most commonly leather but also synthetics and knitted meshes, plus soling materials, laces, metal trims, buckles and eyelets, adhesives and reinforcements.

While in theory, forty component parts could mean forty different countries involved in the supply chain of a single shoe, in practice, SATRA say brands or manufacturers tend to source from a few suppliers where the quality and delivery are known quantities. Countries that have established industrial supply chains are the most attractive to brands, as they promise efficiency.

While labour and materials are the key costs in footwear production, SATRA explain that the cost of materials does not vary as much as labour across the world. It is possible to search around for the cheapest option, but switching around suppliers may not bring any substantial reduction in the cost of materials, and might lose loyalty discounts. Another element that must be taken into account is wear and tear caused by long periods of transit. Leather, for example, is particularly vulnerable to damage caused by heat and humidity.[12]

So while shoes are unlikely to involve a different country for each component part, from cattle farm to retail outlet they are still transnational objects whose production requires easy border crossings. Much of this freight takes place via the shipping container, monstrously large metal tanks filled with food, fridges, shoes and industrial equipment, all circumnavigating the world on their own system of cranes, railways, ports, and ships. Anthropologist Thomas Hylland Eriksen points out that while world GDP is estimated to have grown by 250 per cent since 1980, world trade grew by 600 per cent in the same period, thanks to the low monetary cost of the shipping container system.[13] Within these tanks, shoes and their component parts flow endlessly across lines on maps.

Nor does shoe design care much about borders. In 2014, British shoe designer Paul Smith brought out the 'Robert' range of men's sandals, an imitation of the *chappal*, a sandal that originated in Peshawar in north-west Pakistan and which is now worn across the region.

Chappals in Pakistan sell for around five or six dollars; Paul Smith was selling his replicas for $595. 'I'd say you'd have to be mad to pay 50,000 rupees for chappals,' one local man said at the time. People also pointed out that Paul Smith had copied a design favoured by pensioners. 'My father used to make this design but I don't make it any more as there is no demand for it,' remarked one shoemaker whose family has made chappals in Peshawar for seventy years. 'Only some retired military or police officials come and ask us to make it for them.'[14]

After an online backlash that accused Paul Smith of cultural appropriation, the brand deleted the name 'Robert' from the website and added a line admitting that the shoe was 'inspired by the Peshawari Chappal'.[15] Taking a traditional design from the Global South, copying it and then sticking on an exorbitant price tag is an example of culture being welcomed where people are not. While an equal and voluntary intermingling and sharing of cultures is both an inevitable part of globalisation and something to be celebrated, there are echoes of imperialism when a multinational corporation like Paul Smith uses a marginalised culture to make money without any acknowledgement or reciprocity.

The replication of the chappal also came at a time when British immigration laws had been tightened to require international migrants who wanted to bring their spouse into the country to be earning a minimum of £18,600, a figure which excludes 41 per cent of British people and 55 per cent of British women.[16] This was a law that many British Pakistanis felt was directed at their community. The 'Robert' shoe debacle exposed the hypocrisy of taking culture while rejecting people.

Seeking refuge

If the shoes on your feet told a story of migration driven by terror and loss, would you really want to know where they came from?

A little boy in a red T-shirt lies with the side of his face resting on a pile of shoe parts. He is fast asleep, passed out with exhaustion. His mouth has fallen slightly open and his thin arms rest on the workstation in front of him. The boy is a refugee from Syria. While he was asleep, another child in the workshop took his photo.

The photo was then sent to Ercüment Akdeniz, news editor at the *Evrensel Daily* newspaper in Istanbul. Ercüment has been covering the fate of Syrians in Turkey since the conflict broke out in 2011. He has built a network of refugee contacts, like the child who snapped a picture of his sleeping friend.

For Ercüment, the twenty-first century is already the century of migration. As a journalist, and the son of a migrant worker in Saudi Arabia, a compulsion to find the human stories behind the statistics has already led him to write three books on Syria's refugees. Part of this work has involved documenting the warehouses and basement workshops across Turkey where Syrian refugee children are to be found assembling shoes.

In 1951, the United Nations produced a convention relating to the status of refugees which remains the cornerstone of global refugee protection. In the convention, a refugee is someone who is unable or unwilling to return to their country of origin due to a well-founded fear of being persecuted for their race, religion, nationality, membership of a particular social group or political opinion.[17]

Turkey has recognised the Refugee Convention but with a difference – only those fleeing events in Europe are classified as having refugee status. This leaves Syrian refugee families with no security and facing harsh conditions. Seventy per cent of refugees in Turkey are women and children,[18] many families reach Turkey without a husband or father because the men are fighting or have been killed.

The TCF industry in Turkey contributes $40b a year to Turkey's economy and employs 2.5 million people. According to trade unions, more than half of these employees are casual labour.[19] Until 2016, Syrians were not allowed work permits in Turkey so had to work informally and illegally. These permits are still scarce and difficult to obtain. Many adult Syrians find that even if they get work, they are paid less than they need to support their families.

But while adult Syrian refugees are poorly paid, children fare even worse. A Syrian child in the Turkish shoe sector will earn 150–200 Turkish lira (£25–35) a month. Children work to keep their family from destitution. In a family of seven children, for example, the first three work to pay the rent on their home, the next two work to cover food expenses and the final two provide a little money to send home to Syria.[20]

Child labour in Turkey is not new, but the arrival of millions of refugees has set back attempts to solve the problem.[21] In interviews with the owners of workshops, Ercüment has listened to them complain that Turkish children no longer want to train in shoemaking because the conditions are now too harsh. Before the Syrian refugee influx, children would work in shoe workshops from 8 a.m. until 7 p.m., but for refugees, workshop owners have pushed the hours from 7 a.m. till 10 p.m. or even midnight. No one with any other options wants such a job.

The age of these child workers is also shockingly low. 'We've done stories about eight-year-old refugee workers who started working at the age of six,' Ercüment says. 'One of the bosses told me that parents bring their children at the age of six to work in the shoe production workshops. The reason for that is that when the children are that young, they can get used to the smell of the paint and glue.'

As well as the risk of developmental brain damage and lung disease from glue fumes, these children run a high risk of developing solvent addictions. They are exposed to sharp cutting tools, and the risk of fire from the flammable pots of thinner and glue they work with. These are dangerous conditions for adults, let alone six-year-olds. The litany of horrors faced by refugee children working in the shoe industry includes swearing and verbal abuse, beatings and sexual abuse. It is far easier for a boss to use violence on an unprotected child than an adult.

The TCF industry in Turkey is a tiered industry. Large Tier One factories make deals and accept contracts with brands from all over the world. These large factories generally fall within a framework of inspections and even trade unions. While they have many problems, they are usually free of child labour. The children are to be found in the smaller Tier Two factories or Tier Three workshops which take on work subcontracted from the big factories.

Danielle McMullan is a senior researcher at the Business and Human Rights Resource Centre, where she has worked for seven years. Since 2015 she has been monitoring the conditions of Syrian refugees including children, in fashion supply chains. Danielle says Turkey's subcontracting system is the result of the business model followed by fashion brands, a demanding process that involves orders changing quickly, and huge pressure on factories to cut their costs: 'The model they operate as an industry is essentially exploitation.'

But what if brands do not know their orders are being subcontracted? 'Nobody is saying it is easy to monitor supply chains, but essentially it comes down to brands needing to look at their business model,' Danielle explains. 'The downward pressure on price and the way they are buying is a major culprit of why the undeclared subcontracting happens. To really address it, you need to address the root causes and that means looking at their own model.'

Having surveyed fashion brands about how they combat undeclared subcontracting in Turkey, the Business and Human Rights Resource Centre say they have yet to hear a convincing argument from a brand about what they do to prevent the practice, with many brands falling back on just saying they forbid the practice and take it seriously.

In the spring of 2018 there were an officially estimated 3.9 million refugees in Turkey, a figure which makes Turkey the country with the highest number of refugees in the world. Unofficial estimates put the figure as high as 5 million refugees. While the majority of the refugees are Syrians, there are also Iraqi, Afghan, Iranian and Somali refugees among others.[22]

Research by left-wing trade unions states there are 2 million child workers in Turkey, while official statistics put the figure at 700,000.[23] Neither of these figures includes Syrian child refugee workers, but these children exist and are making the clothes and shoes that end up in our shops and hanging in our wardrobes. These children make millions of pounds of profit for factory owners and brand shareholders, while being paid pennies.

Walking the line

Whose responsibility are these children? Who should step up and end this exploitation? Is that the job of parents, factory owners, brands, the Turkish government, the European Union or the global community?

Ercüment dismisses the idea that it is the families who are to blame, seeing them instead as victims of war who are very often traumatised. Instead he identifies several responsible parties, the first of whom are Turkish factory owners.

Several years after the Syrian war began, Hikmet Tanriverdi, head of the Istanbul Textile and Apparel Exporters' Association, declared that Syrian refugees had 'saved' the Turkish textile industry. In an extraordinary statement Tanriverdi said the industry had been on the brink of importing thousands of Bangladeshi workers to staff factories, but had stopped that plan when the refugees arrived.

'We could not find Turkish blue-collar workers to hire in our factories at the minimum wage, as a majority of them prefer to work in the services sector for the same amount of money in a cleaner working environment,' Tanriverdi said. 'Syrian workers have saved our sector for now. Many sector players had been planning to bring cheap labour from Bangladesh before, and sooner or later we will call them to Turkey to work in our sector.'

In particular, Tanriverdi noted that refugees play a big role in saving the sector in north-west Turkey's industrial region of Marmara.[24] To announce that refugees have saved your industry and yet still treat them so appallingly is a cruel injustice. Turkish factory owners, who directly benefit from the exploitation, are one of the responsible parties in this system.

Then there are the brands themselves. Danielle says it is always the responsibility of brands to make sure children are not making their clothes or shoes. It is no longer acceptable for brands to say they are unaware of the problem. Brands make large profits from sourcing from Turkey and other places where child labour is an issue, so it is their responsibility to say where and how their clothes are being made.

What brands must not do, Danielle says, is cut and run

– abandoning factories where child labour is found to protect their reputation. She says some leading brands take an approach of removing children from workplaces by placing them in education and ensuring the family doesn't end up short. It is vital, she says, for brands to take a child-rights-centred approach and work with local NGOs and stakeholders.

On the wider question of the Syrian war, Ercüment sees plenty of responsibility laid at the door of the international community: regional governments including Syria, the EU and the United Nations. 'All of them are partly responsible. When we look at the political side of the situation we can say that as long as this war continues, this refugee crisis will continue and the issue of child labour will continue.'

There is also a general consensus that the European Union bears a heavy responsibility for the injustices faced by Syrian refugees. In particular, the EU–Turkey deal whereby refugees who arrive in Europe by boat can be sent back to Turkey. The refusal of EU countries to take in people fleeing war and terror makes refugees more susceptible to child labour as they become trapped in Turkey. The EU's desire for Turkey to ingest the overwhelming majority of Syrian refugees means the EU turns a blind eye to human rights abuses.

While many European countries will not take refugees, they still import refugee-made products. Turkey exports $17b worth of clothing and shoes a year, most of it to Europe, and much of it to Germany and the UK. We live in the cruel irony of a world where objects are valued more than people, where shoes are welcomed across borders, but children are not.

A foot in both camps

While money and tradable goods move easily around the world, corporations also hop over national borders, state boundaries and from factory to factory looking for the lowest labour and production costs. This process emphasises cheapness, which in turn incentivises low standards. These low standards cause people to flow.

The fashion system encourages the evading of environmental requirements, the bribing of officials and the cutting of corners. It incentivises destruction. From water pollution caused by factories pumping out wastewater into rivers and lakes, to the burning of forests on a mass scale, big business is destroying farmland, villages and livelihoods.

Free trade agreements and structural adjustment policies pushed by the IMF have, in addition, trampled on traditional occupations like fishing and farming.[25] These factors push people to leave their homes to seek work elsewhere. Arriving in cities where they have no contacts and may not speak the language, migrant workers are often left with no choice but to take on the most dangerous and underpaid jobs.

In an attempt to keep migrants out of their countries, policy makers in the EU and elsewhere are investing in export-orientated jobs in areas where there are lots of people wanting to leave – in Jordan, for example. This investment has tended to focus on creating garment factory jobs, a sector that only really produces extremely low-paid and exploitative roles for people. These jobs, it is hoped, will stem the tide of migration.

Yet as Jennifer Gordon, professor at Fordham University School of Law, has written, there is no consensus that increasing foreign investment and trade decreases emigration, at least in the short term.[26] There are an estimated 750,000 refugees living in Jordan, the overwhelming majority from Syria. In an attempt to stop these refugees moving into Europe, the European Union, the World Bank and other institutions signed a refugee compact with the Jordanian government. The goal was to employ 200,000 Syrian refugees in garment factories, 150,000 of them in special Export Processing Zones. The EU reduced tariffs on exports from factories that met a refugee employee quota. The plan did not work for one critical reason: these factory jobs pay too little and demand too much to be a viable option for most Syrian refugees in Jordan.

Workers in Jordanian garment factories are generally women migrants from Bangladesh or Sri Lanka. Syrian refugee women typically have families so cannot live on site at factories, and unlike in Bangladesh, the wages do not convert into much if sent back home.

The Jordanian industry came into the spotlight in 2011 after an investigation into the Classic Factory by the Institute for Global

Labour and Human Rights found instances of systematic beatings and sexual violence against women.[27] At the time, Sanal Kumar, Classic's managing director, denied the charges and, according to reports, attributed blame to both the United States and Israel.[28]

The ILO list sexual harassment as a major area of concern in Jordanian factories, a challenge made more difficult by the fact that not all types of workplace sexual harassment are illegal under Jordanian law.[29]

The nature of the fashion industry, with its drive for low labour costs, fast turnarounds and long hours, means that if Jordanian factories paid more, they would become uncompetitive. But, Professor Gordon explains, despite huge effort and hundreds of millions of dollars, only a handful of Syrians are employed in the zones today. Instead, the 50,000 or so Syrians with work permits have stuck with the informal agricultural and construction jobs where they have worked since arriving.

A similar situation has taken hold in Ethiopia where 30,000 jobs in industrial parks were reserved for refugees, many of them from Eritrea, in an attempt to stop them leaving for Europe. When refugees were interviewed by policy makers, once again they were found to be uninterested in manufacturing jobs paying $1.25–1.60 per day. For their part, the factory managers were not keen to hire refugees either, preferring instead to look for unmarried women aged between eighteen and twenty-five with a basic education. The World Bank and the Ethiopian government have now agreed the 30,000 jobs need not be in export manufacturing.[30]

Writing about *Human Flow*, Ai Weiwei discussed the fear that people trying to cross borders are 'economic migrants' looking to take unfair advantage of Global North prosperity. Implicit in this argument, he wrote, is the refusal to acknowledge that globalisation has meant some countries, institutions and individuals have grown wealthy at the direct expense of the vulnerable and exploited. The Global North, he wrote, 'which has disproportionately benefited from globalisation – simply refuses to bear its responsibilities, even though the condition of many refugees is a direct result of the greed inherent in a global capitalist system.'[31]

While it is important for wealthier countries to share the financial burden of the refugee crisis with countries like Jordan and Ethiopia, solutions that do not think outside of the box of neoliberalism, and simply reproduce unequal systems and terrible jobs, have little chance of success. Just because people are desperate, does not mean that they will accept, or should be forced to accept, the worst deal. 'Over the long term,' writes Professor Gordon, 'developed countries hoping for less immigration must support decent work in migrant-origin countries, not a seat at a sewing table at any cost.' Without the ability to build lives of dignity where they are, people will continue to flow.

There is also the question of whether more production is actually counterproductive in terms of ending migration. The current economic system that we live under relies upon over-production and over-consumption – the churning out of millions of trend-based and short-lived items that are produced and disposed of at great environmental cost. This system has degraded the environment to the extent that millions of people have already lost their homes and livelihoods to climate breakdown.

More factories, more export zones and more churning out of disposable goods will only lead to more of the same environmental destruction followed by people being forced to leave their homes. Factories in export zones might be a solution that suits Global North governments and institutions, but it may well just compound existing problems.

Climate breakdown is often presented as a danger for the next generation, as something that will impact the children of the Global North. This is to ignore the unequal and racialised nature of climate breakdown that is already wreaking havoc in the Global South. Keeping people safe in the place where they want to live has become ever more important as climate displacement becomes an increasingly serious global issue, leading to millions of people facing migration as a forced and deeply destructive process.

Chinese Lunar New Year

Despite being in the midst of a global refugee crisis, the largest human migration in human history is an event that takes place each year within the borders of one country.

China's Lunar New Year holiday sees an estimated 2.48 billion road trips, 390 million rail trips, 65 million air trips and 46 million boat trips over a 40-day period.[32] The 'Spring Rush' is an annual event that empties cities like Dongguan in central Guangdong province. Dongguan contains approximately 1 million factories,[33] staffed almost entirely by migrant workers. When the Lunar New Year comes around, all of these workers, 70 per cent of the city's population, go home to the countryside. Dongguan is transformed 'from a city of migrants into a city of ghosts'.[34]

'In the holidays all these Chinese cities come to a standstill,' says Professor Kam Wing Chan, at the University of Washington. 'If you want to eat somewhere, or catch a cab, there is no one.' Professor Chan specialises in the study of internal migration in China. While most countries import labour to fuel their economy, China has been able to do this using internal migration.

The figures are startling – while the global count of international migrants is 258 million, within China's borders alone there are an estimated 170 million migrant workers. This has created a set of circumstances unprecedented in scale and importance.

Dongguan is a large prefecture-level city which has been at the core of Chinese manufacturing since the mid-1980s. It grew out of an assortment of towns and villages spread over 2,500 square kilometres on the Pearl River Delta.[35] One of the key products to come out of Dongguan has been shoes. In particular, the town of Houji is famous for its work in branded shoe design and manufacture.[36] Famous factories within Dongguan include Stella International Holdings, which supplies Nike and Timberland, as well as factories run by Yue Yuen, the largest sports shoe manufacturer in the world where 40,000 workers went on strike in 2014.

Dongguang was hit hard by the global financial crisis of 2008 which saw demand for manufactured goods fall. As the region tries to turn itself into a high-tech manufacturing zone, commentators talk of the crash-induced slump which the city has never truly recovered from. Dongguan factories that once employed thousands can be found empty, partially empty or replacing people with automation.[37]

Dongguang, along with dozens of other super-cities across China, is a key site for migration caused by globalisation. Between 1990 and the end of 2015, the proportion of China's population living in urban areas jumped from 26 per cent to 56 per cent.[38] To understand this sudden leap means going back to 1958 when China's Communist government initiated a household registration system to try to control population flows.

The 'hukou system' assigns every citizen of China with a hukou location and classification. Essentially citizens are either rural and agricultural, or urban and non-agricultural. Because their status is for the most part inherited from parents, it is inflexible. The hukou location defines the one place where people are entitled to receive benefits like housing and healthcare; it essentially defines where people belong.[39]

This system made it almost impossible for people designated as 'rural' to move to the city. It kept internal migration to a minimum by tying people to the countryside. In 1979, however, the system underwent major changes. Professor Chan explains how in order to tap into the vast army of very low-waged labour needed to staff factories being set up to supply the world with manufactured goods, China changed its system to allow people to come to the city while still retaining their rural household status.

Poverty was rife in the countryside and the move was welcomed by millions of rural people who uprooted their lives and went in search of jobs and a better life. Urban centres swelled and ranks of workers gained China its 'factory of the world' nickname. By 2013, 62.9 per cent of the world's shoes were being made in China, primarily in factories staffed by internal migrants who had climbed aboard buses and trains to travel in from the countryside.

Over time, the distinction between agricultural and non-agricultural hukou has lost some of its significance. What has remained iron-bound is hukou location which continues to define people's life chances and their access to resources.[40]

Xu Lizhi was a worker poet from the heart of industrial China. Aged just twenty-four he killed himself by jumping from the seventeenth floor of a building in Shenzhen, not far from the Apple-contracted Foxconn factory where he worked. Before his death, Xu Lizhi wrote about the harsh nature of living in mega-cities and working on assembly lines in poems such as 'Terracotta Army on the Assembly Line', 'Obituary for a Peanut' and 'I Swallowed an Iron Moon'. One poem is called 'My Friend Fa' and was written for a migrant worker. In one part of the poem, Xu Lizhi describes the physical hardship of factory work:

> seven years ago you came alone
> to this part of Shenzhen
> high-spirited, full of faith
> and what met you was ice,
> black nights, temporary residence permits, temporary shelter
> . . .
> after false starts you came here to the world's largest
> equipment factory
> and began standing, screwing in screws, doing overtime,
> working overnight
> painting, finishing, polishing, buffing,
> packaging and packing, moving finished products
> bending down and straightening up a thousand times each
> day
> dragging mountain-sized piles of merchandise across the
> workshop floor
> the seeds of illness were planted and you didn't know it
> until the pain dragged you to the hospital[41]

For Xu Lizhi and his friend Fa, life had become a ceaseless cycle of production and exploitation, the promise of a new life having given way to mechanised physical toil and the mental strain of endless repetition. A fate shared by millions of young Chinese workers.

Floating children

A rural worker desiring to swap their *hukou* location runs headlong into an almost insurmountable bureaucratic barrier. They also face the knowledge that swapping means losing benefit rights in their hometown and forfeiting the ability to return 'home' in old age. As a result, most migrants plan to move to big cities for a decade or two before returning to the town or village where they grew up.[42] In this way, the *hukou* system has made transience the key feature of life for hundreds of millions of people in China.

People who live outside of their designated *hukou* location have come to be known as *liudong renkou*, the 'floating population': 'this concept is based on the notion that the *hukou* location is where one belongs and that migration is not considered official and permanent until the migrant's *hukou* location is also changed,' wrote Professor C. Cindy Fan for the World Bank. 'Regardless of when actual migration occurred, a person is counted as part of the floating population as long as his or her usual place of residence is different from the *hukou* location.'[43]

Integral to this transient, floating state is a lack of basic rights for everyone in a migrant family. It is a state that Professor Chan says comes at a huge human cost to the next generation. Since *hukou* status is determined by a person's parents, the children of migrants are classified as rural even if they live in, or were born in, a city.

This has devastating consequences especially when it comes to education. Having a rural *hukou* means migrant children have no right to public schooling in a city, which places a great amount of stress on migrant families. In 2016, one father named Mr Liu became so angry and upset after failing for months to secure a school place in Beijing for his daughter, that he set himself on fire outside government offices.[44]

The lack of public school places means cramped migrant neighbourhoods see children educated in unofficial private schools which the *New York Times* describes as operating in an educational grey zone: without licences or standard curriculums, and with migrant teachers who have the same precarious *hukou* status as their pupils.[45]

These migrant children have become targets for officials seeking to cap their city's population. A 2017 aggressive eviction campaign in Beijing targeted homes and schools in migrant neighbourhoods in scenes the *New York Times* said evoked the devastation of war.[46] By taking away basic services like education, officials hope to push migrants out of cities. 'A number of hostile policies and measures are being carried out,' confirms Professor Chan. 'In a stronger word I would say they basically *purged* all these migrant children from the cities.'

For migrant children who manage to cling on to a school place, another bureaucratic barrier exists to expel them from the city. The post-high school exam, the *gaokao*, must be taken in the province that matches a student's *hukou*. Anyone intending to take the *gaokao* therefore has to leave the city and their family at the end of high school in order to get used to schooling in their 'hometown' before taking their exams.[47]

To deal with this problem, in 2015 China's State Council announced plans to give out 100 million permanent urban *hukous* to rural citizens by 2020. This huge number will still fall far short of the number needed for total reform. The segregation in Chinese society caused by the *hukou* system risks the possibility of growing social unrest, with China's cities growing steadily fuller of displaced young adults who are increasingly angry at being defined, and trapped, by their outsider status.[48]

Left behind

As well as the children growing up in precarious and impoverished migrant neighbourhoods, there is a second issue, that of the 'left-behind children' in the Chinese countryside. Driven by necessity or trouble with visas and housing costs, a percentage of parents globally have had to leave their children behind when they migrate for work. The aim, and often the outcome, however, is for children to eventually move and for the family to be reunited. But in China, institutional and legal barriers mean that nearly 70 million children are permanently left behind.

'If you look at the total number of migrant workers, currently it is at about 170 million,' says Professor Chan. 'We estimated there are roughly 100 million children associated with those 170 million migrant workers. Out of these 100 million kids, only about 35 million – one third of them – are able to be with their parents in the city. The other 66 million are left in the countryside.'

Sixty-six million children is equivalent to the entire population of the United Kingdom. A colossal number of children who are growing up separated from either one or both of their parents. The task of raising small children often falls to grandparents who are ill-equipped to deal with energetic toddlers or increasingly unhappy children.

Photographer Ken Shichen spent three years documenting this generation of left-behind children in order to bring to light the psychological cost of China's economic boom.[49] His photographs show children stood in the classroom with a chalk written message for their parents on the blackboard: *I miss daddy and mommy. Daddy and mommy went out to work. I haven't seen them for three years,* wrote one eight-year-old from Gansu, one of China's poorest provinces.[50]

In a strongly worded critique of the treatment of the left-behind children, Professor Chan believes an entire generation is being destroyed. Transience and this crisis of abandonment might be unintended consequences of migration, but they are a product of globalisation, connected to anyone who wears shoes or owns products that have been 'Made In China'.

Migrant workers were pushed to the cities by extreme poverty, but they were also pulled there by a voracious global desire for consumer items. Beneficiaries of this crisis include each and every multinational corporation that has made mountains of money out of China as a direct result of this unequal system.

China became the most powerful factory in the world because of its phalanxes of rural workers, workers who have never been truly welcome in the cities they helped build. China produces six out of every ten pairs of shoes in the world – mountains of trainers, brogues, ballet pumps, high heels and boots – all made at a huge cost that is only just making itself known in the hearts and minds of 66 million children and the parents who miss them.

Footprints

From makeshift refugee camps to Turkish cellars, shoes tell the stories of the consequences of globalisation. They reveal the millions of people who have been made unwelcome by capitalism. In this way, the refugee crisis is not just about the personal suffering of refugees – it is about the system we live under which prioritises financial gain over people's struggle for the necessities of life. It is a story that leaves us with questions: how should the poor, displaced or occupied exist when their societies are destroyed? Are they expected to simply disappear?

Might it be possible through examining our collective shoes to recognise that accepting and welcoming the continued existence of these millions of people is an essential part of our shared humanity? 'If you're walking down the street and someone is in trouble, you help them. I think it should be common sense for any country that sees people dying, or living in horrendous poverty, to actually want to help them,' said Guy Taylor, reflecting on the current political climate. 'The fact that we're encouraged not to, the fact that we're encouraged to support immigration controls, means the decent, innate helping side of our human nature is forced away. We're encouraged to celebrate being soulless and heartless towards desperate people.'

With millions of people on the move and an ever-increasing pressure on the planet, the next chapter continues to dismantle the belief that any of us can afford the continuation of this system. We might trap children behind barbed-wire fences while welcoming in the consumables they have stitched, but there are some consequences that pay no heed to borders. There are no walls that can protect against the consequences of the desecration of life on this planet, and it is to the unhappy tale of climate breakdown that we must now turn.

CHAPTER 6

Hell for Leather

In the harsh wind of a November morning the sun finally rose on Meadow Lane. It lifted over a dark line of trees, lightened the footpath across the fields and glinted on cars speeding down a dual carriageway. To reach Meadow Lane it rose further still. Tracing a row of lorries in a layby and another line of trees, it lit up the sign for a local football club, the homes of a community of Travellers and the route to a motorway slip road.

Down the dual carriageway came a huge truck; white cabin embossed with haulage insignia, double-decker trailer sprayed dark red. Turning onto Meadow Lane, the truck pulled up at a set of metal security gates that had no sign.

Inside the double-decker container, bodies could be heard skidding into each other and falling, scrabbling on shit-covered steel floors. Throughout the long journey, the wind had blown sharp and cold through narrow air slits. As the truck stopped, eyes tried to see out, heads nudging the low ceiling and metal bars. Wet, rolling eyes so wide with fear they seemed pinned open. White foam hung from mouths and soft whiskery noses gasped for air before blowing out blasts of steam.

The metal gates beeped as they drew open. The truck lurched forward and swung into the facility with a blast of exhaust fumes that temporarily overrode the sharp smell of faeces and urine. It was directed to the end of the yard, past holding pens lined with straw, a line of parked trucks and large white awnings hiding vats of blood.

After a short conversation over clipboards, the driver backed up to the entrance of a single-storey green building. The back of the truck opened and a ramp was lowered. There was no waiting. The walk down the ramp led to the kill sheds. After a first, frightening journey in a metal box, there were just a few steps left.

At the end, they could be heard calling out to each other, to the world, to the last glimpse of anything green or welcome. Metal railings denied the instinct to flee, to return home to restore the bonds of herd. One by one, they were goaded from the truck, their soft fleshy bodies driven towards their end.

When the end came, it was violent, unfair and desperate. Death following a life without choice or consent.

Cows are often transported across countries to whichever slaughterhouse offers the highest price. Once inside, a bolt gun is fired at the cow's head. This is supposed to stun an animal instantly so the cow may not get a second bolt if it doesn't lose consciousness. Chains are then attached to its hind legs and it is hoisted upside down. The cow is then stabbed in the throat to open its arterial vein, and left to bleed out.[1]

Cows are extremely sensitive, social creatures. As complex prey animals they can become alarmed if they are touched, or if they encounter fast movements or loud noises. They display their alarm by flinching or making distressed noises.[2] Just like humans, cows are fully able to feel pain and distress. Studies of cows and calves suggest this extends to protracted emotional distress when subjected to high levels of stress, fear or loss.[3]

Millions of cows continue to be slaughtered for their meat, their bones and their skin. In this process the global livestock industry produces more greenhouse gas emissions than all cars, planes, trains and ships put together.[4]

The intensive farming industry which sees cows repeatedly and forcibly impregnated, is a fundamental pillar of the shoe industry. Leather is not a coincidentally produced by-product of the meat industry, rather it is a co-product, a valuable commodity produced at the same time as meat. Leather typically represents 5–10 per cent of an animal's market value.[5] To talk about shoes, which account for almost 50 per cent of all leather products,[6] but not to talk about the animals whose skin they are made from would be an affront to reality.

Pieces of the dead

'For the animal, it doesn't matter if it is killed for the meat, for its hide, for its fat or bones. The fear, pain and anxiety that these animals feel when they are cut open alive and while conscious is something that is happening every day,' says Frank Schmidt from PETA's office in Germany where he is the head of corporate affairs.

'For calf leather there has to be the slaughter of a young calf that is maybe a few months or a year old,' he continues. 'They are sent to the same slaughterhouses as other cows or bulls so they see what is going on in front of them. They might be stunned several times because the workers aren't working properly, so they might be conscious while they are stabbed in the neck and bled out.'

The existence of slaughterhouses in the fashion and shoe industries is an issue which is tiptoed around. It is taken for granted that millions of animals should die for our clothing and shoes, with the rights of animals seen as a taboo, or embarrassing subject to talk about. And yet the killing is everywhere, hiding in plain sight.

Dr Alex Lockwood works at the Centre for Research in Media and Cultural Studies in the University of Sunderland. Sat on a train one day, watching a group of people rush onto a crowded platform, he had a realisation: nearly all of the people in front of him had been involved in killing by the time they caught their morning train.

Many would have eaten meat for breakfast or prepared meat sandwiches for lunch. Others might be wearing silk ties or underwear. Some had taken medicine or vitamin pills encased in gelatine. Others perhaps had fur-trimmed hoods, hats or gloves, or were wearing down jackets. Then there was the leather: leather shoes and boots; leather bags and briefcases; leather jackets and belts; leather cases for Kindles, diaries and phones; and leather car seats and sofas to sit on. None of which could exist without violent death. From that train window, it was clear that pieces of the dead were everywhere, yet it was utterly unacknowledged, unspoken and unchallenged as an ideology, a way of life.

In Britain, the Victorians moved slaughterhouses out of towns, placing them out of sight and out of mind. Since then, a need has developed to keep some animals close – cats and dogs mostly – and to completely ignore the lives and deaths of all the others. And the extent of what we ignore is horrifying.

So what does it mean to live in a world built on mass death? Are there consequences for society? Much of Dr Lockwood's work involves exploring cultural, psychological and sociological attitudes to the body. He believes moving killing out of sight is based in human attempts to ignore the fact that we are ourselves corporeal, vulnerable animals made of fleshy material. He argues that while we wear clothes and shoes for environmental reasons, they are also part of our sociological need to cover up our vulnerability and our flesh.

'You can trace some of that back to Victorian sensitivities,' Dr Lockwood says. 'If you follow that lineage from the nineteenth century onwards, that's when the civilising process became strongly structured around hiding away the death and killing of other beings. It was considered that we weren't constitutionally strong enough to see that, or to have reflected to us that we are vulnerable corporeal beings.'

Dr Lockwood argues we are scared to acknowledge that we are ourselves animals, that our differences with other species are measured not in totality but in degrees of separation; one of degree and not of kind, as Charles Darwin wrote in *The Descent of Man*. But instead of admitting this, we shun the day-to-day killing of others.

Over in the US, Dr Melanie Joy is an author and animal rights campaigner. She argues that the slaughter of billions of farmed animals each year is a violent atrocity based upon the systemic domination by the strong of those with less power. Oppression mars much of human history, with societies structured around the use of privilege to subjugate and oppress. Humans with power have shown a disturbing ability to exert control over the lives, and deaths, of those they consider beneath them. The farming and killing of animals follows this pattern.

Dr Joy named this ideology 'Carnism', the social belief that humans have the right to kill and eat, or wear, animals. Carnism is linked to 'Speciesism', the belief that humans are at the top of a species hierarchy and have the right to dominate other species. Dr Joy argues these attitudes run deep, their bias embedded in every institution. She argues moving towards a fairer world means exposing shrouded forms of oppression which make us think we have the right to subjugate and kill. The challenge she outlines is to closely examine the world and its structures of power as they relate to humans and animals – not to see different things, but to see things differently.[7]

Carnism sees humans as set up to believe that we have the right to deny rights and freedoms to other animals. 'What we're doing with leather, or wool, or silk, or other material that comes from an animal, is essentially saying, "We dominate you, we can use your skin, we can use the products of your body in the ways that we like",' says Dr Lockwood.

Acknowledging this is not for the faint-hearted: 'If you really wanted to end capitalism, you would end the exploitation of animal labour,' he argues. 'Capitalism is so built upon the exploitation of animal bodies and labour, that to break that element of capitalism, would break capitalism.'

The system we live under now gives us just eleven years to save civilisation from climate catastrophe and as we will see, this is inextricably tied to industrial farming. Unless this is faced and changed, we are not going to have a just and sustainable planet. 'In the end,' Dr Lockwood concludes, 'if your question is, "What is the consequence of this killing in our society?" – well, it's the end of our society.'

Under the ox's hoof

In late 2018, Adriana Charoux found herself afraid to wear a T-shirt she had recently bought. The T-shirt had the slogan #EleNão – #NotHim in Portuguese – on it, a reference to Brazilian presidential candidate Jair Bolsonaro. She was afraid because although the election had yet to take place, it felt like Bolsonaro had already won.

Authoritarian, deeply homophobic, racist, anti-women, promising to fold the Ministry of Environment into the Ministry of Agriculture, and arguing that all citizens should have guns, Bolsonaro was dominating the electoral debate. For Adriana and her friends, it felt like the possibility of dialogue had been shut down. Walking home alone from demonstrations or wearing T-shirts with left-wing slogans no longer felt safe. It was a threat Adriana says felt like a long-reaching shadow, accompanied by the impossibility of knowing whether the danger was from the military, the police or ordinary people on the street.

As a long-term activist and campaigner at Greenpeace Brazil, Adriana's fear went beyond worrying for her LGBT friends and her small son. She feared for the entire Amazon rainforest, the indigenous people living in it, and for environmental activists who were already being killed at a rate of almost four per week.[8] Bolsonaro had even pledged to expel Greenpeace from the country, saying there would be no money for NGOs, and pronounced that indigenous reserves and *quilombolas* (protected settlements for descendants of escaped and freed enslaved people) would be eradicated.[9]

In the subsequent election, Bolsonaro was elected president with 55 per cent of the vote. He had successfully united Bulls, Bullets and Bibles – a coalition of big business, the gun lobby and the religious right.

The last frontier

Adriana's department at Greenpeace Brazil works to stop agribusiness expanding deeper and deeper into the rainforest. Farming cattle for their meat and their skin is a big industry in Brazil, and the number-one cause of Amazon deforestation.

In 2018, Brazil exported \$1.443b worth of leather. This amounted to 181.7 million square metres of leather.[10] These figures represent a drop from previous years, but Brazil is still the second largest exporter of *finished* (dyed and coated) leathers in the world.[11]

A quarter of this leather was exported to China, 17.5 per cent went to Italy, 16.8 per cent went to the US, while Hong Kong and Vietnam each received just over 5 per cent.[12] Brazilian leather is everywhere in the supply chain and it is eating up the rainforest. Even before he had won the election, the effect of Bolsonaro's campaign led to a 36 per cent increase in Amazon deforestation.[13]

Unlike leather, 80 per cent of the meat produced in Brazil is consumed domestically, with many Brazilians seeing red meat as an intrinsic part of their social lives. It has also, Adriana explains, been an intrinsic driver of violent land occupation. '*A base da pata do boi*,' she says, an expression used by the ruling generals during a military dictatorship that only ended in 1985 – 'Under the ox's hoof'. Use cattle to turn land from forest to pasture. Occupy it and do not give it back.

Journalist Sue Branford first went to Brazil in 1971 intending to write a PhD on migration flows and the violent expulsion of peasant families from the land. It was a tumultuous first trip – she witnessed the murders of two people, and wrote increasingly desperate letters to her supervisor that took five weeks to reach the UK.

Eventually Sue dropped her PhD, turned her research into a co-authored book, *The Last Frontier: Fighting Over Land in the Amazon*, and became a journalist. After a lifetime of reporting from Brazil and Latin America, Sue went back to Brazil in 2017 to retrace the steps of a journey she had made in 1974.

The journey began in Cuiabá in the state of Mato Grosso and headed north to the town of Sinop. In 1974 the journey had taken five days of travel on a newly hewn track. Occasionally the party had encountered a peasant family living at the side of the trail. Indians were known to live in the forest but were not seen.

In 1974, Sinop was a settlement that the government was trying to populate with handfuls of families from the south who were seeking land. Families who found themselves 3,000 miles from home, facing rain, heat, mosquitoes and endless forest. The settlement struggled until soya arrived as a 'miracle crop' in the early 1990s. Now it is a boom town of 135,000 people and the frontier has moved north into the forest.

'First loggers move in and take out the good hard timber,' Sue explains. 'Then there's a phase that is quite recent – violent land grabbers who go and clear the land, kick off the peasant families, and push the Indians back. The cleared land is then sold to ranchers. Cleared land costs 100 times more than an area of forest because the hard, dangerous work is done.'

Mountainous terrain usually stays as cattle-ranching land, with farmers gradually pulling up the roots of the trees. Land that is suitable for the mechanised farming of products like soya is sold on again for huge profit, often falling under the control of multinational corporations. Once land is cleared, the loggers push further, erasing the forest.

'We talk about trying to control the way we live so that we produce fewer greenhouse gases,' Sue continues. 'By far the easiest way to reduce emissions is to stop cutting down the forest, yet they go on doing this. It seems very, very difficult to stop it because it's capitalism, it's the search for profit, the short term. It's a great vessel moving north, and we can't seem to stop it.'

It is a tragic change to have witnessed, she says, remembering how far the forest used to stretch. A flight over the eastern part of Amazonia now reveals the rapacious spread of the ranches. All that remains are the green islands of the indigenous reserves where the fight is on to preserve the forest and its biodiversity.

Brazil's indigenous population comprises more than 220 listed peoples speaking over 180 different languages. These 400,000 people living on disconnected indigenous lands totalling 107 million hectares, are now under an even more serious threat of violence and displacement by Bolsonaro's government.[14]

The Guarani people live in Mato Grosso do Sul and have endured sustained violence, rape, murders, and land theft by farmers and agribusiness. 'If Indigenous peoples become extinct, the lives of all are threatened, for we are the guardians of nature,' the Guarani said in a statement regarding Bolsonaro's election. 'Without forest, without water, without rivers, there is no life, there is no way for any Brazilian to survive. We resisted 518 years ago,* we fight in victory and defeat, our land is our mother.'[15]

From Flying Rivers to Apocalypse Now

'There's no more important place for an ecologist to be than here in the Amazon,' says Dr Philip Fearnside from the National Institute

---

* This refers to the Guarani people's experience of Spanish and Portuguese colonialism which led to loss of land, the spread of fatal diseases and mass enslavement.

for Research in Amazonia (INPA). Brazil's Amazon forest is approximately the size of western Europe. Since Dr Fearnside arrived four decades ago, an area the size of France has been cleared.

That the world does not grasp the scale of what is happening is an anathema to Dr Fearnside. 'People have always had this sort of "out" psychologically. They think you can undo these things that are happening, but many of them you can't. In biological terms, you don't get a rainforest back.'

The Amazon rainforest is one of the most biodiverse places on earth, housing at least 10 per cent of the world's known species.[16] Its potential is almost limitless, with scientists believing that less than 0.5 per cent of Amazonia's flowering plants have been properly studied for their medicinal powers.[17]

The Amazon River flows for more than 6,600km, and accounts for 15–16 per cent of the world's total river discharge into the oceans. Along with its tributaries and streams it holds more freshwater fish species than anywhere else in the world.[18] The rainforest also creates vast 'Flying Rivers' as trees draw up billions of tonnes of water from the ground which, once released into the sky, flows as nourishing vapour across Brazil and Latin America.

Dr Fearnside has described Bolsonaro's presidency as an 'Apocalypse Now' moment, a crisis that could cause unprecedented harm both to the Amazon and to the international battle to slow climate breakdown.[19]

Forests are a crucial means of preventing climate crisis because of their ability to absorb and store carbon during photosynthesis. The soil beneath forests also takes in carbon, often three times the amount held by the vegetation above.[20] But because they are such a successful capture and storage system, forests are also sources of huge potential emissions.

Human activity, in this case deforestation, is ending the ability of trees, and the soil they grow in, to store carbon. The carbon stock held by Amazonia is also being released by forest fires, which become more frequent as climate breakdown makes the land hotter and dryer and creates extreme drought. Carbon released from forests and soil is a critical contributor to environmental crisis.

Once global heating passes a certain level, it will become

uncontrollable. 'It becomes what's called a runaway greenhouse effect,' Dr Fearnside says. 'The earth gets warmer, you have more fires, warmer soil, more emissions, and it just keeps going – a snowball effect. That is what we have to avoid, and Amazonia is very important in that because it has so much carbon. Both in the forest and in the soil.'

It is a problem inextricably linked to shoes, because, as Dr Fearnside confirms, cattle is the main thing replacing the rainforest in Amazonia.

Steak, shoes and slavery

All of this destruction for the sake of steak and shoes? 'The planet is shaking,' Adriana says back in her office in São Paulo. She lists the climate-based disasters that have occurred over the last few years – hurricanes, forest fires and floods. 'This is one climate, one world. There is no Planet B.'

In 2009, Greenpeace Brazil were signatories to the Amazon Cattle Agreement which was signed by three Brazilian slaughterhouses: JBS, Marfrig and Minerva. These three corporations accounted for 70 per cent of all cattle slaughtered in Amazonia. They pledged not to buy from cattle farms that were involved in deforestation, human slavery or the invasion of protected or indigenous land.

JBS Couros is a subsidiary of food company JBS. It bills itself as 'the largest leather processing company in the world'. JBS Couros produces leather for cars, furniture, leather goods and footwear.[21] In 2016 an investigation into JBS supplier farms by an investigative journalism NGO and PETA found deeply inhumane conditions on farms at forty-eight sites in four different states. *Repórter Brasil* documented calves pinned down and branded on the face with hot irons, calves with open maggot-infested wounds, cows being beaten, kicked and electroshocked in their anuses as they were driven onto trucks to be taken for slaughter. *Repórter Brasil* concluded: 'Cattle ranches that supply JBS contradict the company's advertising about animal welfare and run counter to the recommendations of the Ministry of Agriculture.' In its defence, JBS said it is 'not responsible for management inside the farms'. The company stated that 'all of the

JBS drivers and third parties are trained in animal welfare, and they all received certificates and have signed a declaration of responsibility with regard to the company policy'.[22]

In part, this is because while Brazil's 1988 constitution says the government must prohibit 'practices that submit animals to cruelty', there is no specific law about animal welfare on farms.[23]

Marfrig is Brazil's second-largest food processing company, supplying 100 different countries across the world. In 2012, four tannery workers were killed and sixteen more were injured in a toxic gas leak at a Marfrig plant in Bataguassu, in Mato Grosso. Marfrig was fined $1m by the Environmental Police for the lethal incident.[24]

Minerva Foods has the dishonourable distinction of being the biggest exporter of live cattle in Brazil.[25] In February 2018, a gigantic livestock ship set sail from Brazil carrying 25,000 cows sold by Minerva to a Turkish client for halal slaughter.[26] Animal rights groups continue to fight the practice of live exports, arguing that sixteen-day voyages in cramped, squalid conditions amount to animal cruelty. In 2015, one of these 'death ships' sank with 4,900 live cows on board. Over 4,400 cows drowned inside the ship, washing up onto local beaches to rot 'in endless rows of bodies on the sand'.[27]

Despite having been formally abolished in 1888, human slavery is happening on cattle farms in Brazil. The Labour Ministry established mobile inspection units in 1995, which have rescued more than 50,000 people being kept in slave-like conditions. A third of them came from ranches. The inspectors have found people being forced to live with cattle, with no bathrooms or kitchens. 'Historically the worst slave conditions in Brazil have been found in cattle ranches in the Amazon where state power is difficult to reach and where exploitation is more violent,' Leonardo Sakamoto, the head of *Repórter Brasil*, told Reuters.[28]

The Walk Free Foundation's Global Slavery Index 2018, estimated there were 369,000 million men, women and children living in modern slavery in Brazil.[29]

In August 2017, Greenpeace suspended its involvement in the Amazon Cattle Agreement, citing corruption scandals in agribusiness, and attacks on human rights and the forest. 'At the moment, no company producing meat or other cattle products in Brazil can guarantee that its production chain is not connected to deforestation or to human rights violations,' states Greenpeace Brazil.[30]

What was taken?

Adriana has a favourite motto: 'the best things in the world aren't things'. She does not want the weight of change to be placed on individual shoulders when it is governments and multinational corporations who must end their destruction. But, Adriana says, there must be a global shift to end the systemic demand for cattle, and a key part of that means people, along with institutions like hospitals, schools and company offices, transitioning away from meat in favour of a plant-based diet.

She also argues that people must connect with what they are buying. With shoes, she says people must think about where they came from and 'what was taken for them to arrive on your feet'. There is a need for a transformation that makes people in cities like London 'really feel like they belong to the forest, just as the person from the forest belongs to London.'

'These connections are something that is really tricky to get,' Adriana concludes. 'We are globalised, but at the end of the day we have globalised the destruction and the poverty, not the wealth, of this model.'

On a hiding to nothing

Humans are the only species known to adorn themselves with a second skin, and are thought to have first started trying to preserve leather in the early Stone Age, around 8000 BCE. It is believed fat was first used to make animal skins waterproof. Later in Ancient Egypt and Mesopotamia, plants, bark and oils were used for tanning.

On the other side of the world, a very different method was used. Communities in present-day Greenland or Alaska would scrape the hair from seal hides, then soften the skins by beating them and soaking them in urine. The next step was for the leather workers, who were most often women, to chew the hides until they grew even softer, before rubbing them with fat and fish oil. Other traditional ingredients used to tan skins have been brains, liver, salt and camp-fire smoke.[31]

An associate editor at *Indian Country Today*, Vincent Schilling has written about being Native American and vegan. There should, he writes, be concern at the energy that comes from factory-farmed animals who have suffered greatly. While he himself chooses never to hunt or harm animals, Schilling wrote, 'I have heard many stories regarding being mindful when hunting. A Native elder once told me, and I have seen similar sentiments elsewhere, this thought: When you hunt, ensure that the animal does not see you. Otherwise you will be feeding fear to your families.'[32]

'When Native people create their regalia, it is done with the mindfulness of the animal. It is done with respect,' Vincent Schilling continues. 'The animal is honored and thanked for contributing to the celebration of Native tradition. The same cannot be said for a leather jacket purchased at a store. In most cases, the leather is left-over from a beef slaughterhouse, and in those cases, the animal is not honored or cared for before it is used for people.'

Today, the leather industry is unrecognisable from balanced and pastoral communal living. According to the United Nations Industrial Development Organization (UNIDO), leather is among the most widely traded commodities in the world, with an estimated world trade value of approximately \$100b per year;[33] in 2015, 23,976 million square feet of leather were produced globally.[34] Despite being farmed at such a high rate, leather is marketed as a luxury product. It is also often referred to as 'natural'. But while cow skin is natural on a cow, once it has been removed from an animal, all illusions that it is a 'natural' product should end.

Turning skin into leather is a complicated and chemically intensive process. Once a cow has been killed, it must be flayed for its skin.* If the skin was left in its natural state it would begin to putrefy and rot away. To prevent this, it must be tanned. In modern factories and workshops, tanning consists of three main phases: the pre-treatment of the animal hides, application of a tanning agent

---

* This process led to the adoption of St Bartholomew as patron saint of the leather industry, a Christian flayed alive for his beliefs.

and material finishing, comprising drying and shining stages. It often also includes any of the following steps: sizing of hides, weaving, bleaching, carbonising and dyeing.

Leather tanning is a system that produces toxic waste on an industrial scale and has resulted in some of the world's worst pollution problems – problems that have been exported to the Global South. A German industrialist, furious at 1990s environmental laws which meant he had to close his tannery, described the situation as: 'It is a crime to export sewage sludge from Germany to India. But it is free enterprise to export hides to India and to produce sludge in tanning them there.'[35]

While countries like India and Bangladesh do have environmental laws, they are less likely to be enforced. Leather is an attractive source of foreign currency, so there is a strong incentive to give a free pass to dangerous practices.[36] Tanning agents can be vegetable-based, but 80–90 per cent of tanning performed throughout the world is done using a specific mineral: chromium. The main chromium compound used for leather tanning is chromium (III) hydroxide sulphate, which risks oxidising into chromium (VI). Chromium (VI) being the infamous chemical from the Hollywood film *Erin Brockovich*, which starred Julia Roberts and told the true story of the environmentalist lawyer taking on corporate polluters.[37]

A thousand gardens

The waters of the Buriganga River run black. A sickly sheen laps the hulls of brightly painted boats. Overcrowded ferries carry migrating villagers past boatloads of timber, ferrymen perch on water taxis and children leap in and out of the water. On the banks of the wide river stand the decaying ruins of nineteenth-century merchant mansions.

The village farmhands climb from the ferries onto the arrival piers in Bangladesh's capital. Hoping for a new life, they have come seeking work in the thousands of factories that web the city, whether that is sewing garments, packaging food or shovelling cement. Some will end up hawking cigarettes, sweeping the streets or becoming prostitutes in Dhaka's brothels. Others may reach the source of this poisoned waterway and find work in one of Dhaka's endless leather tanneries.

In Bengali, Hazaribagh means 'a thousand gardens'. For decades the tannery district of Hazaribagh pumped out 22,000 cubic litres of toxic waste per day.[38] Chemicals such as chromium, sulphur dioxide, formic acid and ammonium chloride were used to tan over a billion dollars' worth of exports each year. The Hazaribagh tanneries killed all the fish in the Buriganga River. They created the fifth most polluted place on the planet.

Syeda Rizwana Hasan is the chief executive of the Bangladesh Environmental Lawyers Association (BELA). As Bangladesh's only environmental law NGO, BELA is not popular among the business community, but very popular among ordinary people. The government, Ms Hasan says, is split fifty-fifty in their support of BELA.

Ms Hasan is an extremely busy individual, constantly required to travel, and overseeing around 350 environmental justice cases. Hazaribagh was supposed to be a residential area and yet it had hardly any greenery, was congested, overpopulated and drenched in pollution. 'They were literally inhaling poison, drinking poison,' Ms Hasan says of the 185,000 residents. 'They complained of losing their sense of smell, of chronic headaches, stomach and skin problems, of losing their appetite and the ability to work.' Residents also found their homes would rust and corrode: 'If this can happen to tin and steel, what is a tannery doing to the lungs of people?'

Working in Hazaribagh meant a 90 per cent chance of being dead before the age of fifty.[39] The situation grew so bad that in 2015 Médecins Sans Frontières (MSF) set up clinics in Hazaribagh to diagnose and treat people's illnesses. It was the first time they had done such a thing outside a war zone or natural disaster area. Human Rights Watch reported: 'Apart from heavy metals like chromium, cadmium, lead and mercury, a conglomerate of chemicals are discharged by the tanneries into the environment. Workers aged eight and older are soaked to the skin, breathing the fumes for most of the day and eating and living in these surroundings throughout the year. Personal protective equipment is not provided.'[40]

No one is counting how many tannery workers are killed or seriously injured each year, nor has there been an epidemiological study on cancer rates among tannery workers in Bangladesh.[41] But when such studies have been done in European nations like Sweden and Italy, where safety standards are far higher, they have found significant links between tannery work and cancer.

The curse of the tannery industry

From the 1990s onwards, the authorities talked of closing or relocating Hazaribagh's tannery district. Having allowed the creation of the fifth most polluted place on the planet, the Bangladeshi government eventually ordered the tanneries to move to specially built plots at a new facility.

The Leather Industrial Park is located in Savar, an industrial district on the outskirts of Dhaka. Chock-a-block with garment factories, Savar is notorious as the location of the Rana Plaza factory collapse, and numerous other deadly industrial incidents.

The new industrial park was intended to open in 2005, but suffered numerous delays until it was officially declared open thirteen years later.[42] Since its inception, the facility created a stand-off between the government and Hazaribagh's tannery owners, many of whom are powerful industrial figures who insisted on receiving compensation and relocation costs. In March 2017, Bangladesh's Supreme Court stated that 43 of the 155 tanneries had moved, leaving 112 still to relocate.[43] The next month, facing international pressure, the government shut down the power to the Hazaribagh tanneries. As of January 2019, they have still not all moved, and tanneries still operate in Hazaribagh.

Nor has the move to Savar solved either the political or environmental problems. The industrial park was designed to include Bangladesh's first ever central effluent treatment plant (CETP), yet where once thousands of litres of toxic chemicals were pumped into the Buriganga River, now they flow into the Dhaleshwari River, which runs alongside the Leather Industrial Park.

Supreme Court documents from 2017–19 describe a worsening situation: the CETP was found to be inadequate and not switched on twenty-four hours a day, disputes sprang up between contractors and ministries, local landfill sites were used as chemical dumping grounds and all the while the Dhaleshwari's oxygen levels fell sharply.[44] Local people say tannery waste is often dumped in the river at night to avoid detection.[45]

Ms Hasan describes the situation in one word: horrendous. 'It is equally as bad as Hazaribagh,' she says. But fixing the problem would not require a major scientific revolution, or huge investment. Bangladesh has no shortage of engineers or money, and Ms Hasan believes this problem could be fixed within eighteen months if there was the political will to do so. Instead, untreated effluent is being dumped into the Dhaleshwari River – the same process that led to the Buriganga being declared biologically dead.

Nowhere to hide

Bangladesh's top three exports are garments, leather and jute. According to Bangladesh's Export Promotion Bureau, leather, and leather goods, were worth $1.13b in 2014–15.[46] With hopes to reach $5b in leather exports by 2021,[47] leather is a powerful part of Bangladesh's impoverished economy. This power kept Hazaribagh uncontrolled in terms of environmental legislation and labour rights. 'We are not doing anything for Hazaribagh. The tannery owners are very rich and politically powerful,' stated Mahmood Hasan Khan, a director at the Department of Environment, in 2012.[48] The residents of the Thousand Gardens on the other hand, were left without their constitutional right to protection from pollution and abuse.

International campaign groups have called upon US and European brands who source leather from or had items made by companies that had tanneries in Hazaribagh to help pay for the clean-up and to prevent further environmental disaster.[49]

This is a call for action that Ms Hasan agrees with. '[Brands] are buying cheap leather from us, but it is actually not cheap,' she says. 'If you consider the environmental cost of producing the leather for them, it is proving to be very costly for Bangladesh. They are giving cheap leather to their customers, but Bangladesh is suffering huge environmental loss and damage.'

Pollution and toxic chemicals are not a problem that stays in faraway places like Hazaribagh or Savar: the leather produced there is destined for export to factories and shops across the world. While the European Union has strict chemicals legislation in place for products either made within or imported into the EU, it is impossible to detect every dangerous item.

EU rules exist to prevent exposure to CMR chemicals (substances classified as carcinogenic, mutagenic and toxic for reproduction). The EU has restricted chromium (VI) since 2015; no leather goods that come into contact with the skin are allowed to have a concentration higher than 3mg per kg.

Member states are responsible for enforcing this legislation, and if they find consumer products that contain hazardous chemicals, they must report them via the Rapid Alert System. Since 2015, the Rapid Alert System has received over 200 reports of sales of dangerous leather products containing chromium (VI), including a pair of 'first-walker shoes for babies' containing dangerously high levels of the chemical.[50]

Drowned on dry land

Having achieved independence from Britain in 1947, India sought to upgrade its leather industry from being a producer of raw hides to an exporter of more profitable finished leather products. Today, 75 per cent of tanneries in India are small businesses, often found in purposefully developed urban export clusters. Approximately 90 per cent are in Tamil Nadu, West Bengal and Uttar Pradesh.[51]

The drive to increase profitability had serious consequences. It required both a far greater volume of skins, and for leather workers to work longer hours, with more hazardous chemicals. It also meant the collapse of traditional rural tanneries run by Dalits.[52] The word *Dalit* comes from the Sanskrit root *dal*, and means 'broken, ground-down, downtrodden, or oppressed'. Dalits were seen as outside other castes, having been born with 'the stigma of "untouchability" because of the extreme impurity and pollution connected with their traditional occupations'.[53]

The concept of 'untouchability' has been abolished by India's constitution, but Dalits are often still socially excluded and restricted to jobs no one else wants. Research by the National Campaign on Dalit Human Rights found that in 38 per cent of government schools, Dalit children are still made to sit separately while eating. In as many as 73 per cent of villages surveyed, Dalits were not permitted to enter non-Dalit homes. In 25 per cent of the villages, Dalits were paid lower wages than other workers. They experienced longer working hours, delayed wages, verbal and physical abuse.[54]

Tannery work – dirty, unpleasant and involving dead animals – has traditionally been an occupation for Dalits, and also for India's Muslim population. When tanneries became industrialised and urbanised, Dalits dropped from being tannery owners to tannery workers because they lacked the resources and capital needed to elevate themselves to export entrepreneurs. The low social status of Dalits, and low pay in the leather industry, reinforce a status quo of poor conditions and wages below the required minimum.[55] Dalits and Muslims have also been targeted, beaten and murdered by hard-line Hindu cow-protection activists, who falsely accuse leather workers of killing cows.[56] Each state in India currently self-regulates regarding cow protection, with twenty-four out of twenty-nine states having some form of legislation restricting or prohibiting the slaughter of cows and other cattle.[57] In Gujarat, killing a cow carries a possible life sentence.[58] As a result of such extreme measures, slaughter often takes place in unlicensed abattoirs and the informal economy. In addition, some 2 million of India's cows are smuggled over the border to Bangladesh each year where they are slaughtered.[59]

Industrialised tannery work in India is, like in Bangladesh, incredibly dangerous. It involves daily, unprotected contact with highly toxic chemicals which seep into the skin, are inhaled into lungs and get splashed into eyes. Fevers, eye inflammation, headaches, bone and muscle pain, asthma, eczema, skin disease and lung cancers are routine. Humans are left to endure poisonous rot from the inside out, and the outside in. With no proper safety training or equipment, toxins cripple internal organs and reproductive systems. Child labour is also rife in India's tanneries with children employed as tannery assistants whose work includes climbing inside tannery barrels and tumblers to scrub them clean.[60]

In a particularly horrible case, ten workers drowned in toxic sludge when an effluent tank collapsed at a waste treatment plant in Tamil Nadu.[61] In the early hours of 31 January 2015, 600 cubic metres of toxic waste gushed out of the collapsed tank, engulfing ten men who slept at an adjacent tannery.

The waste contained toxic and reactive agents like ammonium, chromium and hydrogen sulphide. An engineer stated chemicals in the slurry had produced hazardous gases and exerted pressure on the walls of the tank. The workers were villagers who had migrated to the tannery district in search of work. A report of the incident says the slurry rose 10 feet up the walls of the workers' accommodation, leaving marks clearly visible two days later.[62] Photographs of the incident show a group of rescue workers stood around a plastic sheet at the R.K. Leathers tannery. On the sheet is a small blackened human body, one rigid arm raised above his face.*

Labour casualisation, appalling conditions and rock-bottom wages serve to drive down the cost of Indian leather. This means a long list of countries and brands queue up as customers. They avoid paying the full price of leather because it has been shouldered by the land, animals and human labourers. India's Council for Leather Exports lists the following countries as major markets for Indian leather and leather products: the US, with a share of 14.66 per cent, Germany 11 per cent, the UK 10 per cent, Italy 7 per cent, France 5 per cent, the UAE 5 per cent, Spain 4.6 per cent, Hong Kong 4.5 per cent and China 3 per cent.

Secret Italy

'Premium'. 'Luxury'. 'Clean'. 'From the finest tanneries in the world'. These are just some of the labels that purveyors of Italian leather goods like to attach to their products. In 2017, Italy exported €4b of leather.[63] Tanneries in Italy are primarily located in three areas: Arzignano in the north-eastern state of Veneto; Santa Croce, between

---

* The names of the dead: Shah Jahan Mallik, Qutubuddin Mallik, Sukur Ali Mallik from Phulberia village. Habib Khan, his two sons Ali Akbar Khan and Ali Asgar Khan, brothers Asiar Khan and Agram Ali Khan, and a young worker called Piar Khan – all from Dingapur village. K.G. Sampath, the plant security guard was from Tamil Nadu.

Florence and Pisa in the central state of Toscana; and Solofra in the south. It is an industry fuelled by immigrant workers on temporary contracts. Senegalese workers first found work in Santa Croce, picking up difficult and dirty jobs that Italians no longer wanted.

Tannery owners realised they could exploit Senegalese workers, pushing them to work long hours of often unpaid overtime and keeping them on temporary contracts. Research by the Change Your Shoes campaign found non-EU nationals represented just 16 per cent of people on permanent contracts, while among people on temporary contracts, 53 per cent are non-EU citizens. Overseas workers can find themselves working for over a decade in the same Italian tannery without ever being given a permanent contract. Yet they are unable to get work at another tannery because they are considered the 'private property' of a single firm.[64]

In 2004, Thiam Mamadou Lamine, a thirty-five-year-old Senegalese worker, was killed by a blast of hydrogen sulphide released from a drum. According to the local trade union, the extraction system was switched off and Thiam was not wearing a mask.[65] In addition to fatal incidents, 493 instances of occupational diseases were recorded in Santa Croce between 1997 and 2014. The most common cause was musculoskeletal disorders, followed by cancers which most commonly affected nasal passages and the bladder. There were also high incidences of skin diseases caused by exposure to the chemicals used in the leather tanning process.[66] Between 2009 and 2013, 720 accidents were recorded in Santa Croce, 176 of them serious.

Shoes that don't bleed

With production at 24.2 billion pairs per year, shoes have become an obsession that is jeopardising our future. Nowhere is the shoe industry's lack of sustainability more apparent than in the production of leather.

Predicated on death and the belief that humans have a supremacist right to kill, the leather industry has pain and plunder at its centre. The normalised horror of the industrial death of cows requires the destruction of Amazonia, one of our most precious collective resources. It requires a total disregard for human rights and health, and the imposition of slavery. It also requires vast quantities of toxic chemicals to be pumped into the water and land that we depend upon.

The language around shoe consumption is often one of individual empowerment and enjoyment. With leather, we see this supposed enjoyment and empowerment providing a mask for carnage. But the option exists to collectively step away from complicity in this destructive system, and away from ideas of human supremacy where eradicating animals and the planet is inconsequential.

Responding to this desire for change, the good news is that leather is no longer the only option for shoes. A great many new and sustainable materials now exist which have not been made with the same levels of violence as leather. These new products are durable, non-toxic, more sustainable than PVC or polyurethane leather substitutes, and some can be recycled back into the soil.

Mushroom leather, for example, is strong yet velvet soft. In its untreated state it is tawny brown, with gold and chestnut rings like the concentric haloes of Saturn.[67] Pineapple leather is made using the by-products of pineapple harvests: leaves are degummed and made into a mesh material resembling felt. It is sustainable and needs no extra land, water, pesticides or fertiliser beyond what is already used in established pineapple harvests.[68] Other plant-based vegan alternatives include cork, soya, apple, paper, wine and even tea leather (known as teather).

One brand using pineapple leather is NAE Vegan Shoes. Co-founder Paula Pérez says she stopped wanting anything to do with leather after taking up a plant-based diet over a decade ago. She founded her own brand and now makes shoes from recycled airbags, plastic bottles and tyres, along with pineapple leaves and cork from protected cork oaks.

It is an unlikely fit for a brand based in Portugal, a country famous for its leather goods. 'The first years in the company [were] very difficult for us,' she explains. 'The leather industry was very strong at the time and factories were not used to working with vegan materials. Today things have changed a little bit. Information is much more available, and people are more concerned about the environment.'

Paula is now experimenting with making shoes from bamboo and coconut fibres, still driven by a desire to protect the planet from deforestation: 'In the fashion industry, profit is the driver for companies, regardless of if animals die in a horrible way, or if people are killed because of labour conditions (like at Rana Plaza in Bangladesh),' she says. 'Big companies have outsourced not only production, but also the responsibility of doing things right.'

As we will see in later chapters, transforming the shoe industry requires far more than changing individual shopping choices, but if the decision is made to give up leather, what should be done with shoes people already own? 'It's a very personal decision,' says Frank Schmidt at PETA. 'If you're a sustainable person we would not recommend that you throw them away. But if you feel uncomfortable wearing the skin of another being, it might be better if you donate them to people in need and buy some vegan shoes, because fashion is social and cultural, so you show what you wear.'

The age of extinction

There are many people engaged in trying to actively re-harmonise humanity's relationship with the other beings who live on this planet. Indigenous groups and conservationists, for example, who struggle to preserve land and keep species from extinction. Spending most of her life living in the Australian outback, Professor Deborah Bird Rose worked alongside Aboriginal teachers, elders and historians to study relationships between humans and species on the brink of disappearing forever.

Death is an integral part of life on earth, but Professor Bird Rose identified something particularly wrong with the era we live in. One day, when feeling particularly overwhelmed by witnessing extinction, she wrote that the balance between life and death is being relentlessly overrun.

'Something is happening,' she wrote, 'that involves us as participants, and that we struggle to witness.' Professor Rose named our time a moment of Double Death. An instance of so many losses that ecosystems cannot recuperate their diversity. This leads to the death of resilience and renewal, and sees evolution overtaken. She called Double Death a despoiler, an open secret and an open wound, something that fractures a compact that has been integral to life on earth. It is, Professor Rose wrote, 'an affront to our very being as creatures of earth in the fact that we are doing so much to destroy it.'[69]

In a final blog post before she herself died in December 2018, Professor Rose provided a rebellious antidote to living in an age of extinction. She argued that we must accept kinship and mutualism with the biosphere: 'For humans, saying yes to life is a profound ethical choice. It is a passionate embrace of the living world, a grateful response to the gifts of life, a pledge of solidarity with earth life, and a commitment to participation in the complexities of mutuality.'[70]

We need to overhaul our approach to each other, to animals and to the planet. We need to radically alter the false concept that the biosphere exists to provide shopping thrills, entertainment and profit. As should be clear by now, the people in charge do not have our wellbeing, or the wellbeing of the planet, in mind when they make their decisions, and it is up to us to demand change.

We move now to an integral part of this destruction, a moment we do not think much about, but which will outlast us all. The moment when it all goes to waste.

CHAPTER 7

Getting Wasted

One hundred and fifty years ago, in the borderlands of England and Wales, there was a strange tradition practised by Christian families but considered heretical by the Church. If a person died without receiving confession or their last rights, it was believed they risked being barred from heaven. The solution was to call for a sin eater.

A piece of bread was placed on the dead person's chest, which was believed to absorb the sins of the deceased. When the sin eater arrived, they would consume the bread, thus transferring the sins into themselves.

Sin eaters were shunned outcasts, usually paupers hungry for bread and the few pennies they were paid. This chapter is about sin eating on a global scale, about offloading problems, abdicating responsibilities, and about the people and processes who try to deal with the systemic sins of our world so that we do not have to.

Globalisation has created a system whereby every site of shoe production is in crisis. Factories are full of exploited workers breathing toxic air, millions of cows are having their throats cut, ancient rainforests are being razed to the ground and the planet's waterways are clogged with industrial poisons. This maelstrom produces a yearly dose of 24.2 billion pairs of shoes to be shoved in the faces of consumers who are encouraged to spend beyond their means and buy beyond their needs.

But what happens next, after the meagre thrill of a shoe purchase, after blisters have risen and receded, after a sole has worn through, or a pair of heels have been banished to the back of the wardrobe? What happens after shoes – these complex, handmade, multi-materialled items often made from once living skin – are discarded? What happens when all the pain of production counts for nothing?

This stage in the life cycle of shoes is a little-investigated, deeply underfunded area of research. Post-consumer waste is a grey zone where brands shrug their shoulders and take scant responsibility for what they have produced, where the Global North uses the Global South as a dustbin, and where shoppers close their eyes and pass the problem on.

Re-use

On an industrial estate in the north-west of London is a large warehouse. Metal shelves laden with boxes reach far up to the ceiling, colour-coded sacks form mountains many metres high and trollies stuffed with deliveries are lined up rank upon rank. The volume of discarded stuff is both overwhelming and sickening: sacks and sacks and sacks of discarded clothes and shoes. This stuff has been manufactured all over the world but is now being thrown away because it developed a fault, or because it did not fit any more, because it had fallen out of favour, or because a magazine said it was no longer in fashion. It is a sight that makes you wish for an 'off button' for consumerism.

To deal with this mess, a network of drivers and vans criss-cross southern England, hauling in 50 tonnes of donations a week to fund the work of TRAID, a garment recycling NGO. Donations arrive from charity shops, people's homes and textile recycling banks. Jose Baladron is in charge of operations at the warehouse. Originally from Spain, he once worked in the marketing department at Inditex (Zara's parent company), before switching sides to join TRAID instead. He is now responsible for trying to increase the volume of donations that arrive at the warehouse.

Newly arrived stock is sorted by a team of fifteen people. When a delivery trolley arrives, it is weighed and then labelled with its weight, the area it was collected from and the name of the driver who collected it. The trolley is then emptied and non-clothing items like books, bric-a-brac, DVDs and toys are removed. Collections from houses are regarded as the best; in the depths of clothing banks drivers often find nasty surprises, from dirty nappies to dead animals.

The bulk of the team of sorters work on a platform reached by climbing narrow metal stairs. A conveyor belt carries donations up to the platform where every item is sorted by hand. The items are categorised, and each sorter has been given a different category to look for and pull off the belt as they go past. They all wear plastic gloves and one or two have masks over their noses and mouths. The first category is 'crème', premium clothes with a high resale value. Crème is followed by more expensive high street brands like Zara, and lastly, it's the turn of the cheapest brands like Primark, New Look or Boohoo.

Sorting supervisor Rose Nkore has spent twenty years handling the things that society has thrown away. She has watched the quality of clothes and shoes fall, and found more and more items donated unworn with the label still attached. 'Fast fashion means lower quality,' Rose says. 'Sometimes things are new, untouched, unworn. We get flooded with the lower quality – our lower-grade quality goes mostly to [discount] sales.'

The clothes, shoes and bric-a-brac that arrive at the TRAID warehouse have beaten steep odds to get there. British people throw approximately 350,000 tonnes of used clothing in the bin each year, equivalent to the weight of more than 29,000 London buses.[1] Once in the bin, refuse is headed for landfill or incineration.

Another obstacle is the intensification of gang-related crime. Robbing clothing banks is a surprisingly lucrative business: in the summer of 2018, a tonne of good-quality clothes was worth £1,000–1,200. TRAID say that in the worst months, 2–3 tonnes per week were being stolen from their clothing banks alone.

These textile banks, often found in supermarket car parks, are solid metal boxes, so how do gangs get inside? 'Sometimes they use children to climb in – sometimes our drivers open the bank and a kid runs out and away,' Jose explains. 'Or they take the lock, split it open and get a key cut by paying a bribe.'

Gangs steal the second-hand clothing and take it to their own sorting facilities, hoping to find a haul of crème clothing. In 2016, a pair of shoes implanted with a tracker were put in a clothing bank that was routinely being robbed. The shoes were firstly taken to a farm in Dagenham, Essex. From Dagenham they sat in a shipping container for a week, before being shipped across eastern Europe to Poland, where they ended up in a vintage shop in Krakow.

As well as being angry that charities are robbed so people can fill commercial shops for free, Jose is annoyed by the needless pollution theft generates: 'It really bothers me, the CO_2, transport, petrol, fuel that is needed for a piece that could have been sold a mile from the warehouse. Instead it has travelled all over the world and maybe if it is not sold in that shop in Krakow it will end up in Uganda or Senegal, and maybe if it's not sold there it will end up in Pakistan.'

TRAID say the crime of robbing textile banks is now being taken more seriously, with private detective agencies and police tracking and arresting gangs. But the lucrative nature of second-hand clothes means those arrested just get replaced by new people.

Back in the warehouse, the conveyor belt has been picked clean of everything deemed suitable for sale in a branch of TRAID. 'Shoes used to be 11 per cent of all the stock we collected, 270–280 tonnes a year,' Jose says. 'Now this has dropped to 6 per cent. This is the same across the whole industry. The quality of shoes has got worse, so people just throw them in the bin. This is true for clothing too; fast fashion is killing it. Items get ruined after three washes. It is too easy and too cheap to replace them.'

There is also a gendered difference in what is donated: 'We get lots of ladies' shoes, men don't donate shoes,' Rose says. 'I think they don't buy so many to begin with and they wait until the life has gone out of them for them to donate, so we're always short of men's shoes.'

Clothes and shoes deemed not good enough for an English charity shop end up on a second belt. 'We don't want to dispose of anything,' says Jose. 'If an item ends up on the second belt, it is not good enough for the shops. It goes to the recycling companies who grade them.'

Recycling companies sort rejected donations by style, climate and cultural suitability, and quality. Once sorted, items are packed into bales usually weighing between 40–50kg. These bales are shipped out to eastern Europe, west, east or central Africa, and India and

Pakistan in Asia. It is a market that fluctuates with geopolitics: Ukraine, for example, was a key destination for second-hand exports until the conflict with Russia disrupted the market.

Once they've arrived, bales of clothes or shoes are sold wholesale to warehouses who sell them again to local sellers. Local sellers typically break the bales down into smaller packages weighing 5–10kg. These packages are sold to people who have stalls in markets and villages. In Swahili the bales are known as *mitumba*, which means 'bundles'.

The contents of each bundle is a lottery. Sometimes a market trader will get a good bundle and have enough money to cover their rent and food for the month, sometimes they will not. Kenya's *Daily Nation* paper quoted a twenty-three-year-old second-hand shoe seller in Nairobi who goes three times a week to buy stock. 'In a good week, I can get back everything I put in, plus more,' he said. 'There are some weeks where I make less than Sh5,000 [£38], other times I make nothing.'[2]

The four biggest exporters of second-hand clothing including shoes, are the US who export 19.5 per cent of the world's stock, Britain with 13.3 per cent, Germany with 11.5 per cent and China with 7.9 per cent. Shoes unfortunately are not categorised separately, but are included in the category of second-hand clothing (SHC).[3] Unwanted clothing and shoes flood places like Owino Market in Kampala, Uganda. Owino Market is one of the largest second-hand clothing shopping hubs in Africa, so vast that local safari companies offer market tours.[4]

This deluge of second-hand clothing has been partly blamed for the collapse of East Africa's own clothing and shoe factories, which thrived in the 1960s–80s. In 2016, the leaders of the East African Community (EAC), a bloc comprising of Uganda, Kenya, Tanzania, Rwanda, Burundi and South Sudan, decided to take action. They stated that they would ban used clothing imports in 2019 in order to rebuild their own manufacturing sector.

At the behest of angry recycled clothing exporters, the US government warned the EAC that they risked violating the terms of the African Growth and Opportunity Act (AGOA) if they were to ban importing second-hand clothes. This act gives members of the

EAC easy access to US markets, in exchange for the US receiving preferential treatment. This caused countries, including Kenya, to back away from the boycott, for fear of losing their US market for textiles and clothing. Determined to move its economy away from agrarian roots and create an industrial base for 'Made In Rwanda' products, the Rwandan government, unlike Kenya, hiked tariffs on used US clothing and footwear and was suspended from AGOA as a result.[5]

It is not just second-hand clothing imports that sabotage east Africa's factories. Manufacturing also faces competition from the churn of cheap products from Asia. China already exports $1.2b of new clothing to east Africa and experts warn that any gap in the market left by second-hand clothing bans or tariffs will quickly be filled by China.[6]

Missing shoes

In the TRAID warehouse, everything has now been graded by quality and placed in its correct box. Jose points to one of the large plastic sacks: 'With pain in my heart, this is clothing that is broken, painted, damaged so badly that it cannot be used at all.' These items are compacted into 400kg bales and sent direct to Pakistan where companies promise TRAID they turn the old clothes into car-seat insulation or industrial cloths, rather than sending it to landfill. 'Last year we sent 150 tonnes out of the 2,500 we collected,' Jose says. 'So it is a minimal percentage going there.'

It is now time for one final task on the conveyor belt. At the end of each feed, it is the turn of the missing shoes. Missing shoes are single shoes in a sellable condition which somehow arrived without their other half. Despite the public being asked to tie or strap shoes together before donating them, many pairs get separated during the collection process. At TRAID, the separated shoes have been placed into boxes until it is their turn to be tipped out onto the conveyor belt and sorted.

The jumbled shoes roll up onto the platform. Working quickly, the sorters' hands fly over the piles, spotting shoes by colour and type and matching them back together. This is a lucky run – all the shoes are matched up until a single scarlet baby shoe is all that is left on the conveyor belt. 'Single shoes break my heart,' Rose says. 'We know they cannot have been donated as single, but the process means they're going to get separated. So we end up with lots of single shoes.'

Outside the warehouse are huge bulging white plastic sacks with *SINGLE SHOES* scrawled on the side in marker pen. On their own, these shoes have no retail use, outside of a very small market for people who have just one foot. These white sacks are collected by businesses who have a side-line processing single shoes. From London they will go north to Birmingham or Hertfordshire and then head east, possibly to Poland or Pakistan, where warehouses specialise in matching missing shoes back together.

Missing shoes are drawn into these warehouses from around the world and then an attempt is made to match them back together. Shoes are laid out by type, colour, brand and size. When new batches come in, the shoes are matched as closely as possible. Sometimes an exact match can be found, or sometimes a shoe is paired up with a match that has a close resemblance, then sold at a significant discount. This is shoes returning to their most practical state – their main purpose is to protect feet, and they do not need to be identical to perform this function.

Repair

Once a month, the hall of St John's Church in East London is transformed into the Leytonstone Repair Café. On the wall is a large sheet of paper with three columns, the first column lists a person's name, the second lists the item they have brought and the third states an outcome, often accompanied by a scribbled smiley face. In the second column is written: *briefcase, favourite dress, mobile phone, DVD player, sandwich maker, rug jacket, fan, blood pressure monitor.* Outside the hall a queue of people with bicycles wait in the sunshine to meet with one of two mechanics under a marquee.

Stood at the door, welcoming people into the crowded hall is Oliver Peat, the waste and recycling officer for Waltham Forest

Council. In the last decade, Waltham Forest has gone from being the fifteenth to the thirty-fifth most deprived borough in the UK. It has a diverse population with large Pakistani, Polish and Jamaican populations, a fact reflected in the people eating cake and patiently waiting in the hall.

A woman in a printed cat T-shirt comes in holding what turns out to be a battery-operated cat flap. Oliver apologetically explains that all the electrical repair slots are booked up. The woman sighs and asks if it is possible for her to bring in a broken fridge-freezer next month. 'The waste hierarchy goes – reduce, re-use, recycle,' Oliver says once the woman with the cat flap has left. 'But really we should be focusing a bit higher up – on repair.'

'Repair is better because it means that recycling is what we do when we can't do anything else. If you can keep the thing alive for as long as possible, then it stops you putting it into the bin.' Oliver says there is a growing enthusiasm for events like the Repair Café, prompted in part by a desire to save money: 'We've connected with residents in the area who all seem to get it. They think, "I don't want to throw this away as I've got a connection with it, or I want to save a bit of money, or I want to do something good for the environment, or it worked fine last week so I want to see what I can do."'

Leading the overbooked electrical repair team is Janet Gunter, co-founder of the Restart Project, a growing team of people committed to fixing electronics and teaching repair for free so things do not end up in landfill.

'The moment something goes wrong it should not go to the shredder or landfill. Instead we should try and figure out what is wrong and figure out a solution,' Janet explains. 'At events like this, even if something is end-of-life, at least they've had a go, they've tried.'

Gesturing along the table at a fan heater that has been opened and is trailing wires, Janet is clearly frustrated by the barriers to fixing consumer goods. A lot of the objects on the table are household appliances that were designed never to be opened ever again, locked by safety screws and glue.

Then there is the obstacle of companies not publishing vital information. Janet's team has been unable to get service manuals for any of the objects. The lack of information makes it really difficult for either amateurs or professionals to repair things, even the higher-value objects. It is a situation that leads Janet and her team to spend hours trying to figure out which component parts on circuit boards need replacing. 'Some of it is by design, some of it is the manufacturer squeezing costs out of it,' Janet says. 'A lot of the stuff here is super cheap and made to be thrown away.'

What does she think leads manufacturers, who have to drink the same water and breathe the same air as everyone else, to have such irresponsible practices in place? 'Profit – shareholder capitalism,' Janet says. 'A lot operate on this quarterly treadmill where they have to be seen to be delivering profit to their shareholders.'

Even if an industrial designer wants the product they've spent three years working on to be ecologically responsible, there is always pressure from marketing departments who want products *smaller*, *sleeker*, *sexier*, and from production managers who just want stuff to be cheaper. So how could repair be made easier? 'We'd like to see the barriers to repair reduced,' Janet says. 'Access to documentation, access to spare parts, and some of the worst design decisions being made illegal – like glue. Small electronics are increasingly glued together.'

In 2007, France introduced an Extended Producer Responsibility (ERP) scheme to make clothing, linen and footwear companies responsible for managing the end-of-life of their products. Such schemes are supposed to encourage more environmentally friendly designs as well as give brands public responsibility. In France, the ERP scheme trebled the number of used TCF collections between 2011 and 2016, with 90 per cent of everything collected either re-used or recycled.[7] In the UK, despite the urgency, overhauling the waste system, extending and enforcing producer responsibility systems, and deposit return schemes remain ineffective and stuck at the consultation phase.

While there are clothes being repaired at the Leytonstone Repair Café, there are no shoes, and no one has heard of a community-based shoe repair workshop. For now, shoe repair remains a private business.

Well heeled

In a small town in Cyprus in the late 1950s, Costas Xenophontos's grandfather sat his son down and asked him what kind of apprenticeship he wanted. Conscious of the fact that he'd never had a pair of decent shoes, Costas's father said he'd like to be a shoemaker. Once qualified, he boarded a boat for England with the plan of making some money then heading home.

Instead he founded Classic Shoe Repairs in 1963, got his sons a good education and never returned to Cyprus. From hard-grafted beginnings, Classic Shoe Repairs is now the official repairer for luxury shoe brand Jimmy Choo. In a locked cupboard sit Jimmy Choo own-brand leathers used to create seamless repairs. The Kentish Town shop even once fixed a bag for Lady Diana.

Customers are treated like they've arrived at an exclusive spa. The foyer is large and bright with one wall comprising several hundred small wooden drawers, each containing a pair of shoes awaiting collection. Hidden behind the shiny counter is a flight of steps leading down to a cavernous, low-ceilinged workshop.

The workshop radio is broadcasting sports news, and an air-conditioning unit keeps the air fresh. Every shelf is stacked full of shoeboxes, tools and leather samples. There are containers of zips, threads, glue, paint, heel tips and nails. Classic Shoe Repairs has twenty-four employees. 'Back in the day when we were growing up, all the shoe repairers that were here were Greek,' Costas says. 'If you came to my wedding it was like a Greek shoemakers' convention because my dad knew everyone who was anyone in the industry.' This has changed dramatically: several years ago, Costas's brother got everyone to say good morning in their own language, and counted about twelve different nationalities.

Walking along the aisle, Costas holds up a men's leather shoe: 'This had a big hole in it, so we've re-soled it. The upper is in good condition, and they'll get a good polish, so when the customer gets them back, he's doubled the life of them.' Lifting the tongue of the shoe, Costas points to thinning and discolouring on the inside of the shoe: 'Some people wear the shoe out from the inside out. See how it's changed colour? He's got hot feet, so the insole will need changing.'

Further in, an entire section of the workshop is dedicated to new heel work. High-heeled shoes which have lost their heel tips, or been scraped or even snapped by grilles or cobblestones. In a box is a pair of black suede Valentino heels in several pieces, looking utterly beyond help or hope.

Working in this section is a young Indonesian man named Yon. He started working as a cobbler in 2005 and has been at this workshop for five years. So why would someone bring in such a battered pair of shoes for repair? 'Often this style you cannot buy anymore in the shops, if you love this style you have to get it repaired,' Yon explains. 'Or it is already comfortable, with leather you have to break it, to mould it to your foot. If you buy new shoes you might get blisters.'

On the question of the emotional attachments people form for shoes, Yon says simply: 'One is sentimental, two is comfortable. It is very personal. If they love them, they're going to pay whatever it takes. It could be that they came from their grandma and they got married in them; you can't put a value on it.'

Having spent decades listening to people beg him to restore their favourite footwear, Costas agrees: 'It's all sorts of things – some people have hand-me-downs from their mum, or old wedding shoes, or they're the shoes she first kissed the love of her life in, people have their own quirks. It is more mental than physical. Who are we to question them?'

This particular customer will eventually collect a good-as-new pair of Valentino heels, but not everyone is so determined to resurrect their shoes, and many shoes brought to Costas cannot be repaired. This is because, he says, many shoes were never built for repair in the first place. Trainers, which became popular as dress informalised, have moulded and glued-on soles which are particularly difficult to repair or replace. The team in the basement do attempt to fix trainers and are often successful, but with the cost of repair often being higher than the price of a new pair of regular trainers, they mostly repair designer brands.

'We've become very much a throwaway society, to be honest with you, especially with fashion over the years,' Costas says. 'When trainers became a thing, with even elderly people running around in trainers in the 80s, they were very much buy a pair and throw them away.'

Nor do shoe manufacturers like doing repairs. A factory is a one-way production line, not built for disassembling and remaking shoes. Although factories could fix shoes, if they started to do repairs it would be like putting a spanner in the production line.

It is a paradoxical situation – Costas knows he is running a business built on manufacturers not doing what they are supposed to do. He sees more and more shoes that cannot be repaired but isn't sure what would happen to his business if standards actually improved. What he would like is for more graduates to enter the skilled repair industry: 'When young people go to the London School of Fashion and so on, they want to be designers or manufacturers, there's not a lot of people going into the service side of the industry.' This lack of a British workforce and what the future holds for his multicultural staff after Brexit has become a source of worry.

The shoes people wear take a battering. They are sometimes referred to as 'investments' but no other investment is treated as badly as shoes. 'Of your whole attire – a blouse, a pair of jeans and your shoes – those shoes are going to be the ones that will take the most wear,' Costas says. 'The whole weight of your body is on them, they're going to walk on the street, they'll get splashed with acid rain. From a health aspect, depending on how clean your feet are, you can only carry on wearing shoes for so long. Out of your whole dressage, your shoes are the ones that take the brunt of it.'

But once shoes become worn beyond the point of being reusable or repairable, is the bin really the best we can do?

Recycle

If there is one brain that contains pretty much everything there is to know about shoe recycling, it is the one belonging to Professor Shahin Rahimifard. He is an expansive, generous talker, full of enthusiasm, yet battle hardened after years of arguing with shoe brands who seek to use his research as a smokescreen for business as usual.

Professor Rahimifard started working on the puzzle of shoe recycling fifteen years ago at Loughborough University. He says the research was the result of his wife (also a respected academic) telling him to figure out what to do with a large sackful of shoes she wanted to be rid of.

In his laboratory, shoe recycling is a *Golden Project*, generating more interest than the recycling of cars, mobile phones, laptops or any other high-value item. Professor Rahimifard has no emotional attachment to shoes, he sees them as a utilitarian item that got out of control when they became a fashion product. Rather, the challenge and the lure of shoes for him is that they are very low value in material terms (there is no gold to be pried out of circuit boards) and yet they have been put together with solid complexity.

The question therefore is how to efficiently dismantle a shoe down to its tiniest sections, separate out all the different materials, generate some value from the waste, all while preventing the ecological destruction of the planet.

At the Centre for Sustainable Manufacturing and Recycling Technologies (SMART), the first idea Professor Rahimifard's team considered and discarded was making new shoes out of old ones. If only one part of a shoe had broken, why not just replace the upper or the sole and deliver up a new pair of shoes? But upcycling crumbled, not because of engineering or technology, but because of the problem of consumer and commercial perception.

While assembling shoes from discarded parts may come to pass in a dystopian climate future, in present society fashion makes styles obsolete by the time shoes reach recycling. Then there are the difficulties of quality control and uniformity, plus how to avoid bacterial contamination. In short, few people want to buy and wear shoe waste.

The option that was settled on was *fragmentation, followed by post-fragmentation separation*. *Fragmentation* means dismantling a shoe into its component parts. *Post-fragmentation separation* means separating the parts by material type.

This is no easy feat. A single shoe can be made from as many as forty different types of material: leather, rubber, steel, bronze, plastics of all different weights and densities, polyester, acrylic, nylon thread and so on. There is also the question of scale. This is not a conundrum based on how to slowly dismantle one shoe, but about efficiently dealing with millions of tonnes of discarded shoes, all of which have different assembly methods. At the SOEX recycling plant in Wolfen, Germany, 35,000 pairs of used shoes arrive each day, of which 8,750 (25 per cent) get fragmented.[8]

'Sometimes we see 10–15 different types of materials in one shoe, including four different types of plastic,' says Professor Rahimifard. 'Companies buy insoles and parts of shoes from different companies, and the different companies use different plastics, and some of the manufacturers don't care. If it meets its criteria, it doesn't matter.'

Key factors in contemporary shoe design make recycling really problematic – mixing materials together creates a huge hurdle, mixing colours together also makes huge difficulties and adding metal into shoes as shanks or decorative studs is a calamity because it is so tough to shred. 'The way that shoes are designed and manufactured at the moment doesn't take into account their end of life,' the professor continues. 'The inclusion of metal components in shoes makes their recycling much more difficult. We are calling for a ban on the use of metal in footwear manufacturing.'

The problems brands are creating are urgent and deeply worrying. Put a slice of ethylene vinyl acetate, the shock-absorbent midsole often found in trainers, into landfill and it will still be there in 1,000 years.[9] Times this by several billion and the environmental legacy being created comes into sharp focus. While objects like running shoes promise to take us back to nature and help us achieve well-being, in reality they are destroying the nature they say they connect us to.

Heel to toe

The most recent engineering processes being developed in Professor Rahimifard's laboratory are currently subject to a confidentiality agreement due to the way they are funded, but they mainly involve the use of air, water and vibrating tables to separate out the different materials by their weight.

On a table in the laboratory is the result of this process – small plastic sample bags full of rubber chips, some of which have been bonded together with resin. The sponginess of the rubber makes it ideal for use as underlay in basketball courts, for heat and sound insulation in the wheel arches of cars and as surfacing for athletic tracks.

But becoming an athletic track should never be viewed as a shoe's final destination, because the track surface will eventually wear out and have to be removed: 'Remember that whatever you produce will one day become waste and you'll have to recycle it as well,' says Professor Rahimifard. 'If you do a bad job, the next time it comes to recycling there is nothing you can do and it can only be sent to landfill.'

It is for this reason that Professor Rahimifard looks unfavourably on the term 'circular economy' – the idea of creating closed-loop production in order to keep resources out of landfill for as long as possible. The problem is that a circular economy approach recommends putting waste to the 'best use possible', without defining if this means best environmental use or best economic use. The most economical approach might be to incinerate something but this may make no sense whatsoever environmentally.

'I believe this term at times is misused. The problem arises when economic considerations become the main focus of recovery and recycling,' says Professor Rahimifard about 'circular economy'. 'I've been into companies where they say, "Look, if we were to burn our waste to make energy, we'd get more money than trying to use it as recycled materials." This overriding focus on economy makes people make the wrong decisions based on money, not what is best for the environment.'

Professor Rahimifard's work focuses instead on *Circularity of Material and Resource Use*: the idea that you only ever borrow a resource from the 'bank of resources' and must be able to justify its functionality and then return it back to the bank to be used again. This 'using resources' approach is designed to be the antithesis of 'consuming resources'.

Eat your shoes

An additional plan being worked on in the laboratory is perhaps the most fitting answer to excessive consumerism. Dr Richard Heath, a colleague of Professor Rahimifard's, wants people to eat their shoes. He is currently investigating whether post-consumer leather could be treated like animal hide and broken down into gelatine and fibres which could then be eaten.*

It remains to be seen whether the general public could be convinced to eat shoe waste as part of their daily diet, or whether this is an idea to be kept in reserve in case a climate dystopia does happen and we all end up digging through landfill for food.

Having watched brands churn out hundreds of millions of shoes each year, then show an almost total disregard for what happens to them, Professor Rahimifard has called the industry's response to post-consumer waste 'negligible'. Global footwear manufacturing had an estimated market size of $204.9b in 2020.[10] Although Professor Rahimifard's laboratory is small, it has recently had a dividing wall built down the middle to squeeze in more projects. One thing he would like to see change immediately is for brands to invest in solving the problem of shoe waste by financially backing research.

SMART once calculated that just 5 per cent of the world's shoes were being recycled. It is a figure the professor does not believe has changed much: 'Whichever applications we considered, it was 3 per cent or 5 per cent,' he says of SMART's study. 'There is no new study, I don't think it's more than doubled, if that. I am very confident to say that we are still sending over 90 per cent of shoes to landfill.'

If only 5–10 per cent of shoes get recycled, this leaves billions of pairs headed straight for landfill each year. 'When it comes to landfill, it doesn't matter if it is UK landfill or Bangladesh landfill or Pakistan landfill – if anything it is worse there because there is less monitoring,' Professor Rahimifard concludes. 'We've got to think about a global view of things – not globalisation, but a global view

---

* Acclaimed German director Werner Herzog once ate his shoe having lost a bet to a fellow film director. Herzog dutifully took his shoes to a top Californian restaurant, boiled them for five hours, added lots of seasoning, then ate one on stage at the UC Theatre in Berkeley. Charlie Chaplin on the other hand, pretended to eat his boot in *The Gold Rush*, when in fact it was made of liquorice. Shoes have also been used as serving platters with flip-flops, trainers and clogs used by restaurants instead of plates. Japanese prime minister Shinzō Abe once found himself being served chocolate truffles in a very convincing metal shoe by an Israeli celebrity chef.

of things. Whatever we do, it's somewhere, somebody's landfill and this is humanity's landfill.'

Reduce and rethink

What if one way forward was to transform how we interact with the planet, not just in terms of big-scale thinking about carbon emissions, but with every step we take on the earth's surface?

Dr Kate Fletcher spends a lot of time thinking about re-thinking. Like Cassandra of Troy, the high priestess whose prophecies of doom went ignored, Dr Fletcher's approach to the fashion industry is that 'less is the only way forward'.

Much of Dr Fletcher's work has involved coaching brands on how they can reduce their environmental footprint. Her conclusion is that attempts to lessen the impact of single items are no match for the endless production of stuff: 'The efficiency gains of all of those small-scale reductions are simply not enough to outweigh the accumulative effect of consumption,' she says. What is needed instead is a 'switching of the levers' and an imagining of our world in a different way.

Sat in a train station coffee shop, Dr Fletcher is so intent on her hunt for change that she says we should even fundamentally rethink the way we walk. Sports companies market trainers as protection and enhancement for the body. Part of this message is that this footwear must be replaced regularly to maintain its protection, with running shoes marketed as only being supportive for 500 miles. Nike once intended its Mayfly shoe to last for just 100km before it wore out.

Dr Fletcher argues that rather than protection, shoes create a softening and weakening of the body. In the same way that Erik Trinkaus found human toes became flimsy 40,000 years ago, the modern human foot becomes reliant on splinting. 'Part of the business model is to force a replacement, partly by requiring people to depend on the padding,' Dr Fletcher explains. 'A simple way to circumvent the buying of new shoes is to walk barefoot – take them off. Or develop the strength in the ligaments, ankles and knees to protect your feet if you're walking without a support structure, and then you don't need to replace them.'

There are a variety of companies now offering minimal-soled shoes of just 3mm, which encourage a different way of moving, one they argue brings a greater connection with the physical world. Convincing people to create less waste by walking differently, or even just to buy fewer shoes, is a huge challenge. Not least because the dominance of fashion and cheap production values means many shoes, especially the cheapest ones, are simply not built to last. This is additionally complicated by a knowledge gap around shoes. The manufacture of footwear is shrouded in mystery, leaving shoppers unable to make truly informed decisions about which shoes will last or which can be repaired. This leaves people reliant on trusting multinational corporations.

Dr Fletcher believes there is a need for more education around the things we buy, but she also points towards other, more insidious, problems that produce a rapid turnover of consumer items: 'It's also about a lowering of expectations that these things *should* last, augmented by numerous social and cultural pressures like social media and the pressure to constantly have different things.'

Her approach to consumption draws on work around 'self-defeating choices' by economic historian Professor Avner Offer. Self-defeating choices include smoking, gambling and war, all moments where priorities for the present conflict with priorities for the future. The momentary thrill of the roulette table can destroy the long-term possibility of financial stability; a bloody desire for revenge can plunge countries and regions into decades of chaos. In such moments, Professor Offer talks of a 'divided self' where short- and long-term priorities simply do not match up.[11]

On a societal level this is true of consumption. We are taught to choose shoes over an ensured supply of clean water, clean air and even over planetary stability. This is the result of being caught in a system of market competition which promotes hedonism, individualism and narcissism. Hedonism is easy to package and market, individualism eliminates the social contract we have with other people and with our collective future, while narcissism creates an obsessive interest in the self.[12]

Like cigarettes, fast cars and fast food, the risk of long-term harm from a constant stream of new shoes is initially invisible.[13]

It is a long-term harm caused by structural features, the overuse and under-accounting of natural resources, the destructive model of economic growth fuelled by consumption and a lack of regulations and corporate accountability.

Finding a way out of this trap means figuring out how to better represent the needs of the future in our present-day decisions. It means reclaiming life from just being about each short-term shopping thrill and bringing our collective futures back into focus. In this way we can make a commitment to a positive future, to the things we, and the planet we live on, will need in fifty years' time.

If we cannot collectively mobilise against corporate overproduction and over-consumption, and if we cannot take back the power to treat our planet with the respect of stewardship, rather than the avarice of mercantile ownership, we may all face a bleak shared destiny.

Rubbish

Laboni married at the age of twelve. When she was sixteen, a cyclone destroyed her house and flooded the farmland her village community depended upon. Laboni's family rebuilt but when it happened again two years later, Laboni and her husband left their home in the northern Bangladeshi district of Lalmonirhat and went in search of work. Their three-and-a-half-year-old son stayed in the village to be cared for by his grandmother.

Laboni and her husband followed rumours of work across the country until they reached the capital Dhaka. They ended up in a slum on the outskirts of the city where Laboni heard neighbourhood talk of stitching jobs in garment factories. But the factories she approached weren't hiring and, unlike her new neighbours, she had no experience of sewing machines.

The neighbourhood women told her to head for Matuail, where the work was guaranteed. Matuail turned out to be a vast land of waste, a rubbish dump taking in half of the 8,000 metric tons of refuse produced by Dhaka each day.

The smell rising off the dump was intense enough to turn the stomach. Clouds of eagles circled overhead and swooped down to pick at food. When the rubbish trucks arrived, women and children rushed to get there first – everything was picked over by hand, as people looked for plastic, glass, cloth, tin and animal bone. The materials were stacked into cliff-sized piles of bales, ready to be transported out of the dump and used in industry.

Laboni spent her days sorting and stacking dried animal bones that had been pulled out of the dump, bones that would be sent to China and ground down for gelatine to make medicine capsules. She worked alongside a woman from Gaibandha District whose home had been washed away in a river flood caused by melted Himalayan ice, and another woman who had come from a coastal island, half of which had been lost to rising sea water.

The dump provided work for women who arrived with three or four children to care for, so could not do the twelve-hour shifts required by garment factories, and the women rejected as house-maids because rich people did not want servants bringing children onto their property. Waste picking was self-employed, flexible work. There was even a tiny school run by a charity in a tin shack, and when school ended the children could join in the work.

The other slum-dwellers saw waste-pickers as beneath them. Laboni was lucky to be married already so she could ignore the insults from rickshaw pullers and the sneering factory workers who held their noses and made jokes when she walked home from work.

Even as she grew used to the smell of the bones, Laboni developed abdominal pains. She had had them once before, and would eventually find out they were appendicitis, but she could not afford to stop working so she wound a long cloth round and round her stomach and knotted it tightly to try and lessen the pain.

As Laboni worked, the rubbish trucks sped into the dump, often with two or three teenage boys perched on top of the waste, their feet and sandals black with dirt, their hands gripping the sides of the truck. The rubbish was quickly emptied and shovelled out so the truck could return to the streets and factories of Dhaka. Beside the road an old man made patchwork rugs from the carpets thrown out of houses, offices and hotels. A small child collected piles of plastic and coconut-shell buttons. Cut feet and arms turned septic, while in the heat of the day the eagles and the Salat al-zuhr call to prayer drifted over the waste.

Every now and again death came to the dump. A man with an infected wound; a woman hit in the head by a swinging crane, her crumpled body blended in with the rubbish; a child walking across the dump who fell through a sink hole and was buried alive.

Life and soul

Is Matuail a grim vision of our shared future? A portent of the world where all that is left are giant rubbish dumps where the majority of us scavenge for scraps, where our clothing and houses are made from the remains of a society that shopped and fought its way into extinction. The all-pervasive smell, the mountains of rubbish, the people with no gloves or boots dragging themselves home along narrow, dusty tracks as the speeding metal teeth of heavy machinery graze past.

Matuail may be our shared destiny, but it is not a ghost. Laboni and the other climate refugees have had their lives turned upside-down by environmental disaster, and are already stuck cleaning up the world's mess. Matuail is vast and ugly and dangerous – it is a dystopian future come true.

Since Laboni arrived at Matuail, the world has held climate talks in Paris, Copenhagen and Katowice, where cameras flashed and people in suits discussed what to do. Oil barons have continued to fund 'think tanks' to say climate breakdown isn't real. Scientists have wept as the Arctic burned. Protests have raged as gas pipelines sought to plough through sacred lands. The most powerful man in the world has tweeted that climate change is a myth sent forth by China. Since Laboni became a climate refugee, we have been told the world is about eleven years away from a climatic tipping point that will test the habitability of this planet.[14] At what point do we listen and act?

CHAPTER 8

The Sewbots Are Coming

Imagine the following scenario: six people crouch in the shadows, cloth masks wrapped tight around their faces. In the darkness a match flares, followed by another. It is the signal. No watchmen or soldiers are near.

In tight formation the group runs across the lane, keeping as low as possible. When they reach the mill, they flatten themselves against the rough brick wall. If they are seen, they could hang.

At a whispered word, a broad-shouldered woman steps forward. Raising a huge hammer above her head, she brings it down on the wooden door, twice more and the door splits at the lock and is kicked open. The six run in, a single lamp is lit and raised.

The square wooden frames of mechanical knitting machines stand solidly in the dim light. Without a word six sledgehammers rise and fall, splintering the frames and smashing metal cogs and needles. In a few minutes it is done. One of the six draws a note from his cloth bag and stabs it onto the door as they slip out and run across the fields. Scratched out in a careful hand, the note is signed *KING LUDD*.*

Clogged up

The Luddite Rebellion of 1811–13 was an uprising of textile workers from Nottinghamshire, Yorkshire and Lancashire. Contrary to

---

* While based on historical accounts, these are imagined characters.

popular myth, the original Luddites were not anti-technology, in fact they were often advanced users of mechanical devices. What they opposed was the casualisation of their trade, the reduction of their wages and the degradation of their industry through the production of inferior cloth. In opposing wealthy mill owners, it is little surprise that the impoverished Luddites compared themselves with Robin Hood.[1] They encountered far more violence than they ever dealt out, and were beaten, shot and hanged for their protests.

The Luddites were not the first nor the last group to organise mass dissent against the impact of mechanisation. The French Revolution saw similar protests against machines, and gave rise to a familiar term. The *sabot* is a handmade wooden clog traditionally worn by workers and peasants in France, as well as elsewhere in Europe. These were heavy shoes that clattered over boards or roads as people walked. As labourers began to disrupt work during the industrial revolution by a process of strikes and go-slows, the term *sabotage* was coined to describe the disruption of production lines.[2]

Two hundred years on, we live in another moment of expedited industrial transformation. Whether we call this the 'fourth industrial revolution' or see ourselves as part of one long moment of technological development, we are in the midst of change. Cheerleaders say humanity is on the brink of freeing itself from the drudgeries of physical and mental labour, detractors say this is profit-driven change whose pains will be borne by the poorest members of global society.

In a world where factory bosses push workers to assemble shoes faster and faster, and production is limited only by human endurance and the scant health and safety rules won by trade unions, what would happen if workers on production lines needed no breaks, sleep or holidays? What would it mean for both people and planet if human labour were replaced by robots?

Step it up

Shoe supply chains have long experienced dramatic change as the result of machines: from harvesting cotton with combine harvesters, to gigantic mechanical weaving looms and the printing press.[3] But threshing machines, and of course the ubiquitous sewing machine, are not robots because they require continual human oversight.[4]

Automation is a process whereby machines step in for humans at work, requiring no constant oversight.[5] In a shoe factory there can be over 100 different tasks involved in making a single shoe, from cutting templates from leather and rubber, to gluing pieces together, to attaching uppers to soles. The race is now on to transform these processes which have been the domain of human hands for thousands of years.

Within the world of automation are two overlapping but distinct types of technology: artificial intelligence and robotics. The aim of this chapter is to plunge into the world of robotics and explore its impact on the shoe industry. To keep things simple, this chapter adopts the RSA (Royal Society of Arts, Manufactures and Commerce) definition of what constitutes a robot: *physical machines that move within an environment with a degree of autonomy.* Although in the same field, the robots in this chapter do not have the capacity for artificial intelligence, an area roughly definable as *tasks performed by computer software that would otherwise require human intelligence.*[6]

The world around us is already an automated world, where machines are used to complete repetitive and routine tasks without our intervention.[7] Robots are to be found soldering electronics on assembly lines, searching for miners trapped far underground and lifting bedridden patients.[8] The shoe industry is taking a little longer to become a robot domain, but it is, however, ahead of the clothing industry.

Digital platforms

Getting robots to sew clothes has long been a notoriously difficult task because robots are just not good with floppy fabric. To solve this conundrum, North American inventor Jonathan Zornow created Sewbo, an automation system which aims to transform the fashion industry. Sewbo dips fabric in a plastic called polyvinyl alcohol in order to stiffen it so that it can be worked on by robots before being rinsed.[9]

Jonathan explains why shoes are easier than clothes for robots to assemble: '[With shoes] the materials you're working with are much more suited to mechanical handling – thick leather or plastic material, or anything that has its own kind of structure where it's not going to be skewing or curling up on itself like a knit material would,' he says. 'It's much easier for a machine to handle, you can pick it up and know where the edges are, from a robotic standpoint it's much more straightforward.'

The other reason shoes are easier than clothes for robots to handle comes down to geometry. According to *Guinness World Records*, the biggest feet ever were 47cm long and belonged to Robert Wadlow, who died aged twenty-two in 1940. A typical baby's foot measures around 10cm long. This means that even if a single robot is making everything from huge men's shoes to baby shoes, it still has a predictable shape to work with and less than half a metre in working range. Compare that to differences in apparel sizes – socks to jeans, underwear to an XXL jacket – the shapes are completely different, and the size of the material varies wildly.

These factors have made shoes a far more immediate prospect for automation. So immediate that it may not be long until footwear is an automated industry. 'Within the next 3–5 years, the shoe industry is going to change and people are not going to be sewing shoes together,' predicts Shane Dittrich, the CEO of House of Design, a custom automation firm based in Nampa, Idaho.

Shane had just completed the development of a robot that produces shoes for US shoe brand KEEN. House of Design is what is known as a value provider: they take robots that have been manufactured, in this case by ABB Robotics, and then design and programme them to fit the specific manufacturing process of each client. The challenge set by KEEN was to automate processes involved in its UNEEK line, a shoe with an upper made of two long cords woven together.

House of Design used two ABB IRB 120 robots – a six-axis industrial robot used in a multitude of different arenas, from the oil and gas industry, to warehouses, bakeries and even in medicine as an assembly device.

To be briefly technical, the ABB IRB 120 robot is special because it is capable of 10-micron repeatability. Robot specifications are based on 'repeatability', not 'accuracy'. If you command a robot to go to a certain point on a board, it may or may not be able to accurately pinpoint where you want it to go. But if you place the robot where you want it to go and then tell it to go back to that point a while later, the ABB IRB 120 will hit that same spot within 0.01mm – also known as 10 microns.

The result is that in the KEEN installation, two robot arms tango around each other, darting in with knitting needles to interlock cords around a ready-made rubber sole. The robot arms start at the heel, and mechanically weave back and forth till they reach the toe of the shoe before jerkily dancing back up the other side. It is a shoe based on the sort of highly repeatable pattern which lends itself to robotics.[10]

Shane took on the KEEN challenge in part to disrupt the shoe industry. 'Footwear is one of those industries people say cannot be automated because typically the style changes so quickly that if you were to come up with a manufacturing process it would be obsolete in six months, because the general style of a shoe changes so quickly,' he explains. 'It was a great opportunity to say, "Look, we can come in and automate these and they can be custom."' What they discovered was that robot arms complete the task of interlocking the cords twice as fast as a person doing it manually.[11]

Robot-run world

Automating factories offers many advantages for wealthy shoe brands. Their promise of speed and superiority means robots make for great publicity, flashy adverts and exciting shop-window installations. In an industry marked by catastrophes like the Rana Plaza factory collapse, the Ali Enterprises fire and huge strikes across Bangladesh, Cambodia and China, robot factories promise a reduction of reputational risk – no headlines linking a brand to violent deaths or slave labour.[12] Then there are the financial benefits. After a huge initial investment, a factory of robots promises cheaper production with no labour costs like wages, maternity leave, insurance or pensions; it also promises a consistency of product quality.

In 2015, Nike, for example, collaborated with tech company Flex (makers of the Fitbit) in an attempt to begin automating some of its production processes. At their facility in Guadalajara, Mexico, Flex automated the process of gluing trainers together, traditionally a job done by hand. The *Financial Times* reported Nike could decrease labour costs by 50 per cent and materials costs by 20 per cent using automation for its 2017 Air Max. With Flex producing 30 per cent of Nike's North American footwear sales, savings could be as high as $400m.[13] However, the project ended in 2018 with Flex saying they were 'unable to reach a commercial and viable solution with Nike.'[14]

While the failure of this partnership shows the path to automation will not be a smooth one even for the biggest brands in the world, when it is eventually achieved it will be a truly global issue. Nike is a behemoth employer: 611,120 workers in 13 different countries work on Nike's footwear production lines. Scale this out to include all Nike products and Nike has 1.07 million contracted workers in 41 countries.[15]

adidas is another brand who tried to take advantage of automation. By 1993, adidas had closed nine of its ten German shoe factories as the brand chased cheaper labour costs in Asia.[16] Today adidas predominately sources from ASEAN (the Association of Southeast Asian Nations), an economic area comprised of ten countries including Cambodia, Indonesia, the Philippines and Vietnam.

Collectively, these four countries represent 55 per cent of adidas' overall source market.[17] In 2015, adidas said they sourced 301 million pairs of shoes from around the globe. Their strategic business plan until 2020 includes the production of an additional 30 million pairs of shoes annually.

In 2016, adidas announced it was opening a robot factory in Germany. The 'Speedfactory' opened to great fanfare in Ansbach in 2017. Inside the factory, one production line made soles, and another made uppers. Lacing shoes, however, continued to elude robotic arms.[18]

With an additional automated factory in Atlanta, adidas hyped this development as 'a real game changer'.[19] 'If you look at the production of the shoe itself, this currently takes a few weeks depending on the products as not all components are produced in the same location,' said Katja Schreiber, a spokeswoman for adidas, in 2016.

Add in design, development, selling to retail partners and

shipment, and the production of a regular adidas trainer takes eighteen months from idea to shelf. adidas believed they could reduce this to 5 hours by decentralising production and having robot factories close to consumers.

In 2019, however, adidas announced that it was closing the two Speedfactories and made a hazy promise to deploy some of the technology in Asia where it would be 'more economic and flexible'.[20] At the time of the announcement, TechCrunch commented: 'As other industries have found in the rush to automation, it's easy to overshoot the mark and overcommit when the technology just isn't ready.'[21]

Warning: impact zone

As adidas announced its venture into robotics, the International Labour Organization (ILO) issued a dire warning about ASEAN's heavy dependence on the textiles, clothing and footwear (TCF) manufacturing sector. With the coming of robots that can manufacture shoes and clothes, the ILO have predicted that 9 million garment and footwear workers across ASEAN risk losing their jobs.

The ILO takes this threat so seriously, it is advising ASEAN countries to start diversifying away from garments and footwear to avoid huge setbacks in development. Like the industrial revolution, this technological change will be extremely capital-intensive and will not be an option for small businesses. It will further consolidate power in the hands of the few. For workers in shoe factories, it could be apocalyptic.

Illah Nourbakhsh is a professor at the Robotics Institute at Carnegie Mellon University in Pittsburgh, Pennsylvania. He describes automation as a double-edged sword. The owner of an automated company can make far more money because of two things: they spend less money paying people, and system efficiency is increased as friction falls and production rises.

In the past, a shoe company owner would spend money on labour to increase productivity – she would pay people wages to work in her factory. With automation, money is instead invested in capital to create productivity, in this case robotic factory equipment.

The problem with turning labour wealth (wages) into capital productivity (robots) is that it exacerbates income inequality. While shoes might become marginally less expensive to make, fewer people benefit because a smaller number of people own the capital. 'Capital accumulates wealth by itself, disproportionately faster than labour wealth does,' says Professor Nourbakhsh. 'The people who then become rich, become rich faster than the people who were poor who were getting some money. So you get a double whammy effect on wealth inequality.'

Jae-Hee Chang works out of the ILO's Bangkok office and co-authored the organisation's report on automation, *Textiles, Clothing, and Footwear: Refashioning the Future*. She believes ASEAN's labour-intensive way of manufacturing garments and shoes will inevitably be disrupted by technology. 'While some jobs in the sector will stay, many – especially the lower-skilled jobs that can be automated – will no longer be needed,' she said after the launch of the report.

Another problem is the threat that sewbot factories will not be built in Asia, rather they will be installed in destination markets like Europe and the US. Shifting production back to destination markets, known as reshoring, is a reversal of globalisation trends but it does not herald the return of manufacturing jobs that people like President Donald Trump have promised. adidas's CEO has made it very clear he does not see reshoring happening in the US in any major way because it is financially 'very illogical'.[22] The shuttered 'Speedfactories' each employed just 160 people.[23]

No diamonds on the soles of her shoes

As we have seen, workers in shoe supply chains already tend to be low-waged, overworked, exposed to injury and ill health, plus face working conditions that risk death by fire, cancers and factory collapse. Added to this list is now the risk of being replaced by faster, cheaper, less rebellious sewbots. The question of what will happen to workers in the TCF sector is becoming more urgent every year as tens of millions of people face an uncertain future. Once again, this is a gendered issue.

Consider this list of ASEAN countries: in Cambodia 81 per cent of TCF workers are women; in Laos that figure is 86 per cent; in Thailand 76 per cent; in Vietnam 77 per cent; and in the Philippines 71 per cent. This overwhelmingly female workforce is young, with an average age of thirty-one. In Cambodia this falls to a youthful twenty-five. It is a workforce that faces being wiped out as the jobs of nearly 90 per cent of garment and footwear workers in Cambodia are at risk from automated assembly lines.[24]

In the factories of the future, there will be a need for engineers, supervisors and robot programmers, but for women factory workers to take on such roles will take investment in education and training by governments and stakeholders. It will require dismantling the sexist systems that prevent women from obtaining such roles. Without urgent diversification and training, millions of women face being sent back to domestic servitude.

Across Asia, young women, usually with scant access to advanced education, have found themselves engaged in factory work. Work means wages, which means food, housing and transport. It means the opportunity for greater autonomy – for not marrying young; for not having so many, or even any children; for not having to stay with an abusive partner; for paying for schooling, or supporting elderly parents. To point this out is not to let brands and factory owners off the hook – there is no excuse for the gross exploitation that characterises the industry – but we must question where these women can go if robots take their jobs.

So what is it like to be inventing machines that could wipe out millions of jobs for the poorest people in the world? Jonathan Zornow is well aware that the threat of job losses is the big question for automation, and says he spends a disproportionate amount of time worrying about it and trying to square his conscience with his work.

He lists three reasons why, despite this, he is still striving to make automation happen. Firstly, he argues we should compare automation to previous technological leaps like the loom or the sewing machine which inspired fear of job losses and protests. Would we now, Jonathan asks, argue to ban sewing machines? 'I just don't think that's what we are as a species, we make tools and move forward,' he says. 'We're saving ourselves labour and ultimately that's going to be good for everyone in the long run.'

Secondly, Jonathan takes issue with factory work: 'These jobs, they're important in developing economies and the people take them for a reason, they take them because they're better than the alternative, but even so, they suck.

'You'll be hard pressed to find a single garment worker who would ever say they want their kids to have this job; they're doing this job so their kids won't have to,' he continues. 'On the one hand it does play on the conscience to take that opportunity away, but on the other hand these aren't good jobs. They're incredibly tedious, they pay nothing, unfortunately they're rife with human rights violations, worker safety issues and environmental damage.'

Spending a lot of his time travelling the world explaining the possibilities of his sewbot, Jonathan frequently finds himself in India and Bangladesh where he tries to prepare people for what is coming: 'It won't be surprising to hear that those who make our clothes, the ones who have the most to gain or lose from all of this, are the ones who are the most interested in it in a practical sense – how much does it cost, when can we get one?'

It is to Bangladesh that Jonathan turns for the third reason, the argument that automation is not the biggest problem facing Global South economies. Most importantly, he says, the jobs at sewing machines that stand to be affected by robot factories are not going to exist by the time the technology is ready.

Jonathan's point is that Bangladeshi garment jobs will already be in decline or will have gone by the time robot factories are up and running. As labour costs rise in Bangladesh, factories are opening in other countries in Asia and now in Africa. Yet Bangladesh remains extraordinarily and dangerously dependent on a single industry, with textiles and garments regularly accounting for 80 per cent of all exports. Rather than diversify, the lives of 100 million people are gambled on Bangladesh's attempt to become a world leader with a $50b TCF industry.[25]

Ones and twos

For years Professor Nourbakhsh worked in robotics when it was an abstract field, something he describes as being like theoretical maths – fascinating but with scant impact on the world around us. Gradually this began to change until in the early 2000s robots were putting people out of jobs and changing the way war is fought. What bothered him was the lack of public debate about the role of this technology and how it changes society.

As a response, he wrote the book *Robot Futures* and now teaches robotic ethics at Carnegie Mellon. We must, he says, engage with the reality of advancing technological influence on our society and not just thoughtlessly go forward assuming technology is always good. This, in part, means not accepting the narrative around job losses.

'Often, your average robot consumer or robot manufacturer will make these statements about how people shouldn't do jobs that are dirty, dull and dangerous – ironically these are usually people who are multimillionaires and who take Learjets to travel,' says Professor Nourbakhsh. 'They're making this statement in the position of some world where we have an economy where everybody has what they need because the robots do all the dull work and the dirty work. What usually these people don't understand is that a large proportion of humanity makes its way through life and finds some form of dignity, and certainly some form of sustenance, by doing work that others would consider dirty or dull or dangerous.'

Another clog in the machine

Globalisation scattered the production of easily assembled items like shoes around the world, as brands hunted for ever cheaper manufacturing locations. This led to the creation of thousands of new factories across the Global South. This path has not ended inequality, with trickle-down economics being little more than a trick. Even within the thirty-six higher-income countries of the Organisation for Economic Co-operation and Development (OECD), most countries are facing their highest levels of wealth inequality in thirty years, even while they generate gigantic ecological footprints.[26] Yet manufacturing has traditionally been the key approach for countries wanting to industrialise.[27] In particular, the TCF sector has been a notable means for countries to transition from informal agricultural jobs to formal wage employment.[28]

Industrialisation has been aided by three factors. The first is that technology is easy to move. Cars, or shoes, can be constructed on factory lines just the same in the US or Thailand. Secondly, manufacturing is an arena that can absorb millions of unskilled people and turn them into highly productive workers who add huge amounts of value to an economy. This is what happened in China where Chinese shoe factories were launched using peasant labour because basic eye–hand coordination was all the skill required to start work. In moving from fields to factories, people's productivity leapt upwards.[29]

Thirdly, the shoes made by these new factory workers can be exported to the world market. This leaves no need for an internal market, or domestic demand, for shoes to make a sector profitable, which in theory allows countries to master one type of manufacturing at a time. The problem with being dependent upon a domestic market is it means there needs to be a lot of well-off citizens within a country's borders. Creating these well-off citizens can mean that every sector of an economy needs to grow at the same time.[30] Citizens must also want to buy domestically made shoes over international brands, which is not always a given.

Economist Dani Rodrik is concerned that industrialisation is about to disappear as an option for growth, in part due to automation. He calls this process *premature deindustrialisation*, with countries running out of industrialisation opportunities sooner and at much lower levels of income compared to countries which industrialised earlier in history.[31] The ability to provide an army of low-skilled but low-cost labour is simply not going to matter so much in a world of automation, where tasks need fewer people and require high levels of skill. Rodrik points to economies in Latin America and Africa as places that could find the drawbridge being raised in front of them.[32]

Within the means of the planet

But is more industrialisation and growth the answer? The economic system we live under, that of giving primacy to shareholder profits and GDP growth (the cost of all goods and services sold in the market), is already pushing our planetary society to breaking point.

This is what happens when statistics do not take the cost of doing business into account. A move away from GDP to GPI – genuine progress indicator, which takes into account pollution and other costs of production – would give a clearer picture of what is happening. It would mean, in the words of economist Kate Raworth, having a new goal of meeting the needs of all, within the means of the planet.[33]

But if we accept that we must live within the means of the planet, does that mean we must accept vast economic inequality between and within countries? If a community is poor now, is that their lot for good? Or does it mean moving beyond growth to a more equalised society?

Since the financial crash of 2008, economists have been working on a programme called the Green New Deal. This plan for radical transformation is championed most famously by New York congressional representative Alexandria Ocasio-Cortez, and involves rapid decarbonisation while raising living standards and creating green jobs. Fundamentally, a Green New Deal means rejecting neoliberal economics and business as usual. Ending dependence on economic growth will have to start with rich nations accepting that progress is not just producing and selling more than last year. Some sectors, those that do the most damage, will have to shrink and be transformed. This does not mean life gets worse. We are lucky enough to have a planet that provides more than enough food and resources for all of us – the reason it does not seem like this is the case is because resources are unfairly distributed.[34]

Ensuring that a Green New Deal is global and centres the Global South will be the key to its success. The shoe industry runs on the same tracks as colonialism and slavery – the richest nations of the world plundering the Global South for labour and resources. Decarbonising the global economy must not mean continuing along this track either by further mineral extraction, or by hoarding all the opportunities for green jobs and wealth creation in the Global North.

In this sense, we should not blame all of our problems on robots and automation.[35] The real problems we have are structural: monopolised of ownership of the means of production, hoarded profits, record levels of wage inequality between those who own companies and those who work in supply chains, pitifully low taxation on billionaires and corporations and a lack of political commitment to environmental protection.

This is not to say robots will automatically make things better. Until now, technological ability has not been tempered by any moral or cultural barriers saying there might be consequences to producing 24.2 billion pairs of shoes a year. If production is going to become even faster through robotics, there is nothing in place to safeguard our futures, or to allow us to say enough is enough. One thing that can, and possibly will, halt production is the point at which the living systems of the earth become so scarce that they are unaffordable. But is that really what we want, or is there a better priority for our technology?

Full of uncounted costs, the production of shoes is a long way from GPI thinking. An entire layer of humanity survives on subsistence factory wages, the true cost of their lives ignored; the planet is counted as a free resource, with fresh water, rainforests, animals, the air we breathe and the wellbeing of society, all treated as expendable. The only thing that counts is the profit made by corporations and their shareholders.

Nobel Prize-winning economist Joseph Stiglitz wrote that efficiency in production does not necessarily correspond to systemic efficiency, or efficiency in consumption. Throughout the history of shoes, faster means of production has just meant more shoes being made, often of a worse quality. Under capitalism there is no reason to believe more technology, in the form of robot factories, will reduce the volume of shoes being made, nor make them more sustainable. More likely, under present conditions, it will mean an escalation of over-production and over-consumption for some, meaning more income inequality and exacerbated poverty for everyone else.

Robots, however, continue to evolve, becoming cheaper and more competent. 'Whatever they can do today, tomorrow they'll be able to do even more,' reasons Professor Nourbakhsh. 'It's a one-way road that we're on, sometimes we walk down that road, sometimes we run.'

What we face now, he concludes, is the question of how to protect global citizenry. 'The public good depends on the protection afforded by government in this case. I really don't see corporations as being self-governing in this matter.' Far from believing in the fantasy that corporations will implement their own standards, our shared environmental future depends upon a global programme to decarbonise and de-corporatise the economy, while redistributing wealth and creating green jobs.

Trump's America, Trump's world?

Back in Idaho, Shane Dittrich is not overly worried about the consequences of automation in the US and Europe: 'I visit a lot of manufacturing facilities and I can tell you, greater than 90 per cent, I might say greater than 95 per cent, they have a labour shortage,' he says. 'It used to be that automation was justified by direct labour savings, so we would go in and say you're going to eliminate three jobs and you're going to be able to pay for the automation in three years, and after the third year you're just making money because you don't have the labour any more. That's how the cost used to be justified.' Now, Shane argues, US companies struggle to find and retain employees, and it is this shortage of labour that drives them towards automation.

The forty-fifth president of the United States, Donald Trump, has professed himself an opponent of globalisation, preferring instead to deregulate domestic markets while regulating and imposing tariffs upon international ones. His 2016 election campaign promised to 'Make America Great Again' in part by returning well-paid manufacturing jobs to communities who feel weakened by the slow bleed of jobs going overseas.

While not much of a reality, it was genius rhetoric as jobs are not just at risk of automation in the Global South. In 2018, three Oxford University academics published a paper entitled *Political Machinery: Did Robots Swing the 2016 US Presidential Election?* The paper's hypothesis was that voters who have lost out to technology are more likely to opt for radical political change. Using this as a starting point, the academics examined the impact of robots on the Trump–Clinton race for the White House. They found support for Trump was higher in local labour markets that were more exposed to automation.

One of the authors of this paper was Dr Chinchih Chen, who says she is fascinated by the possibility of industrial robots triggering political unrest. Could political behaviour be driven not by beliefs but by automation? The data analysis results were striking, with the paper concluding that Michigan, Pennsylvania and Wisconsin would have swung in favour of Hillary Clinton if exposure to robots had not increased in the immediate years leading up to the election. This would have left the Democrats with a majority in the Electoral College, and made Clinton the president.

The question of automation causing political unrest becomes even more stark in the light of findings that suggest 24 per cent of US men aged between twenty-five and fifty-four could be out of work by 2050.[36] It is a spectre that brings to mind the work of photographer Dorothea Lange who captured the mass unemployment, migration and suffering of 1930s America, her black-and-white photographs allowing us to glimpse the hardship of migrant farm workers in the Depression Era dust bowl.

Access to money and skills is essential for keeping up with the pace of change; this has never been more true than with automation. Studies in the US found a lack of education increases job automation risk, with certain demographic groups being most susceptible to job automation, including Hispanics, African Americans and the young.[37]

Eventually was nonetheless a long time

Automation is often slotted into the category of 'creative destruction' – the argument goes that while workers may be made redundant, new employment opportunities will also be created. But this path is neither smooth nor equal. Take, for example, the mechanisation that took place from 1780 to 1840. This was a period of great upheaval for British workers as tens of thousands of people lost their jobs.

As wealthy industrialists sat on piles of gold which grew into mountains, the impact of unemployment made itself apparent in the physical health of the workers. British men in 1850 were shorter than in 1760 because they had less to eat. The Oxford paper points out that, 'almost by any measure, material standards and living conditions for the common Englishman did not improve before 1840.'[38] When new jobs did arrive there was a stark difference – the earliest machines were simple enough to be tended by children, who swiftly made up half the textile workforce during the 1830s.

Looking at the challenges of automation today, Dr Chen is not put off by the thought of technical change: 'Since ancient times technology means we suffer in the short term but in the long run, if you put the timescale into one hundred, or two hundred years, we benefit.' But what happens to today's people who have been born at the 'wrong time'? If automation takes her job, what should a thirty-year-old shoe factory worker in Cambodia do for the remainder of her working life? Why should progress once more require the suffering of those who have the least?

Political planning is needed on a global scale to mitigate mass unemployment. This will involve creating a skills switch on a generational level. It will mean retraining people so they are educationally equipped for more than just assembly lines. The challenge ahead is to reimagine a green global economy where jobs are meaningful, well-paid and in harmony with the natural world.[39]

This is an urgent challenge. As wages rise and companies become ever more tempted by the profit margins that robots promise, automation in the labour-intensive shoe industry looms alongside climate breakdown.

Transitioning to a green global economy will not work if demands and economic plans remain behind the borders of individual nation states. Transforming the world will take a huge global effort. It will mean the richest countries helping the poorest to transition to renewables – not as an act of charity but as an act of reparation in recognition of centuries of colonialism, exploitation and unfair trade deals. Only then can we start to see a global deal that works for people and planet – a just transition to a brighter, fairer new world.

The pace of a machine

Of the billions of items sold online each year, shoes are big business for web giant Amazon. During a single promotional discount day in 2016, Amazon sold over a million pairs of shoes to shoppers around the world.[40] Since they do not have physical retail stores, all of Amazon's stock is shipped from gigantic warehouses, which Amazon like to call 'fulfilment centres'. These warehouses have part-human, part-robot workforces.

The introduction of robots into this part of the supply chain has not resulted in job losses. Alongside people, thousands of small, orange, floor robots which look like automated vacuum cleaners navigate round Amazon warehouses collecting stock, while larger axis robots take things down from higher shelves.

Nigel Flanagan spent seven years as a senior union organiser for the global trade union UNI Global Union. As well as interviewing hundreds of Amazon workers, Nigel gained access to an Amazon fulfilment centre in Poland and was taken aback by what he saw: 'It made me think of a *Dr Who* episode where the Daleks are in charge. It's not as super-shiny or futuristic as you would imagine, there's still humans there and the floor robots look a bit fragile and crude moving around, but they're basically leading all the work.'

Amazon has long been highlighted for operating question-able working practices. In 2013 the *Financial Times* reported on Amazon's strict 'three-strikes and you're out' regime, with workers discouraged from talking to each other in warehouses,[41] and in an in-depth investigation in 2015, the *New York Times* detailed work-ers' movements being electronically monitored to speed them up.[42] Amazon maintains that it works 'hard every day to ensure all of our employees are treated fairly and with dignity and respect'.[43]

The robots have added an extra layer of surveillance to this regime. Equipped with cameras, they monitor workers and film whether or not they are doing their job properly.

'I wondered why the workers don't smash them up,' Nigel says. 'They said they dare not do it because the robots are all equipped with surveillance equipment. If they damage it or sabotage it, Amazon have access to recordings, and they'll know how it happened.'

As well as providing constant surveillance, the robots have brought another change to work in the warehouse: a truly me-chanical pace. Although they need recharging, robots do not get tired and they do not change their pace during long shifts. Despite needing human 'co-workers' to complete their tasks, the robots are impervious to requests to slow down or break for a moment. 'It's tiring because you can't say to a robot, "Can you just stop, I need to go for a piss" or "Ow, I hurt my knee",' Nigel says. 'You just have to keep running after the robot and if you're not there, the robot can provide evidence to management that you're not doing your job.'

This creates a system whereby the workers become an assistant to the robot rather than the other way around. 'There's a lack of autonomy, no freedom of movement or decision making,' Nigel continues. 'The robots are not enhancing the working lives of the workers in any way at all. They're just making it more intense, speeding it up and making it more difficult to get a rest.'

The fact that Amazon's system reverses the traditional relationship between humans and machines has led one writer to describe people as 'meat algorithms', reduced to their ability to move and follow orders, and easy to 'hire, fire, and abuse'.[44]

This robotic pace has serious consequences and is a cause of concern for many, especially workers' representatives. A GMB trade union inquiry into injury rates at Amazon warehouses in the UK said ambulances had been called 600 times to 14 sites in a 3-year period – 116 of these emergency calls were made from Amazon's Rugeley site in Staffordshire, including emergency calls made for 3 pregnant women, and 3 for major trauma. People also needed treatment after falling unconscious or suffering electric shocks. In comparison, a supermarket depot nearby had just 8 call-outs in the same period.[45] Amazon said it was 'simply not correct to suggest that we have unsafe working conditions based on this data or on unsubstantiated anecdotes', adding that they did not recognise these allegations as an accurate portrayal of the activities in their warehouse.[46]

Made to last

In Amazon warehouses, technology is not being used to make people's lives better, rather it is being used to make profits greater. There is existing technology, however, that could be utilised to raise standards of living. The shape of a foot depends on multiple factors: heel-to-toe length, foot height, ankle wrap, plus the width and girth of instep, ball and heel. It is a complexity that makes your foot shape as unique as your fingerprint. This complexity is not reflected on the high street where feet are reduced to numbered sizes, a regulation system so flawed that there can be up to four size differences between the same stated size of shoe, depending on the brand.[47]

The fact that people's feet are unique was a question traditionally solved using lasts, a wooden model of each customer's foot that was used to create perfectly fitting shoes. Today such bespoke treatment can cost thousands of pounds per pair of shoes. Technology, however, has the potential to democratise this process by using laser scans, along with specialised treadmills, to determine the perfect shoe fit for every foot. These measurements could then either be 3D printed or sent for production. Each shoe could be bolstered to take into account gaits or weighting that would normally cause a shoe to wear through.[48] This technological fix has the potential to slash shoe consumption by providing access to top-quality and individualised products. The problem however is that technology is not channelled into the common good.

A post-work society

For inventor and roboticist Frances Gabe, automation was a specific means to free women from drudgery. Born in 1915, Gabe was a visionary who designed and built a self-cleaning house in Newberg, Oregon. 'You can talk all you like about women's liberation, but houses are still designed so women have to spend half their time on their knees or hanging their head in a hole,' Gabe told the *Baltimore Sun* in 1981.[49]

In the self-cleaning house, crockery cupboards doubled as dishwashers so there was no need for endless loading and unloading. Clothes were laundered and dried in their storage cupboards, and at the touch of a button sprinklers would wash down walls and floors before everything was blown dry. This was a political statement wrapped up in a genius invention, a move to release women from thankless, unending housework.

It is possible to envisage this kind of freedom in the shoe industry. Looking into the future of automation and shoes, ILO economist Jae-Hee Chang envisages a best-case scenario whereby 'robots take on board the most repetitive, mundane and non-cognitive tasks of apparel and footwear manufacturing. They would also assume more of the dangerous and dirty tasks, like mixing of chemicals which can be hazardous to human workers.'

But how to get there when the history of industry shows it has not been designed with people's wellbeing in mind, when there is no democratic control over the focus of robotics, or in deciding who and what robots benefit. When artist Lily Benson visited Frances Gabe in her self-cleaning house in 2007, she found it in a state of disrepair. Reflecting on the absence of support for Gabe, Benson wrote that the lack of investment in the project was because 'venture capitalists weren't interested whatsoever in liberating women from doing housework.' A woman ahead of her time, Gabe had struck out on her own. 'Despite the lack of financial support, Frances just went for it and built the entire house with her own funds and her own hands,' Benson writes. 'While the prototype didn't function perfectly, it provided her with shelter and contained a life-size model of her vision and dream.'[50]

So how might we ensure the benefits of automation are available for all? Could robots help us escape the pantheon of endless growth and vast inequality? What if automation could be used to redistribute work in a more equitable manner, to ensure the overworked get to work less, and the unemployed find meaningful occupations? What if robots can be used to generate other ways in which people can get an income beyond just their wages?

Ideas already on the table include reducing the working week from five days to four in order to give people a three-day weekend while paying them the same. This is an idea backed by the Trades Union Congress (TUC) and adopted by the Labour Party in the UK. In the US, Congresswoman Alexandria Ocasio-Cortez has floated the option of taxing robots or automated productivity gains by as much as 90 per cent. The reason people are not excited about automation, she rightly says, is because 'we live in a society where if you don't have a job, you are left to die. And that is, at its core, our problem.'[51]

A tax on robots could be used to fund a universal basic income which seeks to replace poverty with financial security. This involves the state providing everyone with a no-strings-attached payment which supplies them with the minimum amount of money needed to survive. This idea has been trialled in Canada, the US, India, Namibia and most recently in Finland where a trial group of 2,000 people receive €560 (£516) a month for two years.[52]

As well as tackling poverty, the universal basic income is a key means for letting people have more to life than just work. It would allow greater access to art, literature, music, theatre, sport, politics, travel and community rather than reducing life to market-based production.

Organisations like Fixfest alongside economists like Niko Paech are championing the role of citizen-led change which turns 'consumers' into 'prosumers' whereby people work 20 hours a week then use 20 hours a week to repair, produce and share goods completely independent of industrialised production systems. Crucially all these ideas must be applied around the world – made applicable and available to citizens in the Global South, not just the Global North.

If you are wondering where the money for such plans might come from, the TUC has estimated that artificial intelligence, robotics and automation could boost economic output in the UK by £200b over the next decade. The problem is that money is not fairly distributed, rather it is currently concentrated in the hands of a few Silicon Valley billionaires. The challenge therefore is to make sure wealth is distributed fairly. Plus, as proponents of the Green New Deal are fond of saying – this is something we can't afford *not* to do.

The challenge of fair distribution, like the challenge of working fewer hours for the same pay, is one that rests upon a battle between two forces: those who would benefit from equal distribution, versus a small minority who are better served by hoarding wealth. The shoe industry, with its encapsulation of handmade items, Global South labour and gender inequality, is set to see overwhelming change in the near future. It is a space ripe for proving that we can uncouple economic activity from human exploitation and ecological destruction. Robots will create opportunities, we must not allow corporations to be the only beneficiaries.

CHAPTER 9

If the Shoe Fits

Under grey skies in London, 2,000 people are gathered outside the Polish embassy. On the eve of the twenty-fourth UN Climate talks in Katowice, Magda Oljejor climbs onto a makeshift stage to read a message from Polish activists.

'We're repeatedly told the most important things are business and money,' she says. 'More important than people, more important than the environment, health, love and friendships, more important than our future. It's time these people understand that what they're doing threatens our existence.

'This is the tricky bit,' Oljejor concludes. 'I hope we have some Polish speakers in the crowd to help me. It goes like this: *Razem Dla Klimatu! Razem Dla Klimatu!*' The crowd takes up the chant, stamping their feet against the cold. People hold up blue placards printed with the slogan *Razem Dla Klimatu*; Together For The Climate.

Taking to the stage, MP Clive Lewis tells the crowd Britain has a duty to be at the forefront of tackling climate change as it was the first country to industrialise. Britain's industrialisation was fuelled by conquest and slavery, he argues, with people taken from Africa to islands in the West Indies to make sugar. The irony of climate change, Lewis says, is that people in the West Indies, where his father comes from, are now battered by hurricanes caused by industry and climate breakdown.

People wave homemade placards: 'Earth's Future Is Our Future', 'Stop Killing Our Mother Nature', 'System Change Not Climate Change'. Pink, orange and blue flags flutter in the cold wind, stamped with the black symbol of Extinction Rebellion.

'We're in a system,' announces Asad Rehman from War On Want. 'An economic system that says that black and brown and poor people can be sacrificed in the interests of profit. We're in a system where the interests of corporations and big business are put ahead of the interests of ordinary people.'

After the speeches and the cheering, the demonstration left the Polish embassy and marched towards Oxford Circus, London's most famous shopping precinct. It marched past the stuffed retail units of Nike Town, H&M, Burberry and Topshop and past bemused shoppers looking for Christmas presents, past stressed retail workers, past the pretence of choice, past the endless flow of billions of pounds to corporate bank accounts. Down Regent Street, past Clarks, Camper, Apple and another H&M, the demonstration turned into Trafalgar Square and headed for Downing Street, the heart of political power in Britain.

Lost world

The decisions made over the next decade will determine the fate of tens of thousands of species on planet earth, including humans.

Shoes are far from the only destructive item in this system, but how does such a basic object cause such havoc? Where are the checks and balances to protect people and the planet? Where is the accountability? To answer these questions, it is necessary to step away from the limits of the shoe industry and unpick a cluster of issues that illuminate why the world is in such a mess. Here we unravel the rise of corporate power and the inability of the legal system to cope; how corporate social responsibility programmes have subverted progress; the side-lining of trade unions and the impact of gendered exploitation; and the criminalisation of protest. As well, of course, as examining the constraints placed on progress by the capitalist economic system we live in.

Many of the environmental and labour rights crimes in this book have been carried out by corporations, free to act as they wish because they are often more powerful than many countries. Part of the problem is that globalisation is characterised by a series of dramatic power imbalances. The first of these is between nation states and corporations.

Gross domestic product, GDP, is calculated by measuring the total value of all goods made, and services provided, within a country during a specific time period. Based on this calculation, the top five economies in the world at the start of 2019 were the US, China, Japan, Germany and the UK. GDP ranking currently only applies to nation states, but what if it included corporations? If Nike was ranked as a country, it would be the world's ninety-sixth largest economy, bigger than that of Cameroon. Walmart would place higher than Belgium, ranked twenty-fourth in the world by its GDP of $485,873 million.[1]

Yet corporations are not held to the same account as countries. Giant companies are not simply multinational but 'postnational, transnational and even anti-national' because of their opposition to anything that restricts their ability to do business.[2]

Shouldn't there be a law against all this?

Daniel Simons and Charlie Holt work together at the Greenpeace International Legal Unit, constantly kept on their toes by the battle of corporations versus the environment. 'You've got this huge expansion in corporate power that happened over the last few decades,' Charlie explains. 'But the international community hasn't been keeping up in terms of accountability mechanisms. We've been making much slower progress in ensuring that responsibilities are commensurate with powers.'

Without checks and balances, corporations are able to dominate nation states, particularly in the Global South. 'If a country needs the employment, corporations have a lot of leverage,' Daniel adds. 'They can ask for taxes not to apply to them, they can lobby for labour conditions or environmental rules to be adjusted to their liking.'

Then of course there is the money that flows from corporations in the Global North to feed and foster corruption so that they can buy whatever standards they want. This undue influence also exists within countries.

But couldn't a global law enshrine environmental standards and prevent rich countries or corporations from opening up poor countries, using them as trash cans, then facing no consequences?

Under current international law, each country gets to decide which agreements it signs up to and which ones it rejects. Countries rush to sign up to free trade agreements, hoping for economic growth and business dynamism, while often sidestepping pacts on the environment or labour rights. It is still held as a question of national sovereignty that enforcement mechanisms cannot be imposed onto countries. Ultimate political power and legal authority, it is argued, must rest with national governments who set their own rules and regulations within their own borders.

Countries do not want to sign up to basic environmental standards or worker protections because of the need to attract foreign investment. Unlike an oil refinery, a shoe factory is mobile and can be shifted between countries or continents. Corporations look for the most lucrative manufacturing option and go wherever labour costs are cheapest and environmental standards are most profitable.

This is 'the race to the bottom' that we've seen throughout this book. The collision of globalisation and inequality that means poorer countries, in an attempt to climb out of poverty, must keep themselves open for business – which in turn means being vulnerable to abuse.

Global trade is characterised by greater or lesser degrees of state intervention. States might impose stringent regulations or tariffs on goods crossing their borders, or they might adopt a so-called 'free trade' approach by minimising or doing away with regulations and tariffs altogether.[3] 'The problem is, if you liberalise trade you make it attractive for countries to lower their environmental standards, so that they can attract more investment and export more,' Daniel says. 'Economic activity will move to the country with the least resistance in terms of environmental law, tax law, labour rights, etc.' Liberalised trade not matched by agreements about protecting labour and environmental standards spells disaster.

Blocs like the European Union have developed protections around the environment, workers' rights and consumer rights which have led to a decrease in dangerous practices within the EU. But instead of disappearing off the face of the planet, polluting industries were instead exported to countries where there are less robust protections. A prime example of this is the devastation the leather industry has wrought in Bangladesh.

From the Caymans to the courts

Until now, the international system has been reliant on voluntary initiatives like the UN Guiding Principles on Business and Human Rights. This 2011 agreement is touted as a historic breakthrough, and the moment the world acknowledged it was no longer just governments who should take responsibility for human rights. The principles are a set of expectations for how corporations should behave, but given their voluntary nature, the private sector is as unethical as ever.

A UN intergovernmental working group is hoping to change this by exploring options for a binding treaty to regulate corporate human rights obligations. It has, however, been very slow to get off the ground as it is supported overwhelmingly by the Global South, but opposed by industrialised countries and the Global North, in particular the US and the EU.

It would be a mistake, however, to believe that corporations are averse to legally binding agreements – they like them so long as they work in their favour. Corporations were aided in their quest to become multinational by the removal of restraints on capital flowing across national borders. This process was accompanied by the gradual creation of thousands of investment treaties around the globe, including the North American Free Trade Agreement (NAFTA) or the now defunct Transatlantic Trade and Investment Partnership (TTIP).

In the shadowy world of investment treaties and free trade agreements lurks the Investor-State Dispute Settlement (ISDS) system. This system allows corporations to sue countries they claim damaged their investment by, for example, trying to protect a natural habitat or suspending a dangerous mining licence. ISDS provisions were intended to avoid states coming into conflict with each other – without ISDS provisions, an investor would rely on intervention by its home government, to protect overseas citizens and to boost the rule of law. It has become normal for this mechanism to be built into trade and investment treaties to allow corporations to protect their assets, but not all agreements give countries the same option if a corporation violates their laws.

'The sorts of laws and measures that have been attacked under the ISDS have disproportionately been laws designed to protect human health, to address labour standards or to protect the environment,' explains Carroll Muffett, president and CEO of the Center for International Environmental Law (CIEL). Thousands of these agreements now exist. In New York, CIEL's recent case files bear witness to wealthy Global North corporations who have set up subsidiaries in the Cayman Islands to avoid taxes, in Global South countries to conduct advantageous surveys and finally in whatever country gives them the best shot of suing under any given free trade agreement. Unlike people or governments, corporations get to choose whether they exist in a country, or not.

Proponents of globalisation often argue the key to success is a self-regulating global free market, yet what we have is not a *free* market, but one regulated in favour of corporate interests. Joseph Stiglitz has said: 'we have a system that might be called *global governance without global government*.'[4] It is a system dominated by financial institutions and commercial interests, where those most affected are left almost voiceless. Without a global mechanism, protection of people and the environment comes down to domestic laws, which corporations can far too easily overwhelm.

'This has led to a system where multinational corporations are largely unconstrained by the law in many countries,' Carroll says. 'We've seen this over and over again under the ISDS process. Because of the way these treaties are set up, a multinational corporation that doesn't like how a new environmental regulation has been adopted, or labour standards have been enforced against it, or doesn't agree with the protection of these particular health standards, will turn around and sue the government of a host country under a set of provisions that are designed to pull the suit out of the normal judicial and political processes and into a secretive environment heavily tilted towards the companies themselves.'

Getting rid of the ISDS phenomenon would involve cancelling or renegotiating thousands of trade treaties. Going forward public pressure is vital for preventing the ISDS system being attached to any new agreements. The corporations who enjoy the ISDS system very often originate in and are sent forth by the US and Europe. A fundamental solution Carroll proposes is to 'rehome' companies, enforcing a system whereby every company has to identify the one home country, and state, where they exist. This would allow anyone who needs to sue that company to do so because they exist in a single identified place.

Brought to heel

The late British barrister and campaigner Polly Higgins called climate ecocide 'the missing international crime of our time'. She argued ecocide was excluded at the eleventh hour from the treaty that founded the International Criminal Court (ICC).[5] Had it been included, could it have provided a means to hold states and corporations to account?

Ecocide can be defined as the loss, damage or destruction of an ecosystem or territory in such a way 'that peaceful enjoyment by the inhabitants has been or will be severely diminished.' A growing number of campaigners argue ecocide should be included in the Rome Statute, the treaty which founded the ICC and established its remit of dealing with what are considered the worst international crimes: genocide, crimes against humanity, aggression and war crimes.

But again, environmental protection encounters the problem of voluntary agreements and arguments over definitions. 'The Rome Statute only has four core crimes at the moment. One of those is aggression,' Charlie Holt explains. 'It is enforceable against all states as a result of a Security Council referral, but when it comes to state referrals or self-referrals, or the prosecutor's own powers, that is only enforceable against thirty-four countries.'

The level of disagreement over the meaning of 'aggression' implies it would be extremely difficult to create an internationally agreed definition of ecocide. A growing camp believes, however, that the Rome Statute can be used as it is currently worded to prosecute for ecocide.

In 2016, Fatou Bensouda, prosecutor of the International Criminal Court, released a policy paper which stated the ICC would pay particular attention to crimes committed by means of, or which resulted in, environmental destruction. The paper set out the types of cases the ICC will prioritise for prosecution, including the illegal exploitation of natural resources, cases of environmental destruction and instances of land grabbing where investors buy up vast areas of poor countries.

This allows for the prosecution of individuals accused of human atrocities carried out by environmental destruction. It opens the door for CEOs and politicians joining warlords in the dock at the ICC,[6] and marks growing public pressure to recognise corporations as having the ability to threaten human rights in a way that has historically been associated with governments.

A judgement is coming

Direct action protests and school student climate strikes on Fridays have ramped up pressure on governments to act on climate breakdown. Another thing breathing life and optimism into the climate movement is the rise of climate liability lawsuits, where groups of people file human rights lawsuits demanding protection of their rights, or asserting their rights have been contravened by corporations or government action or inaction.

'As climate change becomes less of an abstract issue, and more an issue with direct and concrete implications for human lives, it becomes more an issue of justice and not just an issue of environmentalism or conservation,' says Charlie. Scientific progress means tangible harm can be properly determined, bringing into play the tools of tort or criminal law. As a result, lawsuits have been filed across the globe with more expected to follow.

'These cases are very important in stopping "business as usual" thinking,' Daniel Simons explains. 'A lot of corporations up to now had the mindset that they could weather this, but I think it's become clear this is a tobacco industry moment.'

In the same way Big Tobacco was eventually held accountable in the lawsuits of the 1990s and 2000s, fossil fuel corporations may find themselves in the dock having lost deniability that they are doing grievous harm. Daniel says while corporations may be able to tackle current cases, it will become increasingly difficult for them to defend themselves if they show inaction. 'It's a very similar pattern, where the science was probably clear to them much before it was clear to policymakers and the general public,' he concludes. 'They tried to cover it up, with dire consequences. That's now become clear, there's really no way back for them, they have to start changing their practices or they will be held liable for the damage their business has caused.'

Some environmental groups, and even countries, have also been experimenting with the idea that nature itself has rights. This strategy, often inspired by the beliefs of diverse indigenous people across the world, has been adopted by groups from Chile to India. Can a river, for example, obtain legal personhood? Could the Buriganga be recognised as having rights? In 2008, Mother Earth, known as Pachamama, was included in Ecuador's constitution, with Bolivia quickly doing the same thing.[7]

But how to remain cheerful when leaders like Trump and Bolsonaro reign at perhaps the most critical moment in human history? When powerful countries, including the US, Russia, Saudi Arabia and Australia, are run by administrations actively working against environmental progress?

Charlie and Daniel maintain public pressure is the key to change. 'We tend to treat countries as being monolithic blocs where everyone operates in the same way, but that's not really true,' Charlie says. Even if an individual president seems entirely resistant to any type of pressure, governments are made up of lower-level politicians and bureaucrats who are more susceptible to public pressure.

There is also leverage to be had with corporations, who rely upon a social contract to operate and who are susceptible to public pressure. As they increasingly operate on a global level, their shops and offices can become the focus of campaigns and protest. But, as we shall see, even if this leverage prompts action, it does not necessarily result in the best outcome.

CSR: What is it good for?

Having moved their manufacturing to countries with fewer labour
or environmental rights, and having contracted with factories that
operated on the worst kinds of exploitation, famous brands ran into
trouble. Travel and communications meant human rights groups and
journalists were also globalised and on the hunt for wrongdoing.
Child labour, violence, unsanitary conditions and inhumane wages
were all found in the supply chains of some of the biggest brands in
the world.

The response to bad publicity was to develop Corporate Social
Responsibility (CSR) programmes, a trend that took off in the 1990s
and which persists to this day. CSR departments promised ethical
business practices which would take social, human and environmental concerns into account. It was a strategy that promised to improve
conditions, factory by factory. It would be done on a voluntary basis
and not involve any binding agreements or legislation. It comes as
little surprise that critics insist that despite twenty-five years and
billions of dollars, CSR programmes have failed to improve supply
chain workers' lives either on the job, or in society.[8]

Professor Beth Rosenberg is a specialist in occupational and environmental health at Tufts University. A descendent of a Massachusetts
shoe factory owner, she is a former member of the United States
Chemical Safety and Hazard Investigation Board. In the summer of
2005, Professor Rosenberg visited a string of factories in China and
Vietnam as part of an attempt by several large shoe brands to improve standards in their factories. The trip left Professor Rosenberg
deeply sceptical of the entire premise of CSR to this day.

Conditions in the factories varied greatly, but the worst were
appalling. In a Korean-run factory in northern China, sixteen young
women shared bare dormitory rooms, the toilet-block stench hitting
the nose from 50 feet away. The owners of the factory had hired an
art student, who knew nothing about health and safety, to oversee
CSR requirements.[9]

Professor Rosenberg describes a truly farcical moment. Some
of the factories she toured were only producing for one brand, but
some were so enormous, each production line was making shoes

for one of three different brands: 'All these different shoe brands had different codes of conduct, so if one brand's CSR programme outlawed solvent-based glues in favour of safer, water-based glues, others maintained solvent-based glues. The good intentions didn't matter, everyone was breathing the same crap because the lines were 20 feet apart.'

'It just shows you how ridiculous CSR programmes are,' Professor Rosenberg continues. 'They're voluntary, there's little to no enforcement or monitoring and the monitoring is done by people who are paid by the brands so there is serious conflict of interest.'

It is even possible for something as seemingly simple as targets for reducing the number of injuries to hide sinister practices. Professor Rosenberg discovered workers and their supervisors being *blamed* for their own injuries and fined nearly two-thirds of a day's salary. This is a sure way to discourage the reporting of injuries. It is a practice known in the US as 'bloody pocket syndrome', where low injury rates are seen as a measure of success but are actually the result of underreporting, allowing unsafe conditions to continue.[10]

Slipper-y slope

Another major problem is that CSR programmes tend only to cover consumer-facing companies who are susceptible to public pressure, this excludes the vast majority of shoe production. Professor Rosenberg has described walking into a large, state-owned factory compound outside of Ho Chi Minh City in Vietnam. Most of the buildings in the compound were producing trainers for a top sports brand under a CSR framework. Although there were issues with overtime, protective equipment and long hours of standing up, the buildings were at least well ventilated and lit.

In the same compound was a building leased to a slipper company. With no famous clients, the factory was a disgrace: 'There was no ventilation and the temperature was in the humid 90s,' Professor Rosenberg wrote. 'Windows were blocked by shelves of material, there were no fans, the stench of glue was dizzying, a single, dim, light bulb was hanging in each of two rooms, and the workers looked anxious.'[11]

With nothing but piecemeal brand-led CSR agreements to govern standards, factories next door to each other can vary wildly. While CSR agreements may raise standards in a few factories, labour rights should not be left to this kind of chance, with the majority of workers abandoned. Take, for example, the component parts of shoes made by companies no one has heard of – who is watching those factories?

'If you're interested in making workplaces safe, you don't regulate brand by brand,' says Professor Rosenberg. 'It's only factories at the end of the supply chain that are vulnerable to any kind of consumer boycott or consumer attention. When you think about an athletic shoe and what goes into it, you're not going to have a consumer boycott about working conditions in the glue factory, or in the shoelace factory, or in the factory that makes grommets.'

People will not join a boycott over emissions from a glue factory that supplies a famous brand, she argues. Which is why shoes, and their obscure component parts, need to be regulated and monitored by governments.

Goody two shoes

CSR programmes have generated thousands of identikit websites, glossy brochures, well-paid jobs and lofty slogans.

But is CSR a failure or just a façade or just a snapshot of a point in time?

In an article about serving ten years in the CSR industry, one consultant claimed brands: 'create a department in charge of "sustainability" – or human rights, or corporate citizenship, or social responsibility, pick your buzzword – whose job is to keep the NGOs at bay . . . The fifteen other departments of the company, meanwhile, do exactly what they always did. Only now, they've got a guy whose job is to dress it all up as "sustainability" and sell it to consumers.'[12]

Take a different example. In May 2012, a British corporate research company ranked Puma as the number one brand for sustainability. The report stated that despite operating in a sector at high risk for human-rights abuses, Puma had a strong environment record and showed improvements in supply chain labour standards.[13] Ironically, just three months earlier in February 2012, Reuters reported that Puma executives were flying to Cambodia after a woman had been shot during a protest by workers at a Puma supplier factory. The protest had been calling for better working conditions and increased pay. The year before, a different Puma supplier in Cambodia was placed under investigation when it was hit by a mass fainting epidemic (of the kind described in Chapter Two).[14] However, in 2017 Puma told the *Guardian* its recommendations to combat mass fainting included the provision of energy bars and medical checks, maintenance of ventilation systems and worker management committees. Puma stated: 'The causes for mass faintings seem to be multiple and often complex. Only when there is a collaborative approach between the brands, factories, the workers and the government will the situation improve.'

Soul traders

The Südwind-Institut is housed in an office block next to a railway line in Bonn, Germany. Südwind carry out some of the most persistent and detailed research into the global shoe industry, acting as a watchdog on brands and their CSR claims. Anton Pieper has been researching the shoe industry on behalf of Südwind since 2015. Passionate about his work, Anton is constantly exasperated by the difference between the image and the reality of big sportswear brands.

'There is a big, big gap between what the industry is saying, what people know about those brands and what the workers' reality is in the factories,' Anton says. 'That goes for all the big brands. If you go into Tier One factories that are supplying big-named brands, you will hardly find any massive labour rights violations. But if you have a closer look into subcontracting companies further down the supply chain you will often discover that the sector as a whole is not compliant with international labour law and environmental regulations.'

Most of the big brands, he says, rely upon a supplier market that is not wholly transparent. Raw materials such as leather are often not traceable as to which small tannery has produced them. So if the supply chain is taken as a whole it shows a very different picture from the one projected by brands. Anton has seen the CSR industry mushroom as a result of increasing pressure on brands. 'More and more companies have CSR departments, or at least employ one person,' he says. 'It is still really rare, but the bigger companies are getting there. So you can sell it as a success and it's certainly good that we have people to talk to in the companies.'

On the downside, however, Anton finds that having a named individual to speak to in a CSR department is sometimes where it ends. Brands keep organisations like Südwind-Institut busy by talking, but in reality, they often do nothing.

Anton lists more problems with this broken system – CSR teams being far below managers and buyers in company hierarchies; departments skilfully filling in questionnaires sent by ethical consumer organisations to ensure they place highly. He names a large shoe brand who do well in 'ethical rankings' thanks to having an office full of people dedicated to CSR.

CSR has become the masterful use of greenwashing, projecting a responsible image to obscure the reality of production. Any good done with CSR consultants is quickly outweighed.[15] But if CSR was a strategy that never intended to change the industry but instead wanted to make corporations look good, then it has been a huge success. How else could Nike, a behemoth that guzzles oil, plastic, cotton, rubber, metals and chemicals, be ranked No. 1 in a survey that asked people to name a sustainable brand?

The CSR system is not just about misdirecting consumer attention, rather it has been set up in direct competition with robust institutions that could inspect and enforce standards. Over the past few decades, at the very time when courts and lawmakers should have been strengthened, government institutions and the very rule of law have been sidelined.

When the Rana Plaza garment factory complex collapsed in 2013 and killed 1,138 people, it emerged that it had not once, but *twice*, been given a clean bill of health by Primark's auditing system. What the workers who died needed was not meaningless corporate box-ticking, but rigorous government factory inspectors and an independent trade union. For their part, Primark say that before 2013, ensuring buildings were structurally sound was not part of their auditing process.[16]

Whereas shoe production used to be based in countries with robust conventions governing labour and the environment, these countries have been left behind for cheaper production sites in the Global South.

Multinational corporations have no place having the final say in factory standards. Not just because they are unqualified to do so, but because the aim of any corporation will always be profit, and so trusting them to regulate themselves is, and has been shown to be on a number of occasions, a catastrophic mistake.

Big shoes to fill

'Globalisation has brought about job opportunities for groups of workers that were traditionally and historically marginalised and did not have access to waged employment,' says Arianna Rossi at the International Labour Organization (ILO). 'This is perhaps most evidently young women workers that didn't have any opportunities to participate in the formal workforce before this export-oriented production started to take off in developing countries. This also applies to many other groups such as migrant labour and unskilled labour – of course there's a lot of intersectionality among these groups.'

But, Arianna points out, for every opportunity there were challenges. Nowhere is this clearer than in the garment and footwear sector, where job opportunities very often took the form of exploitative working conditions.

Arianna works on the Better Work programme, a collaboration between the ILO and the International Finance Corporation. Better Work aims to improve working conditions and competitiveness in the global garment and footwear industry by being a bridge between trade unions, employers, manufacturers, governments, brands and retailers. The programme operates in Bangladesh, Cambodia, Vietnam, Indonesia, Jordan, Nicaragua, Haiti and Ethiopia, and a pilot scheme running in Egypt from 2017 to 2018.

But despite big labour rights institutions working to try and protect people, the global labour market still seems like the Wild

West. Where are the protections for ordinary people, the checks and balances that could enshrine trade union rights and counteract corporate power?

'From a labour regulation perspective, globalisation poses intrinsic challenges, because it is just by definition transnational and historically labour regulation is within the boundaries of a nation state,' Arianna explains. 'Global supply chains have presented challenges for national governments because they are just not equipped with the legal instruments to enforce legislation beyond the boundaries of their own country.'

She points to recent transparency legislation, like Britain's Modern Slavery Act 2015, as examples of the world slowly waking up to the fact that supply chains are now complex and global. But again, corporations have the flexibility of being able to hop from country to country in a never-ending chase for the cheapest, closest, most adaptable production site. This has transformed the consumer market into a superfast whirl where people expect new product lines to constantly appear.

A thousand watchful experts

It is entirely possible to end this situation of exploitation and have every point of the supply chain full of watchful experts who ensure standards on health and safety, wages and hours are upheld. These best-placed experts are the very workers who are currently underused and exploited. Working in factories all day long, tending to machines and caring for buildings, they see everything. In this sense, preventing problems in factories is not an issue that needs a new invention, rather it needs the best resources a company has – its staff – to be properly motivated and respected.

What it requires is for workers to have a voice, a voice that has historically been found in trade unionism. It was workers gaining this voice that ended the worst exploitation of the industrial revolution in Britain. Without a collective voice, workers in supply chains are left atomised and vulnerable. 'Labour unions in general give workers a voice at the table which they do not have in CSR programmes,' says Professor Rosenberg. 'CSR doesn't change the hugely imbalanced power dynamic, whereas unions do.

'I would like to see workers have more power and more say in their working conditions. I would like to see more democracy in workplaces,' she continues, before listing some of the things blighting the shoe industry that a trade union could bargain over: working hours, working conditions, wages, what materials are used, how toxic those materials are, the recyclable nature of the product, the pace of work, the amount of product that is made and the safest way to carry out each production task. Labour struggles for better conditions are not always successful but they do at least establish a forum for bargaining and discussion.

No more princes, no more money

This lack of workplace democracy has had a particularly negative impact on women. As we have seen, some 80 per cent of garment workers and an unreliably estimated 46 per cent of shoe workers are women. While the data is wobbly, due to few countries recording accurate employment data for women, we do know that women are routinely paid less than men.

A regional study of Asian textile, clothing and footwear (TCF) worker wages by the ILO found that while non-compliance with minimum wage regulations was widespread, women are more likely than men to be paid less than the minimum wage. The largest wage gap between men and women was found in Pakistan where 86.9 per cent of women in the sector are paid less than the minimum wage, compared to 26.5 per cent of men.[17]

The exploitation of women does not end with wages. The #MeToo movement has swept the world after originally being founded in 2006 by US activist Tarana Burke to encourage survivors of sexual abuse to speak out. The movement has become most famous for exposing the imbalance of power in Hollywood where moguls like Harvey Weinstein have been accused of abusing women for decades.

The fashion industry has also been subject to scrutiny, in particular regarding the treatment of fashion models. Similarly, after #MeToo hit Nike, a slew of top executives left the company amid widespread accusations of a corporate culture of discrimination, bullying and sexual harassment.[18] Nike maintained throughout that it was opposed to discrimination and was committed to diversity and inclusion. They said the vast majority of Nike employees live by their values of dignity and respect for others.

Far from just existing in corporate boardrooms, gendered power imbalances run right throughout supply chains. Sexual harassment or abuse at work is when men exploit the power they already have over women in workplaces. This power protects perpetrators from the consequences of their actions, as women who accuse men of abuse risk losing jobs or being publicly shamed. Sexual abuse in the workplace is therefore the reassertion of male dominance through the humiliation of women.[19]

Studies on sexual harassment specifically within factories are inconclusive. There is a lack of accurate data on how many women exist in these supply chains, let alone data on their experiences. The Fair Wear Foundation believe 60 per cent of garment workers in Bangladesh have experienced some form of harassment, though a study by BRAC University may point to a more accurate figure. The study found that 94 per cent of women commuting on public transport in Bangladesh have been subjected to sexual harassment, with men aged forty-one to sixty identified as the overwhelming perpetrators.[20]

Women in the TCF sector work in factories owned and managed by men. They are surrounded by a social context which considers women to be inferior, caught at the intersection of gender inequality and inequalities of class, race, ethnicity, age and migrant status.[21] Add to this the fact that fashion and shoes have historically not been taken seriously and have been dismissed instead as women's interests. This attitude further sidelines the production of fashion and shoes as 'women's work', devaluing the work of women in workshops and on production lines, and lessening the chances of calls for change being taken seriously.

It is a sad truth that the shoe industry would not be possible without gendered exploitation. Footwear is an industry swamped with money and yet shoe workers are dirt poor and exploited. This is not a coincidence, it is a deeply gendered issue, with sexism inextricably linked with racism and class exploitation. We live in a world where women are paid less and treated worse than men, a world where the lives of people in the Global South count for less than rich white lives and where the poor are seen as an open goal for exploitation. That the shoe industry feeds at this point of intensity is again no coincidence.

Industrial struggle is one area where women can change not only their conditions at work, but their position in society. Case studies abound, from Mary Macarthur's chain workers of 1910, to the Dagenham factory workers of the 1960s, the two-year Grunwick Dispute of the 1970s and the present-day women of the Garment Labour Union in India. But this vital pathway to end gendered exploitation, and create social change, is nearly always blocked whenever calls for increasing workers' rights are silenced.

This barrier to change particularly intensifies within export processing zones (EPZs), also known as free trade zones (FTZs). There are over 3,500 of these zones, with more than 900 located across Asia.[22] Some of the oldest EPZs are in Latin America, set up to churn out clothes, shoes and toys.[23] These zones are established to attract export-orientated industries and foreign direct investment. Within an EPZ, multinational corporations are offered even more privileges and control than usual: tax breaks, relaxed regulations, means to circumvent minimum wages by offering 'apprenticeships' and crucially, limitations on trade union rights.

Workers in EPZs may encounter a total ban on unionisation, or find that union leaders are unable to access the EPZ; strikes may be outlawed, collective bargaining repressed and anyone challenging the status quo risks being summarily fired.[24] With the path to social progress blocked, globalisation has created and maintained a system stacked against factory workers in order to keep the profits rolling in.

Criminalising protest

One of the most depressing pages on the *Guardian* website is called 'The Defenders'. It lists all the people who have been murdered for trying to protect their community's land or natural resources. Chances are, the page reads, four such people will be killed somewhere on the planet this week.[25]

The most dangerous places to be an environmental defender are Brazil, the Philippines and Honduras. Typically, killings occur in places where there are deep intersections between poverty, indigenous peoples, marginalised populations and where extractive resources are located.

'When conflicts arise the people who are working to defend their land and their communities are often by definition among the most vulnerable people in their country,' says Carroll Muffett. 'This leaves them particularly exposed, often in countries where official impunity is already a problem. This is why we see over and over again, and with increasing severity in recent years, the rise in attacks on human rights and environmental defenders. Companies have seen over and over again that they can get away with it.'

Building international solidarity movements is vital for protecting people at risk of violence. It must be demonstrated that environmental defenders have a visible global support base behind them. But this is something that is becoming more of a challenge as campaigners in the Global North increasingly face harassment and arrest.

'We're seeing the echoes of this same hostility to environmental and human rights defenders even in countries that are supposed to be beacons of democracy and free speech,' Carroll Muffett says. 'We've seen the increasing criminalisation of protest, the militarisation of policing from the Keystone XL pipeline to the Dakota Access Pipeline and Bayou Bridge. Peaceful protestors severely prosecuted for what has historically been the exercise of one of the most fundamental freedoms that this country has afforded – the freedom to criticise your own government.'

Greenpeace say they are fighting the use of SLAPPs, Strategic Lawsuit Against Public Participation, essentially a means of using civil lawsuits to harass environmental defenders. This backlash in the Global North has led to the rise of the #ProtectTheProtest movement. But this leads to movements having to fight on multiple fronts – protesting against climate breakdown, fighting to maintain basic freedoms in supposedly democratic countries and in addition advocating for stronger protections for activists in countries where the price of resistance can be death.

The rich are on the deck of the *Titanic* while the poor drown in the hold

As the December wind harried demonstrators outside the Polish Embassy, Asad Rehman told the crowd about his experience attending previous climate talks: 'There are people at those climate talks who used to say to me, *You're too radical, we have to live within the system, we have to work within the system*, I used to say back to them: *That's easy when you're not dying from that system.*'

This is a system Asad describes as sacrificing 'black and brown and poor people' in the interests of profit. A system where the interests of corporations and big business are put ahead of the interests of ordinary people. This is the economic system not just of capitalism, but of globalised neoliberal capitalism. It is why the shoe industry is ultimately in such a state.

Capitalism established itself as the dominant economic system and class structure in Britain in the eighteenth century, and soon spread across the world. It is a system of private ownership of the means of production – resources like factories and the land. A system where people have to sell their labour to survive, and are paid less than the amount of wealth their work produces. The fact that workers are underpaid, and the earth is treated as a free resource, creates a surplus for the small minority of people who own the means of production.

Shoes illustrate this scenario perfectly. Independent shoemakers under feudal or early capitalist systems would make a small profit on each pair of shoes they made, the surplus coming from selling shoes for slightly more than they cost to make. In contrast, production facilities in the current factory system can employ tens of thousands of people.

The aim of the game is to make as big a margin as possible between production costs and the amount a shoe is sold for. This means two things: reducing labour costs as low as possible and sourcing materials as cheaply as possible. Unless companies are using slave labour, people need to be paid wages, but what characterises the shoe industry is the hunt for and maintenance of the lowest possible wages. So it was that globalisation opened up a whole new world of possibilities for reducing the cost of labour as the Global South came online.

Along with profit, the other defining aspect of capitalism is competition. As soon as one or two companies jumped ship from old production centres in Europe and the US, it was game over for the industry. Being in competition with other companies meant even brands reluctant to close down their factories felt they had little choice, once their competitors had found the means to greatly reduce costs. As capitalism globalised, it demanded sacrifices to extreme liberalism. Nothing should stand in the way.

Neoliberal capitalism and putting people before profit are inextricably linked with climate breakdown. We have seen how the shoe industry characterises the neoliberal, hyper-destructive short-termism of treating water, oil, animals, air and the rainforest like they are a free or inconsequential resource. 'Ultimately the formulation of neoliberalism, of unfettered corporate power, of deregulation, of this idea of a small state and the power of corporate power, is what's driven the climate crisis,' Asad says.

Under neoliberalism, and particularly under austerity, we have seen the transfer of wealth from the poor to the rich, with those least responsible being the most impacted. Carbon inequality is also so extreme that the top 10 per cent of the world's population are responsible for 50 per cent of emissions, whereas the poorest 50 per cent of people are only responsible for 10 per cent.[26] From the War on Want office in London, Asad describes climate breakdown as the greatest inequality of them all, chillingly calling it 'the transfer of life, from the poor to the rich.'

'We're told climate change affects everybody and we're on the *Titanic* and it's hit the iceberg,' he says. 'Yes, we're all on the *Titanic* but there's a difference. The rich are on the deck of the *Titanic*, still listening to the orchestra, still sipping cocktails and hoping there's going to be some miracle answer. In the hold are the poor who are already dying, and they're prevented, when they try and escape the water, from being able to get out.'

The global legal system has not been allowed to catch up with the realities of corporate power, corporations have proffered snake-oil solutions to make themselves look good while they tear up the earth, workers have been denied their right to freedom of association and women blocked from finding equality in this supposedly global village.

The answer to why shoes cause so much havoc, is because the footwear industry is a deregulated and subcontracted part of capitalism. It makes billions of dollars from massive over-production based on the hyper-exploitation of Global South people and the planet. Bonded to this out-of-control production is over-consumption of short-lived commodities that are destined for landfill once the thrill fades. The cradle for this mayhem is capitalism and the globalised capitalism that we inhabit today. The question now is how to deal with it.

CHAPTER 10

Kick Back

At twenty, Kristina Ampeva had long left school, endured a violent, unhappy marriage and been plunged into a custody battle. Reaching for her lighter, she describes how the courts told her she needed a job if she wanted to take care of her baby daughter. Kristina's phone rings and she answers it, standing up to pace around her living room. On the phone is a worker in the midst of suing his former employer. He needs advice.

The view from Kristina's balcony is of Štip, a red-roofed sweep of a town that curves along a green mountain valley. Brightly coloured primary schools bustle with children and the streets are tree-lined. The city's 16,000 university students walk the river promenade and hang out in cafes.

High on a hill, overlooking Štip, is a giant metal-girder cross. The steep trail of steps up the hill serve as a memorial, flanked by white marble blocks carved with the names of young men who died fighting in the Second World War. The hill has become a hangout spot. Marble memorials to the war dead are covered in graffiti about sex, drugs and the spurious advantages of not having feelings. In red, someone has written: 'I AM A BO$$ U A WORKER BITCH.'

With its industrial heritage, Štip has been called the 'Manchester of Macedonia'. Approximately 80 textile factories employ between 15 and 200 people each. From the top of the hill, you can see the town's factory district, buildings one or two storeys high, built in the boom time of Yugoslavia.

It was in one of these factories that Kristina found a job many years ago. Hanging up the phone, she describes how all of a sudden she had health insurance, a pension and a salary coming in on the fifteenth of each month. 'It was good, I had a job, I could raise a child, I could show the court,' Kristina says. 'But even after a few days I was telling myself, what are you doing here? All that yelling: "You stupid woman, you can't sew, you don't know anything, you can't work with machines."'

For four months Kristina took home a tiny trainee salary of under €60. She kept quiet, doing what she was told to keep her job. She lights her next cigarette with a smile, describing how over the next four years she met her husband Denis and became pregnant with her second child. Though things were better, the work was relentless. She argued with the women she worked alongside, telling them they should refuse to do overtime or work Saturdays.

'I said let's have a strike, let's leave from this place – our working time is from 7 a.m. to 3 o'clock,' Kristina recalls. 'But the women next to me said, "They will fire us. Where will we work? We are older women, this is how it works in textile companies. We're sorry you're pregnant and young, but this is how it is, you'll get used to it."'

'But I never got used to it.'

Her phone rings again and she answers it, talking excitedly before returning to her story. In the summer after the birth of her second daughter, her older colleagues started fainting from high blood pressure. 'We did thirty days with no break or rest because the partners in Europe were waiting for their order. Sunday, Saturday, national holidays, we were there. In September when my pay cheque arrived I got a salary of little more than €100 and I said – that's it.'

Her next job was in a factory where 50 workers churned out 500 car seats a day. It was a big step up in terms of salary, but the work was gruelling and she still hated being yelled at all the time.

Experiencing more and more injustices around her, in healthcare and schooling for her children, Kristina became a community activist. 'It was like, boom!' she says, describing how all around her she suddenly saw social problems that were shrouded in silence. She was approached by a political opposition party to run a campaign on behalf of garment workers. In 2017, Kristina decided to found the independent Association Glasen Tekstilec, meaning Loud Textile Workers.

The small Association Glasen Tekstilec office in Štip is lined with red posters, its frosted glass door leads out onto a busy roundabout. There is a tiny bathroom and a gas stove with a coffee pot on a desk. Constantly scraping money together, with more work than twenty people could do, Kristina is leading the fight to overhaul the garment and footwear industry in this small pocket of eastern Europe. She has organised protests, implemented official factory inspections and coordinated collective challenges to the worst exploitation. She is advised and supported by trade unionists from other eastern European countries and by campaigners in Germany.

The idea of pushing for change is catching on. Arriving at the office is twenty-six-year-old legal advisor Simona Maneva Zivkova. Simona gives free legal advice to factory workers. She acts as a conduit between intimidated workers who need to remain anonymous and the government-run Labour Inspectorate who can scrutinise factories and fine owners who break the law. Simona can also help workers navigate the gauntlet of legal documents needed to hold a strike.

Most importantly, however, Simona trains workers to deal with these responsibilities themselves. While factory owners would prefer for their workforce to remain ignorant of the law, Simona is creating a small team of worker paralegals.

So far, five factory workers have signed up to be secret legal representatives within the industry. One worker paralegal arrives to visit Simona and explains that they are motivated by a desire to learn about their rights and to help their colleagues. To maintain secrecy, worker paralegals tell people they have a friend who can help workers.

Issues already being challenged include a factory making workers return part of their wages in cash and a factory that makes orthopaedic shoes paying significantly beneath the minimum wage. Both Kristina and Simona are up against powerful industrial magnates, the biggest brands in Europe and a mostly unsympathetic political system, but as their base grows, so do their chances of success.

The triangle

Shoes help explore the characteristics of globalisation: production by Global South factory and homeworkers, rampant consumerism and the mountains of waste it produces, the illusions conjured by capitalism, migration flows and barriers, biosphere exploitation, the lack of legal protections and the onset of a techno-future. Tracing the production of shoes reveals how we came to face such crises today.

But there is one further characteristic of globalisation. Where there is oppression and destruction, there is also resistance. This book would be incomplete without an exploration of the fact that people are pushing back against the erosion of their rights and are challenging transnational corporations, oppressive factory owners, environmental violations and unjust governments.

Changing the world is no easy task. With the shoe industry lagging behind the rest of the fashion industry in terms of transparency, accountability and standards, there is a complicated road ahead. To address this, this chapter looks at three issues: individual, political and system change. The diagram opposite is of a triangle of change, a means of thinking about possible methods for transforming the world. In the diagram, individual change is placed at the top of this triangle of change as it is generally where people start when they begin to think about shifting the balance of power. But as you can see, it only impacts the tip of the problem.

Because our object in question, the shoe, is a consumer item, emphasis is often placed on changing ourselves, rather than the world around us. Individual change is the most inward-looking and singular set of solutions as it focuses on working on yourself and your own personal wardrobe, food cupboard, make-up bag and so on. Individual change is not invalid, but it can function as a trap. The trap is thinking that as long as the top of the triangle is fixed, everything will be fixed. The trap is becoming stuck on this level and never progressing beyond it.

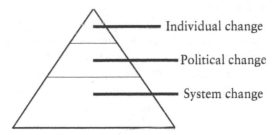

The second level is political change, and it is here that questions of power begin to be examined. This level covers regulation, legislation, freedom of association and taxation, all elements that involve placing political pressure on governments and institutions and pushing them to regulate capitalism. This section involves collective activities and discussions about power. By its very nature it is collective and covers a far greater number of factories and countries.

The third level is by far the biggest and is often the unspoken elephant in the room. This is quite literally the basis of the problem. It is here we find the most intransigent problems of capitalism: the systemic exploitation of women, the exploitation of the Global South, the creation and maintenance of racism and the imposition and exploitation of class and poverty. This third level means confronting capitalism and moving towards system change.

On discomfort

The aim of this book has been to provide an accurate snapshot of the shoe industry and to illuminate the systems of globalisation. Having read it, however, you may feel a sense of discomfort when you look down at your shoes, or even just out of the window at the world.

This discomfort is an important feeling to experience. It is not something you are alone in feeling. In fact, the sense that there is something wrong with the world is more widely felt than ever before. This is in part because the questions humanity faces are huge: how are we going to stop climate breakdown, redistribute our resources and make the world a fair and peaceful place?

The enormity of these questions makes it very tempting to ignore them, to retreat into a cocoon of your house, or room, or bed, and ignore reality. This is where allowing yourself to feel discomfort comes in. Embracing discomfort means waking up. It means accepting that something is wrong with the world and that you have a part to play in finding solutions. Discomfort means you care about the state of the world, which is the first step in driving change.

Discomfort also means you have the power to connect with what you care about. Whether that be the rainforest, or tannery workers, or refugees, or cows facing slaughter. Your discomfort means you can build a bridge and connect with people and things other than yourself. So don't push it away. Neoliberalism would love for you to retreat to your cocoon, to focus only on yourself, to perfect your little space and to feel comfort and pride in your personal choices, but where does this leave everyone else, and eventually where does it leave you?

Individual change

As a species we are overusing the world's resources. It is already necessary for consumption to be made sustainable – this will mean more for those with very little and a reduction for those with far too much. This is not about making life worse for anybody, but making it better for all.

To counteract the social weight of consumerism, Dr Kate Fletcher, the calmly wise academic from Chapter Seven, has developed an idea called 'the craft of use', a way of interacting with the things we wear which is not about constantly buying more.

Because capitalism needs us to keep shopping, we are taught to disregard rather than value the memories and stories contained in the things we wear. This is becoming more acute as 'fast fashion' speeds up consumption and disposal cycles. In opposition to this, a craft-of-use approach is about replacing consumption with action, developing the skills needed to maintain what we have and finding enjoyment in repair and maintenance. It is a strategy based on tending to the things around us rather than buying more stuff: it means stewardship, not ownership.

Dr Fletcher describes a pop-up shop run by a friend where no clothes could be bought, they could only be swapped for things people were already wearing. To complete the purchase people had to fill in a card describing the item they were discarding, explaining the story of its purchase and why they liked it. The result was that once people rediscovered the value of their own belongings, very few swaps were made.

Navigating this change in mindset involves acknowledging that, as Dr Fletcher says, there is satisfaction and creative flourishing to be found within the limits of the things we already have. It is an approach that acknowledges each of us as being part of the planet's ecosystem and is explicit about the responsibility that comes with that. Shoes are handmade objects that are quite literally the product of tens of thousands of years of human ingenuity. We are each connected to, not separate from, this entire process, to both the good and to the bad, to the people who make our shoes and the materials they are wrought from.

While there is value in trying to reset our relationship with consumerism, there are limitations to an individualised approach. There is a drive under neoliberalism to make us believe our value is in our ability to shop, and that it is at the cash register that we make change. The theory goes that if we all shopped 'better' we could transform capitalism. As well as keeping us shopping, this theory assumes that all shopping options are open to all people, and that we all start off equal. To believe this is to ignore the inequalities of class. It is no good telling people to just save up to buy more robust shoes when, far from having money to save, by the end of each month many people are surviving on payday loans. Real change is never based upon excluding people, it must be accessible to be effective.

Another problem with solutions based on shopping is that they encourage us to limit our potential. Andrew Morgan, director of *The True Cost* documentary, is fond of saying that he has never met 'a consumer'. A far more powerful identity than 'consumer' is citizen, or teacher, or staff member, or trade unionist, or activist or whatever word places you as having agency. It is a shift that makes ordinary people extraordinary, and powerful. It is here that the possibility of widespread change really exists.

It is also important not to spend too much time at the top of the triangle because individualism distorts the placement of responsibility for the ills of this system. Rather than blaming people for owning shoes made of carcinogenic materials, we must ask why there are any shoes on the market that have been produced using such dangerous means. The production of shoes begins at the design stage and continues down into the sourcing of materials and factories. The question is not why people buy shoes that have been made by refugees (often having no idea of, or means to discover, their origins), but why brands and retailers have such unconscionable supply chains.

Political change: Restructuring an industry

The second level of the triangle is political change. It is here that the move away from individualism begins. The challenge for the shoe industry is how to keep 7.7 billion people shod, while avoiding exploitation or destruction. This is not a challenge that can be overcome by a few tens of thousands of people, or even a few million people, changing their brand of shoe. What is needed is an end to the shoe factory system being deregulated and unpoliced.

This is the transformative work of generations, of citizens and their elected representatives coming together to demand change. It involves governments regulating the activities of corporations at every stage of their supply chain. It involves legally binding environmental and animal rights regulations on a global level and the creation of regional and global living wages to end the race to the bottom. It involves iron-clad health and safety for every factory and homeworker – both in fire and building safety and in the chemicals and materials used to make shoes. Finally, it involves ensuring total freedom of association for workers in the form of trade unions.

This is no easy task and it often seems like the world is set up to put people off becoming engaged in political processes. But because the changes needed are global, it will take everyone becoming politically active and joining in.

Three-point shopping list

Deborah Lucchetti is the coordinator of La Campagna Abiti Puliti, the Italian branch of the Clean Clothes Campaign. Living in Genoa, she is a leading specialist in workers' rights within the shoe industry.

Deborah outlines the three things needed to transform the shoe industry: the first is for brands and retailers to change their purchasing practices and stop forcing suppliers across the world to meet ridiculously low prices. Exercising the most influence in supply chains, brands and retailers hold the greatest responsibility for conditions. It is their insistence on rock-bottom prices that sees suppliers bypass laws, squeeze wages and pollute the environment.

Secondly, Deborah argues, structural power within global value chains must be rebalanced in favour of workers instead of shareholder profits. At the moment, everything from wages, to health and safety, is made subservient to increasing profit.

Thirdly, binding legislation should be brought in to force the shoe industry to respect basic human and labour rights in every country it operates in. This legislation would need to be actively enforced by prosecutions and penalties at a national and international level. This legislation would need to include mandatory supply chain transparency, to allow public scrutiny by journalists, politicians and citizens. Disclosed data would need to include accessibly published information on production facilities, employment statistics, factory accounts and product information.

This three-point shopping list should not be a lot to ask. Yet the shoe industry remains deregulated, unmonitored and murky. 'To change the shoe industry is possible but totally unrealistic without the political will to do so,' Deborah says. 'The political will of transnational corporations comes only through public pressure, and if they know they will be under scrutiny and will pay high sanctions if they breach the law.'

The creation of a groundswell of public pressure is also vital with regard to global climate talks. Without national movements holding politicians to account and demanding they deliver on their promises, where is the urgency? With the future of the planet at stake, why are the buildings that host climate talks not surrounded day and night by millions of concerned citizens?

Finally, there is consensus among those trying to change the shoe industry that there can be no improvement without a dramatic increase in trade union membership and collective bargaining agreements. The right to freedom of association is rightly regarded as crucial. It is not possible to create genuine and sustainable structural change without directly involving those on the sharp end of the factory system – the workers themselves. These are the people who are best placed for detecting problems, preventing violations, advising on long-lasting solutions and monitoring how solutions are implemented.

This remains a big problem in the largest shoe-producing country of them all. In China, there is no freedom of association for workers, who are instead supposedly represented by the state-controlled All-China Federation of Trade Unions.

People power

Taiwanese company Yue Yuen is the biggest producer of sports shoes on the planet with over 400,000 employees.[1] It makes shoes for big-named brands: Nike, adidas, ASICS, New Balance, Puma, Converse and Timberland, and its factories are found in countries including China, Indonesia, Vietnam, the United States and Mexico. In 2014, Yue Yuen employed approximately 60,000 workers in Dongguan in southern China.[2] It was here, at one of its colossal facilities, that Yue Yuen became the site of the most serious situations of social unrest in China for many decades, and became a symbol of what can be achieved when factory workers say enough is enough.

Workers at the Yue Yuen facility became angry at the chronic underpayment of state-mandated social insurance and housing provident funds. They also wanted a pay rise and the right to organise. In 2014, a colossal 40,000 Yue Yuen workers walked out of their workplaces and went on strike.

Social insurance contributions are compulsory under Chinese labour law. They evolved from China's attempt to make individual employers, instead of the state, responsible for contributions to pensions, and insurance for unemployment, medical fees, work-related injury and maternity cover. But social insurance coverage remains piecemeal, with many workers receiving no benefits whatsoever. This leaves the looming spectre of old age – many of the workers are women whose wages are too low to save for retirement, the One-Child Policy means their families are small and after thirty years of work they face ending up without a pension.[3]

The unrest at Yue Yuen lasted for many weeks, with footage posted online of riot police attacking peaceful marches.[4] The workers held their ground and Yue Yuen eventually caved in and promised to properly compensate the workers' social insurance and housing fund. While many such workers joined the factories as girls, they are now mature women who have realised their strength and are not easily intimidated. Yue Yuen went on to post that as a result of the strike, and because it was no longer able to deprive workers of their benefit payments, its net profit for the first half of 2014 fell 48 per cent to $101.4m. This was down from $194.45m in the same period a year before.[5]

In a matter of weeks, the Yue Yuen workers held one of the biggest shoe companies in the world to account over unpaid benefits. If the strikes could have been coordinated with other blocs of Yue Yuen workers in Vietnam and Mexico, the company could have been brought to a standstill.

These strikes characterise a period of increasing industrial unrest and social discontent in China. A similar strike took place the next year in March 2015 at a Dongguan factory owned by Stella International Holdings, where 5,000–6,000 workers went on strike. They had been making shoes for Nine West, Nike and Kenneth Cole, among others, and were also angry at a lack of proper social insurance and housing payments. The strike was met by heavy repression, with many workers reporting being bitten by police dogs.

When industrial action occurs, national governments tend to come down on the side of the factory owners, as they are keen to protect foreign investments. The Chinese government has met the rise in strikes by cracking down on labour rights groups in an attempt to prevent social instability from spreading. There have been arrests, disappearances and trials. In November 2016, workers' rights activist Meng Han, from the Panyu Workers' Centre in Guangdong, was sentenced to nearly two years in jail for 'gathering crowds to disrupt public order'.[6] Meng had previously helped shoe workers engaged in a dispute at the Lide factory to win over 120 million yuan ($18m) in compensation. Workers have also been supported by a new generation of Marxist university students who have also faced arrest and punishment by the authorities.[7]

Fuelled by anger and without much faith in the state-run All-China Federation of Trade Unions, many of the recent strikes have been spontaneous and fiery. It has been argued that without the structure provided by workers' rights groups, spontaneous strikes could turn violent, and that structural problems like industrial restructuring and factory relocation will not be solved by repressing civil society.[8]

Dissident

Han Dongfang was born in Beijing and raised in the countryside before he became an electrician and worked on China's rail network. Dongfang developed an interest in politics and participated in the pro-democracy movement of the late 1980s before being imprisoned for two years without trial for his activities in the Tiananmen Square protests. Gravely ill in prison, he eventually received treatment in the US before being expelled from China. In 1994, he founded the China Labour Bulletin in Hong Kong.

Seeing no current route for reducing state control, the China Labour Bulletin focuses instead on negotiating for collective bargaining rights in the workplace. Full freedom of association is seen as too dangerous by the government so they have gone for another approach, Han Dongfang explains. 'We want to have the right to bargain with our employers for better salary, for better working conditions, for a reasonable leave and working hours. That doesn't "harm" the government, and it achieves better benefit rights for workers, and makes employers better regulated,' he says.

Because of repressive attitudes in China, and because he does not believe change can happen in one country alone, Dongfang and his colleagues have been working with Indian unions also looking to transform their factories. For Dongfang, the importance of collective bargaining cannot be overestimated – he calls it 'the beginning of the end of globalisation, the revision of globalisation.'

For Dongfang, it is workers on the frontline, most often women, who are the game-changers. They pay the price physically, financially and psychologically, but have the best chance of creating change. 'When you talk about globalisation, and ask where's the changing point, that's where it should start. That doesn't mean university research, journalist attention, brand CSR programmes and global trade unions are not important, but all the effort should, as much as possible, focus on helping these workers, particularly women, to become fighters [instead of] victims.'

Though Dongfang is far more inspired by India than the land of his birth, he sees room for hope in China because, he says, workers are not waiting. Strikes continue to happen, not just in the shoe sector but right across industry. After forty years of economic reform, Dongfang explains, 'some people got rich, but the majority of people remain surviving and poor. The crucial thing is that ten to twenty years ago, people were poor but they did not really know what caused them to be poor.'

A new element is allowing people to connect the dots as to why they remain impoverished. Social media lets people see their own situation reflected in the experiences of other people across the country. When information and images of successful strikes spread, people now ask, why shouldn't that be me?

Dongfang scoffs at the reports he reads by international commentators on internet control in China. Such reports place China as a country of total control, where people cannot find out news from around the globe. But this, he argues, is not a true picture. News from Washington or London is of less importance to people than workplace safety, social security payments and wage levels. He describes a landscape of people willing and able to share their cases and success stories on social media, beaming photos and videos around the country, with simple-to-use apps, Weibo and WeChat, being common tools for people trying to stay ahead of the authorities. The idea of struggling and fighting for fairness is now in the public consciousness.

'You can say: China is a black hole without freedom of association, with political complications, control of everything, monopoly of trade union organisation – that is the negative part,' Dongfang says. 'But the positive part is that workers' strikes started in the early 2000s. Now it's nearly twenty years and social media is carrying these ideas, images, all over the country and this will change the country. The shoe industry, electronic industry, or whatever industry cannot ignore this.'

For international brands and investors, this means the possibility of strikes has been added to the list of risks alongside rising wages. This has in part led to some investors looking for alternative opportunities elsewhere in Asia, and in Africa. To be truly successful, industrial activity by workers must be as connected and global as the transnational brands who dictate the terms.

Uniting students and workers

This is not to say that political change is only something for people working in shoe factories to engage in. A good example of civil society coming together to take on a shoe brand is the case of United Students Against Sweatshops (USAS) and Nike.

In October 2015, Nike announced that it would no longer allow US labour rights group the Worker Rights Consortium (WRC) to monitor its subcontracted factories. This was seen as a huge blow to supply chain transparency and angered many American students who had campaigned for years to ensure that their university-logoed apparel was not being made in sweatshop conditions. Based on its past performance, the students did not see Nike as having any credibility in independently monitoring its supply chains.

They pointed to the example of Nike's Hansae Vietnam supplier where WRC had uncovered serious violations including mass fainting due to illegally high temperatures, and women being fired for being pregnant – all issues that Nike's own monitoring had not 'noticed' despite strikes about these issues at the factory.

The Just Cut It campaign was launched to stop Nike from 'turning back the clock on factory transparency'. For two years, students at twenty-five universities battled with Nike, demanding the brand be expelled from their campuses until the WRC was allowed back into its factories. Over 600 university faculty staff signed an open letter to Nike, national tours were held with union leaders from Cambodia and Thailand visiting the US and demonstrations were held outside Nike shops and factories. Rutgers University and UC Berkeley ended multimillion-dollar sponsorship agreements with Nike and other universities rescinded Nike's licence to produce university-logoed apparel.

Under pressure, Nike eventually caved in and announced in August 2017 that it would reinstate the right of the WRC to access its supply chain factories.[9] In a statement, Nike added that it remains committed to independent monitoring. But of the WRC, it said: 'We respect the Worker Rights Consortium's commitment to workers' rights while recognizing that the WRC was co-created by United Students Against Sweatshops, a campaigning organization that does not represent the multi-stakeholder approach that we believe provides valuable, long-lasting change.'[10]

Structural change

All the toil and struggle needed to bring about political change can right some of the wrongs of the shoe industry. It can slightly raise wages, improve conditions, get polluting practices outlawed and ignite social change. But these advances will always be under threat. There is no end point where hard-won rights can be taken for granted because history is not a linear march towards progress but a tug of war between the exploited and those who profit from exploitation.

Deborah Lucchetti, and many others like her, argue that the system we live in is so immoral, it should be taboo. What we see is the extraction and draining of human and natural resources in order to feed the greed of a few billionaires. The millions who make up the working poor are unable to access fundamental rights or wages to live on, while CEOs, managers, designers, celebrities and shareholders become richer than ever.

This absurd situation is the result of a pact based on competition and profit. It is an arrangement that encourages vast over-production and over-consumption while billions of people live in poverty.

Surrounded by so much evidence of a broken system, and with little household objects causing so much havoc, it is necessary to question not just the consequences of this economic model, but the very model itself. The final element is to add in a structural critique of capitalism, and to work towards a way of organising society that replaces, rather than sticky-tapes, the current system.

Battle for Seattle

World peace, cancelling 'third world' debt, protecting land rights, fair trade, environmental justice, anti-corporatism and sweatshops were just some of the myriad of issues that made up the anti-globalisation movement of the 1990s and early 2000s. Farmers joined forces with socialists, anarchists and church groups. Environmentalists allied with consumer protection and labour rights groups. Peace campaigners marched alongside students, animal rights activists and the leaders of indigenous and peasant communities.

This period became characterised by the Battle for Seattle, a series of demonstrations that successfully disrupted a 1999 gathering of world leaders at the World Trade Organization (WTO) conference in Seattle. Even the opening ceremony was cancelled as delegates found they could not leave their hotels.

After Seattle, in response to the need for global coordination, the World Social Forum was founded in 2001 as a gathering for civil society. It stood in opposition to the World Economic Forum held in Davos each year. The first World Social Forum was held in Porto Alegre, Brazil and attracted activists, campaigners and civil society groups from Latin America and across the globe.

It was a period of internationalism where the ills of Nike trainers, Starbucks coffee and McDonald's burgers could be debated alongside the threat of nuclear weapons; where pesticides and land rights were discussed in the same breath as feminism and the HIV epidemic; where links of solidarity and action were made across every continent.[11]

This global justice movement vocalised a sense that the world was leaving millions of people behind, that the promise of progress and wealth was hiding a system shaped by the Global North to further exploit the Global South at the expense of the planet.

Occasionally, as in Seattle, world leaders had no choice but to listen, but for the most part the anti-globalisation movement was decried and dismissed. With the global stage the property of corporations and financial institutions, what could peasant farmers and village fisherfolk possibly have to say about how the world was being run? As long as the money was coming in, why listen to conservationists or indigenous people when they warned of an impending planetary storm?

'Globalisation' had become a buzzword in the 1980s, and by the end of the 1990s 'anti-globalisation' had taken root right next door as a global force expected to grow exponentially as it united more and more people.

But this did not happen. The major turning point took place on 11 September 2001. The terror attacks of 9/11 prompted Bush and Blair's 'War on Terror', with war swiftly launched upon first Afghanistan and then Iraq. Millions of people who had been active in the many threads of the anti-globalisation movement found their energies necessarily compelled towards anti-war activities.

The 'War on Terror' was also a direct challenge to the principles of internationalism and solidarity as global leaders, local politicians and major media outlets began to carve the world into 'us' and 'them'. Security fears, terrorism, war, the demonising of Muslims and the rise in nationalism undermined the global unity of the anti-globalisation movement. Asad Rehman, who was at Porto Alegre and later threw himself into anti-war work, recalls, 'the ability for us to be talking about the "we" became much, much more difficult after 9/11.'

Another factor that led to dissipation was the global financial crash of 2008. The crash led to the bailing out of banks on the one hand, and on the other, foreclosures on thousands of homes, the imposition of national austerity budgets, the proliferation of food banks and the debt crisis in Greece. It was a period that led to further isolationism as progressives in the Global North reeled from the shockwaves of recession and dedicated themselves to localised campaigns. Global links faded as people faced battlegrounds in their home countries.

This is where the risk of a warped anti-globalisation movement now lies. The biggest recent challenges to globalisation have not come from the progressive-Left, but from the Right. The upswell of support for Trump and for Brexit is based, in part, on the idea of pulling up the drawbridge against 'others', and trying to do better alone. They involve mindsets based on walls and fences, of competitions to be won at any cost. This is no longer about solidarity with the Global South, but hatred for others and fears for the prosperity of the Global North.

Building a movement

So how to win back this ground and construct a movement with internationalism at its core? The key may well be in the climate.

The story of climate breakdown is the story of capitalism, of unchecked corporate power, of the sidelining of regulations, laws and democracy, of profit and growth deified and implanted in every aspect of life. Following the track hewn by capitalism, climate breakdown exacerbates the inequalities and injustices of racism, gendered exploitation, conflict and obscene wealth inequality.

Yet because the stories of capitalism and climate breakdown are so intertwined, the solutions to climate breakdown are also the solutions to a fairer world. Take energy, for example: the world cannot afford to base its energy supply on extractable, carbon-intensive fossil fuels like oil and gas. Instead it is generally accepted that we need to transition to 100 per cent renewable energy. In order to fully tackle issues like energy poverty (urgent because 2.7 billion people still have no access to clean cooking facilities and instead have to cook on polluting, open fires or inefficient stoves),[12] this renewable energy will have to be locally produced and democratically owned by communities.

Such an energy system would place the needs of the planet and people at its heart, but it would not exactly be popular in the boardrooms of BP, Shell or ExxonMobil. In this way, when we take any issue and apply the pressing question of climate breakdown, we come up against questions about the economic model we are living under. We have been told this is the best we can do, but who is the system really working for? Is it designed to feed, shelter and enrich people's lives while moving in harmony with the biosphere, or is it designed for something else?

There are a lot of big questions about capitalism, but the simplest ones hold the key. Is it worth destroying the rainforest to make trainers? Is it right that factories churn out 24.2 billion pairs of shoes a year, yet wealth is distributed so unequally that tens of thousands of kids get sick walking barefoot to school? Should people tanning leather have a life expectancy of fifty? If in our hearts we know the answer to these questions is no, then we have to ask ourselves what we are doing in a system where the answer is yes.

The economy is currently designed to prioritise profit-fuelled over-production and over-consumption, rather than a dignified life for all. Redesigning it to switch these priorities immediately gets rid of the worst practices of capitalism. With different concerns, come different results. This is by no means an exhaustive list, but imagine how a dignified and sustainable shoe system could look:

Shoes shift to plant-based materials, and animals are freed from the suffering and death of intensive farming and footwear supply chains. Materials are easily recyclable; materials like metal, which make recycling extremely difficult, have been removed. All glues and dyes meet the highest environmental standards and are non-toxic.

Digital scanning allows every shoe to be a bespoke object, made to augment the body rather than be a burden on the feet. Production is localised and automated, staff in safe workshops rotate through different jobs in society to allow the spread of craft and the valuing of what was made. Every part of the supply chain is a collectively and locally owned resource. Workshop hours are democratically decided.

Production standards are rigorous, with shoes designed to last as long as possible. Design is modular, allowing for easier shoe repair, which is free. Design is democratised so every individual can access the ability to create their own shoes, allowing creativity to flourish.

Shoe libraries exist in every community so people can access a variety of shoes without the need for ownership. Everyone is guaranteed shoes and replacement shoes when theirs are ready to be recycled. Access to shoes is equal, shoes are made according to the needs of people, and are free.

Look into the earth

There have been previous systems that felt eternal and impervious to change: feudalism and slavery were both means for a tiny minority to control wealth and populations. These systems eventually became intolerable to enough of society that they were overthrown. What is needed again is for a sufficient amount of people to accumulate enough collective power to rebel. Climate breakdown may create these conditions if it seems like there is nothing left to lose, but it would be obviously preferable if it took place before the earth becomes uninhabitable.

Under slavery and feudalism, there was no shared blueprint for how to transition, or what to transition to; all that was clear was the need to change and end the ownership of resources and people. What is clear now is that we cannot continue along a destructive path that profits the few at the expense of the many.

It remains true that the root of all wealth in this world is human labour and natural resources.[13] This knowledge carries with it a sadness that these two things have been warped and stolen for exploitation. But equally, were they to be reclaimed, we would have the means to create a society that is equitable, sustainable and which provides for all. As with climate breakdown, the solution is in our hands. It involves overhauling the energy system, the food system, the housing system, land rights and ownership of national resources. This is what needs to happen to save the planet, and at the same time, it is the foundations of a fair world.

> Then I remember my shoes,
> How I have to put them on,
> How bending over to tie them up
> I will look into the earth.

So reads the poem by Serbian-American poet Charles Simic at the start of this book. Great change can only ever bring great challenges.

Our shoes have been with us for 40,000 years. They have both witnessed and propelled our journey through the ages, beholding humanity at its best and at its worst. Perhaps they are as good an object as any to lead us into a brighter, fairer future. If not, they should be a reminder that in them, we carry the world.

Foot Notes

Many of the issues in this book are deeply urgent. We face a series of environmental, social and ethical questions which require us to act collectively. Though not exhaustive, this list is your guide for changing the world, not just your wardrobe:

- Educate yourself. Join your library and read up on human and labour rights, the environment and capitalism. Attend talks, listen to podcasts and radio shows, watch documentaries and follow informed sources on social media.
- Work with other people. Connect with organisations already engaged in pushing and demonstrating for progressive change. The good news is that organised campaigns already exist: Clean Clothes Campaign, Labour Behind the Label, TRAID, War On Want, United Students Against Sweatshops, Greenpeace, Extinction Rebellion plus many more. These groups are waiting for you to join in. Also, if there is a trade union at your workplace make sure to join it, and if there isn't, then talk to supportive colleagues about launching one.
- In addition to NGOs focused on the TCF industry, in every country there are organised groups of people critiquing and challenging capitalism itself. These networks offer you the chance to link issues together and push for systemic change. Remember that social change never happens by accident, it only happens when we organise.
- Work with these movements to build power. Make sure decisions, demonstrations, campaigns and actions are intersectional

and rooted in solidarity with the Global South.

- Collectively apply critical leverage directly to corporations. Use your social media accounts to speak directly to brands by asking questions about supply chains, wages and workers' rights. One thing brands fear is the disruption of their image. As they move more and more online, they become extra vulnerable to disruption. If you cannot find information about your shoes, ask for the relevant data. If you do not like how a brand is behaving, tell them. Don't let them get away with greenwashing.

- Offline, people in the Global North have access to something many workers in the Global South would love to have: the headquarters and shops of brands and retailers. Political pressure and media coverage can be sparked by protests and civil disruption at these sites. Protest is your right – use it.

- Use organised campaigns to demand that politicians stand up to industry by changing the law to protect workers' rights, animal rights and environmental standards. Self-regulation and voluntary initiatives within the shoe or wider garment industry have failed; we need legislation with teeth. This may mean finding and electing people who will champion these causes while fighting hard to hold corporations to account. Perhaps for you, change will mean standing for public office.

- Actively support those on the sharp edge of political change – the campaigners, activists, lawyers and democratic trade unionists who are risking their lives at every point of the shoe supply chain. These people are organising workers, surveying factories, piecing together lawsuits and defending land rights. Part of demanding a sustainable shoe industry means international solidarity: listening to what is needed, raising funds, sharing news stories, signing petitions, writing letters to politicians and police chiefs and protesting vociferously on the streets for the rights of other people to protest.

- It is vital to go beyond centring your own wardrobe, but what about the next time you need to buy a pair of shoes? Much of this decision will be based on what you can afford, but you have the option to research and test the claims of small shoe brands that offer alternatives to leather, environmental destruction and sweatshop labour. Many of these small brands are providing a design blueprint for a future where shoes are not made via a process of death and destruction, so if you want to give them your custom, then go for it.

- Or you might decide to get all your shoes repaired, or undertake a public pledge not to shop for a year, or dive into the world of upcycling. You could also pledge to buy second-hand, then hunt down pre-loved pairs in markets, charity shops and online forums.

- Other options include organising a swap-shop (an alternative shopping event where everyone brings items to swap with each other), or a free-shop (a pop-up shop of 100 per cent free donated items for people to take as they need), or arranging loans among friends. These activities can serve to make you conscious of the pressures of consumerism or they may reset your mindset for life. While they do not necessitate spending money, they do depend upon access to resources, time and physical spaces, so aren't available to everyone.

- Part of changing the world means bringing people together. A good way to find other people interested in the same issues as you is to run film nights, book events, open mic nights or cultural events at your school, college, university, workplace, place of worship or community centre.

- And finally, develop your creative skills to show that the alternatives to crisis and neoliberalism are far better than the corporate mess we are in – create art, make films, pitch articles, post blogs, write books, take pictures and make music. Good luck, take courage and remember that collectively we can do better than this.

ACKNOWLEDGEMENTS

I would firstly like to extend my heartfelt thanks to all the people in these pages who gave up their valuable time to talk to me. Their combined gracious goodwill and enthusiasm made writing this book feel like a collaborative and often profound experience. Some people took a chance by revealing personal stories, while others risked serious consequences just by talking – there would be no book without them and I am indebted to their courage.

My special thanks for additional kindness and help to Kristina Ampeva, Jose Baladron, Syeda Hasan, Scott Frederick, Clare Moseley, Bettina Musiolek, Anton Pieper, Professor Shahin Rahimifard, Asad Rehman, Dr Juliet Schor, Rebecca Shawcross and to activists from the Save Movement. I also want to give a large thank you to Michael Wiedemann and Denis Ampev. Parts of this book were only made possible with the time and help of Khalid Mahmood and Jalvat Ali at the Labour Education Foundation in Lahore, and Om Thapaliya from HomeNet Nepal – you have my sincere gratitude.

Nor could I have put this book together without some serious translation, fixing and journalistic help from Usman Ali, Elaine Lu, Dina Mitrovikj, Tuğba Tekerek and an Italian journalist who prefers to stay anonymous. Thank you also Elly Badcock for many hours of transcription. Special mentions to Sweta Tapan Choudhury, Leigh McAlea, Sam Maher and Gus Alston for helping me bring this book together.

Away from the nuts and bolts of book research, when Yanis Varoufakis came to speak at the Union Chapel in Islington, a chance encounter in a nearby pub led me to one of the most important and inspiring working relationships of my life: thank you Andrew Gordon at David Higham Associates for believing in me and in this project throughout. Your insight, faith and encouragement have been completely crucial. My extended thanks also goes to the entire DHA team for their tireless work and support.

This book would also not exist had it not been championed, in various incarnations, by editor Holly Harley – thank you a thousand times for your encouragement and enthusiasm. My sincere thanks also go to Jenny Lord at Weidenfeld & Nicolson, from whom I continue to learn so much. It is a real pleasure to see how a book strengthens and transforms under the intellect of brilliant editors. Thank you also to Jo Whitford for your skill and patience in keeping this project contained and managed ahead of publication, to Felicity Price for an in-depth legal read, to Loulou Clark for fabulous art direction and to Simon Fox for brilliant copy-editing. I also remain incredibly grateful to Maddie Mogford at Hachette for her timely help with this project.

My unofficial guide to making things beautiful in ink has always been Anne Aylor, an author and teacher from whom I continue to love learning. Thank you especially for smoothing the bits of this book that hurt to write. Thank you to Anne, Jan Woolf and friends for an inspiring writers' retreat in November 2018 when many of these stories first saw the cold light of day. Thank you also Mark Kramer for appearing at just the right time to answer my questions and conundrums about long-form journalism.

I would also like to say a very warm thank you to Natalie Fay, Delilah Jeary and the team in ITN's best corner. It has been an honour to learn from you and I often replay your advice and reasoning in my head.

Outside of work hours, I am indebted to friends who keep me smiling. A special thank you to Jennifer Ahlkvist, Emma Barrett, Jennifer Braunlich (for never being a brick), Emily English, Lisa Fox (for keeping the ship steady), Laura Harvey (for the past twenty years), Samir Jeraj, Huseyin Kishi and Tony Reiss. Tom Sanderson also appeared in a different pub towards the close of this book – thank you for everything, especially the terrible shoe puns. My heartfelt thank you also goes to Angela for wisdom and insight that resonates over the years. Finally, to my dear friend Robin Beste, RIP, you are very much missed.

To my parents Kay and Gareth, thank you for all your love and encouragement, it means the world to me. Likewise to my brother Bryn, thank you for being there for some of the more difficult chapters of this process, and for convictions that help me see our place in the world differently.

Because writing has the potential to be months of lonely toil, I want to wholeheartedly thank the team at Sands Film Studio for keeping me going with invaluable good cheer, advice, lunches, cups of tea, printer ink, political analysis and encouragement. I don't know where I would be without them and would like to sincerely thank Olivier, Christine, Annabelle, Kay, Graham, Kay, Barbara, Neale and co. An especially sky-high thank you to Richard Goodwin for constant encouragement and for helping me navigate the machinations of the 'great production manager in the sky'.

And finally, I want to recognise the dedication, creativity and passion of people round the world who are fighting to change the textile, clothing and footwear industry. The inspiration for this book is the chanting outside embassies, the activists who sticker and lock-on to clothing stores, the factory workers who strike and blockade roads despite phalanxes of armed police, the bloggers and vloggers and tweeters, the journalists who never let up, the groups holding vigils outside abattoirs, the organisers of events and panel discussions, the academics, teachers and fashion students who crave change, the trade unionists who keep going and make a difference despite the odds and the people who risk everything for justice. You are the fashion industry's conscience and its necessary future.

ABOUT THE AUTHOR

Tansy E. Hoskins is an author and journalist based in London. She can be found writing about the textile, clothing and footwear industries for the *Guardian*, Al Jazeera, *i-D* and the *i* paper, or making TV documentaries. This work has taken her to Bangladesh, Kenya, Macedonia and to the Topshop warehouses in Solihull. Her first book, the award-winning *Stitched Up: The Anti-Capitalist Book of Fashion*, was placed on Emma Watson's 'Ultimate Book List'.

REFERENCES

Preface to the Paperback Edition

1 https://www.mckinsey.com/industries/ retail/our-insights/state-of-fashion.
2 https://www.worldfootwear.com/news/ rowthiproductioaccumulatedovera decadewipedawayi2020/6879.html
3 https://asia.floorwage.org/wp-content/ uploads/2021/07/Money-Heist_Book_ Final-compressed.pdf
4 https://www.theguardian.com/ global-development/2020/ dec/10/i-thought-about-killing-my- children-the-desperate-bangladesh- garment-workers-fighting-for-pay
5 https://www.ituc-csi.org/violations- workers-rights-seven-year-high
6 https://www.opendemocracy.net/en/ oureconomy/report-says-soldiers-shot- three-dead-myanmar-factory-making- us-cowboy-boots/
7 https://www.mckinsey.com/industries/ retail/our-insights/state-of-fashion
8 https://www.theguardian. com/business/2020/oct/07/ covid-19-crisis-boosts-the-fortunes-of- worlds-billionaires
9 https://www.workersrights.org/ wp-content/uploads/2020/11/Hunger- in-the-Apparel-Supply-Chain.pdf
10 https://www.worldfootwear.com/news/ growthiproductioaccumulatedovera decadewipedawayi2020/6879.html

Introduction: What's Shoes Got to Do with It?

1 https://classical-inquiries.chs.harvard. edu/herodotus-and-a-courtesan-from- naucratis/ [March 2019]; https://www. ancient.eu/article/1038/the-egyptian- cinderella-story-debunked/ [March

2019].
2 https://web.archive.org/ web/20110903190535/http://www. endicott-studio.com:80/rdrm/forashs. html [March 2019].
3 https://www.nytimes.com/interactive/ projects/cp/obituaries/archives/hans- christian-andersen [March 2019].
4 https://www.theguardian.com/ environment/2018/oct/08/ global-warming-must-not-exceed-15c- warns-landmark-un-report [March 2019].
5 Paper: Trinkaus, Erik and Shang, Hong, 2008, 'Anatomical evidence for the antiquity of human footwear: Tianyuan and Sunghir', *Journal of Archaeological Science*, 35(7), 1928–33, 10.1016/j.jas.2007.12.002.
6 Ibid.
7 http://staffscc.net/shoes1/?p=228 [March 2019].
8 http://www.bbc.co.uk/history/british/ abolition/africa_article_01.shtml [March 2019].
9 M. B. Steger (ed.), *Globalization: The Greatest Hits*, Paradigm Publishers, 2010, p. 1. Plus: https://www.nytimes. com/2006/07/06/business/06levitt.html [March 2019].
10 D. K. Vajpeyi and R. Oberoi, *Globalization Reappraised – False Oracle or a Talisman*, Lexington Books, 2018, Introduction.
11 Ibid., p. 31.
12 E. Cazdyn and I. Szeman, *After Globalization*, John Wiley & Sons, 2011, p. 1.
13 Alexis de Tocqueville, *Journeys to England and Ireland*, first published 1835: http://www.pitt.edu/~syd/toq. html [March 2019].

14 R. Wolff, https://truthout.org/articles/ richard-d-wolff-capitalisms-deeper- problem/ [March 2019].

15 P. Newell, *Globalisation and the Environment*, Polity, 2012, pp. 10–11.

16 https://www.theguardian.com/ commentisfree/2018/sep/26/donald- trump-globalisation-nation-state [March 2019].

17 P. Newell, *Globalization and the Environment*, Polity, 2012, pp. 10–11.

18 Ibid., p. 4.

19 https://www.theguardian.com/ commentisfree/2018/sep/26/donald- trump-globalisation-nation-state [December 2019].

20 P. Newell, *Globalisation and the Environment*. Polity, 2012, pp. 4–5.

21 D. K. Vajpeyi and R. Oberoi, *Globalization Reappraised – False Oracle or a Talisman*, Lexington Books, 2018, p. 31.

22 Ibid., p. xviii.

23 https://www.theguardian. com/business/2019/jan/21/ world-26-richest-people-own-as-much- as-poorest-50-per-cent-oxfam-report [March 2019].

24 R. Wolff, https://truthout.org/articles/ richard-d-wolff-capitalisms-deeper- problem/ [March 2019].

25 J. Stiglitz, *Globalization and Its Discontents*, W. W. Norton & Company, 2002, pp. 5, 10.

26 https://www.theguardian.com/ commentisfree/2018/sep/26/donald- trump-globalisation-nation-state [March 2019].

27 https://www.marxists.org/archive/ marx/works/subject/quotes/index.htm [March 2019].

Chapter One: Lust for Kicks

1 G. Riello, *A Foot In The Past*, Oxford University Press, 2006, p. 19.

2 J. H. Thornton (ed.), *Textbook of Footwear Manufacture*, The National Trade Press, 1953.

3 http://www.mirror.co.uk/news/ uk-news/revealed-actual-number- shoes-british-9660645 [March 2019].

4 *World Footwear Year Book 2016*, https://www.worldfootwear. com/publications/?documento= 14081877/37615558&fonte=ISSUU [March 2019].

5 https://www.worldfootwear.com/ tag/world-footwear-yearbook/184. html [March 2019]. The *World Footwear Yearbook* is part of an initiative developed by APICCAPS (the Portuguese Footwear, Components, Leather Goods Manufacturers' Association) https:// www.apiccaps.pt/

6 http://www.who.int/lymphatic_ filariasis/epidemiology/podoconiosis/ en/ [March 2019].

7 https://twitter.com/AFP/status/ 1045135025673396225 [March 2019].

8 Article: Zygmunt Bauman, 'The Self In Consumer Society', *The Hedgehog Review: Critical Reflections on Contemporary Culture*, 1(1), Fall 1999.

9 https://www.youtube.com/channel/ UCh7ttG6-bf3XMsv1CkZLI6Q [March 2019].

10 https://www.npr. org/2017/05/10/527429299/ dont-be-fooled-generation-wealth- is-more-about-wanting-than-having [March 2019].

11 From: P. Bourdieu, *Distinction, A Social Critique of the Judgement of Taste*, Routledge, 1979.

12 J. H. Thornton (ed.), *Textbook of Footwear Manufacture*, The National Trade Press, 1953.

13 http://inspiredeconomist. com/2012/09/20/the-greatest- invention-planned-obsolescence/ [March 2019].

14 The quote is attributed to industrial designer Brooks Stevens, from an April 1958 interview with *True, the Man's Magazine*. J. Wall, *Streamliner: Raymond Loewy and Image-making in the Age of American Industrial Design*, JHU Press, 2018.

15 https://akongmemorialfoundation.org/ about/ [March 2019].

16 http://someone-else.us/stories/joanne- eicher-fashion-studies/?fbclid=IwAR2

FOlrumTtXUCy159zeQaVhHnYm2z
1diMcloWo03IHsgX6MIj29-23UYKY
[March 2019].

17 T. Hoskins, *Stitched Up – The Anti-Capitalist Book of Fashion*, Pluto Press, 2014, p. 58.

18 Z. Bauman, *Work, Consumerism, & The New Poor*, Open University Press, 2005, p. 30.

19 Ibid., p. 25.

20 Ibid.

21 J. Schor, *Plenitude: The New Economics of True Wealth*, Penguin Press, 2010, p. 41.

22 Exhibition guidebook: A. Veldmeijer, *Stepping through Time: Footwear in Ancient Egypt*, BLKVLD Uitgevers/ Publishers, 2017, https://issuu.com/ blkvlduitgeverspublishers/docs/fw_1lo [December 2019].

23 Jacob Nacht, 'The Symbolism of the Shoe with Special Reference to Jewish Sources', *The Jewish Quarterly Review*, vol. 6, no. 1, 1915, pp. 1–22, JSTOR, www.jstor.org/ stable/1451461 [December 2019].

24 A. Sherlock, https://www.sheffield. ac.uk/polopoly_fs/1.102578!/file/ TranscendingTheMindBody DualismInFashionTheory.pdf [March 2019].

25 E. Semmelhack, *Shoes: The Meaning of Style*, Reaktion Books, 2017, pp. 10–11.

26 Ibid., Conclusion.

27 H. Koda (Introduction by Sarah Jessica Parker), *100 Shoes: The Costume Institute / The Metropolitan Museum of Art*, The Metropolitan Museum of Art, 2011.

28 E. Semmelhack, *Shoes: The Meaning of Style*, Reaktion Books, 2017, p. 216.

29 https://www.newyorker.com/ magazine/2011/03/28/sole-mate [March 2019].

30 Elizabeth Semmelhack, phone interview with the author, November 2017.

31 E. Semmelhack, *Shoes: The Meaning of Style*, Reaktion Books, 2017, p. 161.

32 Ibid., p. 169.

33 C. McDowell, *Shoes: Fashion & Fantasy*, Thames and Hudson, 1989, p. 9.

34 D. Ging, 'Well-heeled women?', http://webpages.dcu.ie/~gingd/ articleslectures.html [March 2019].

35 Ibid.

36 https://www.theguardian.com/ commentisfree/2009/sep/17/why-i- threw-shoe-bush [March 2019].

37 https://brooklynrail.org/2018/10/ artseen/Ivy-Haldeman-The-Interesting- Type [March 2019].

38 https://believermag.com/an-interview- with-dian-hanson/ [March 2019].

39 S. Freud, 'Fetishism', 1927, https://cpb-us-w2.wpmucdn.com/ portfolio.newschool.edu/dist/9/3921/ files/2015/03/Freud-Fetishism-1927- 2b52v1u.pdf [March 2019].

40 B. Barber, 'Shrunken Sovereign Consumerism, Globalization, and American Emptiness', *World Affairs*, 170(4), Spring 2008, pp.73–82.

41 Z. Bauman, *Work, Consumerism, & The New Poor*, Open University Press, 2005, p. 30.

42 J. Schor, The Overspent American, HarperCollins, 1999, Introduction.

43 B. Barber, 'Shrunken Sovereign Consumerism, Globalization, and American Emptiness', *World Affairs*, 170(4), Spring 2008, pp.73–82.

44 Line from a poem by Muhammad al-Maghout. Quoted in M. Hisham and M. Crabapple, *Brothers of the Gun*, One World, 2018.

Chapter Two: Factory Gates

1 https://www.hyllanderiksen. net/blog/2018/12/13/ whats-wrong-with-the-global-north- and-the-global-south?rq=global%20 south [March 2019].

2 Ibid.

3 *World Footwear Yearbook 2018*, https://www.worldfootwear.com/ news/the-world-footwear-2018- yearbook/3292.html [January 2020].

4 *World Footwear Yearbook 2016*, https://www.worldfootwear.com/ yearbook/the-world-footwear-2016-

Yearbook/103.html [March 2019].

5 http://www.panarub.co.id/profile/
   company-profile [September 2019].

6 https://cleanclothes.
   org/news/2018/03/14/
   clean-clothes-campaign-files-
   complaint-against-adidas-for-
   breaching-oecd-guidelines-in-indonesia
   [March 2019].

7 https://www.adidas-
   group.com/en/media/
   news-archive/press-releases/2005/
   update-actions-taken-pt-panarub-
   worker-rights-consortium/ [December
   2019].

8 https://cleanclothes.
   org/news/2018/03/14/
   clean-clothes-campaign-files-
   complaint-against-adidas-for-
   breaching-oecd-guidelines-in-indonesia
   [March 2019].

9 https://fashionunited.uk/news/
   business/adidas-faces-compliant-
   for-breaching-oecd-guidelines-in-
   indonesia/2018031428643 [December
   2019].

10 https://www.adidas-group.com/
   media/filer_public/69/1d/691d6520-
   d1f9-4549-8a94-744dc49ab6ca/
   adidas_response_to_clean_clothes_
   campaign_open_letter_on_panarub_
   dwikarya.pdf [December 2019].

11 https://www.fairwear.org/
   wp-content/uploads/2016/12/
   CountryplanVietnam2016.pdf [March
   2019].

12 https://www.theguardian.
   com/business/2017/jun/25/
   female-cambodian-garment-workers-
   mass-fainting [March 2019].

13 https://www.phnompenhpost.com/
   national/mass-fainting-kampong-cham;
   https://www.khmertimeskh.
   com/542730/dozens-of-workers-faint-
   at-shoe-factory-2/
   and https://www.khmertimeskh.
   com/514897/more-workers-faint-in-
   kampong-cham-factory/ [November
   2019].

14 https://www.sciencedirect.
   com/science/article/pii/
   S2590113319300082#bb0010
   [November 2019].

15 World Footwear Yearbook 2019,
   https://www.worldfootwear.com/
   yearbook/the-world-footwear-2019-
   Yearbook/213.html [November 2019].

16 http://www.independent.co.uk/news/
   business/news/ivanka-trump-shoe-
   factory-china-workers-physical-
   beating-verbal-abuse-ganzhou-huajian-
   international-a7812671.html [March
   2019].

17 https://www.washingtonpost.com/
   graphics/2017/politics/ivanka-trump-
   overseas/?noredirect=on&utm_term=.
   d74355c40107 [September 2019].

18 SACOM Report: 2016 Garment
   Campaign. Reality Behind Brands'
   CSR Hypocrisy: An Investigative
   Report on China Suppliers of ZARA,
   H&M, and GAP, http://sacom.
   hk/2016/06/20/investigative-report-
   reality-behind-brands-csr-hypocrisy-
   an-investigative-report-on-china-
   suppliers-of-zara-hm-and-gap/
   [January 2020].

19 Ibid.

20 http://www.chinadaily.com.cn/
   china/2015-07/05/content_21185707.
   htm [March 2019].

21 Ibid.

22 World Footwear Yearbook 2017,
   https://www.worldfootwear.com/
   yearbook/the-world-footwear-2017-
   Yearbook/209.html [January 2020].
   Please note that production and export
   are not the same thing.

23 http://labourbehindthelabel.org/
   the-realities-of-working-in-europes-
   shoe-manufacturing-peripheries/
   [March 2019].

24 Ibid.

25 http://www.industriall-union.org/
   towards-living-wages-in-north-
   macedonia. Data from: Trade Union of
   Workers in Textile, Leather and Shoe
   Making Industry (STKC). This data
   was for the second quarter of 2018.
   [December 2019].

26 https://www.esiweb.org/
   enlargement/wp-content/
   uploads/2009/02/swf/index.
   php?lang=en&id=156&document_
   ID=86 [March 2019].

27 Ibid.

28 https://www.falcotto.com/en_gb/about-us [November 2019].

29 http://www.falc.biz/brands/ [November 2019].

30 http://www.restorankajgino.mk/for_us.htm [March 2019].

31 https://twitter.com/carloromeo70/status/796771979017777152 [November 2019].

32 J. Murray, *Murray's Handbook for Travellers*, J. Murray, 1878.

33 J. Swann, *Shoemaking*, Shire Publications Ltd, 2003, p. 11.

34 BBC: 'Mechanisation and Northampton's shoemakers', http://www.bbc.co.uk/legacies/work/england/northants/article_4.shtml [March 2019].

35 Ibid.

36 J. Swann, *Shoemaking*, Shire Publications Ltd, 2003, p. 9.

37 http://www.northamptonshirebootandshoe.org.uk/wp-content/uploads/2013/07/Boot-and-Shoe-Industry.pdf [March 2019].

38 J. Swann, *Shoemaking*, Shire Publications Ltd, 2003, p. 19.

39 J. Waterer, *Leather and the Warrior*, Museum of Leathercraft, 1982, p. 146.

40 BBC Look East, 'Northampton Factories Made Millions of WW1 Boots'. https://www.bbc.co.uk/news/av/uk-england-northamptonshire-26353846/northampton-factories-made-millions-of-ww1-boots.

41 J. Waterer, *Leather and the Warrior*, Museum of Leathercraft, 1982, p. 138.

42 P. Russell, *100 Military Inventions that Changed the World*, Hachette, 2013, chapter: 'Let The Sweat Pour Out (The Jungle Boot)'.

43 Richard Goodwin, interview with the author, May 2018.

44 https://www.yadvashem.org/articles/general/shoes-on-the-danube-promenade.html [March 2019].

45 http://www.ilo.org/global/about-the-ilo/newsroom/news/WCMS_008075/lang--en/index.htm#n2 [March 2019].

46 Ibid.

47 T. B. Kazi, 'Superbrands, Globalization, and Neoliberalism: Exploring Causes and Consequences of the Nike Superbrand', *Inquiries Journal/Student Pulse*, 3(12), 2011, http://www.inquiriesjournal.com/a?id=604 [December 2019].

48 https://cleanclothes.org/resources/publications/asia-wage-report [March 2019].

49 https://cleanclothes.org/resources/publications/follow-the-thread-the-need-for-supply-chain-transparency-in-the-garment-and-footwear-industry [March 2019].

50 http://www.nyu.edu/pubs/counterblast/issue1_nov01/media_art_review/collins.html#_ednref3 [March 2019].

51 https://www.counterpunch.org/2008/06/28/nike-s-bad-air/ [March 2019].

52 https://www.oregonlive.com/playbooks-profits/2014/06/post_40.html [March 2019].

53 https://ipc.mit.edu/sites/default/files/2019-01/02-007.pdf [March 2019].

54 https://www.nytimes.com/1997/11/08/business/nike-shoe-plant-in-vietnam-is-called-unsafe-for-workers.html [December 2019].

55 https://www.nytimes.com/1998/05/13/business/international-business-nike-pledges-to-end-child-labor-and-apply-us-rules-abroad.html [March 2019].

56 Forbes real-time calculator: https://www.forbes.com/profile/phil-knight/#433a3d9f1dcb [March 2019].

57 https://purpose.nike.com/human-rights [December 2019].

58 Nike received a 'C' rating the 2017 *Ethical Fashion Report*; the 2018 *Foul Play* report by Clean Clothes Campaign found Nike factory wages remain poor; Nike scored 36 out of 100 in Fashion Revolution's Transparency Index; Nike was rated 'Not Good Enough' on GoodOnYou. eco; in 2016 Greenpeace described Nike's 'commitment to Detox' as 'not credible'. Nike does, however, score positively in other reports. For example, in 2015 Morgan Stanley ranked Nike the most sustainable apparel and footwear company in

North America for environmental and social performance, including its labour record.

59 ILO/IFC Better Work Programme 2018–2022, http://um.dk/~/media/UM/English-site/Documents/Danida/About-Danida/Danida%20transparency/Documents/U%2037/2018/ILO%20Better%20Work.pdf?la=en [pdf, March 2019].

60 ILO Research Paper: P. Huynh, *Developing Asia's garment and footwear industry: Recent employment and wage trends*, October 2017.

61 Ibid.

62 Dominique Muller, phone interview with the author, May 2018.

63 World Footwear Yearbook 2019 , https://www.worldfootwear.com/yearbook/the-world-footwear-2019-Yearbook/213.html [March 2019].

64 According to Ethiopia's Leather Industry Development Institute, http://business.financialpost.com/pmn/business-pmn/amazing-china-documentary-more-fiction-than-fact [March 2019].

65 https://www.ilo.org/wcmsp5/groups/public/---africa/---ro-addis_ababa/--sro-addis_ababa/documents/genericdocument/wcms_573550.pdf [March 2019].

66 https://issuu.com/nyusterncenterforbusinessandhumanri/docs/nyu_ethiopia_final_online?e=31640827/69644612 [October 2019]

67 http://africachinareporting.co.za/2017/01/inside-the-chinese-factory-in-ethiopia-where-ivanka-trump-places-her-shoe-orders/ [March 2019].

68 Ibid.

Chapter Three: Living on a Shoestring

1 Report: A. Pieper, P. Putri, *No Excuses For Homework – Working Conditions in the Indonesian Leather and Footwear Sector*, Südwind-Institut, March 2017.

2 http://www2.unwomen.org/-/media/field%20office%20eseasia/docs/publications/2016/05/pk-wee-status-report-lowres.pdf?vs=5731 [March 2019].

3 http://www.ilo.org/wcmsp5/groups/public/@asia/@ro-bangkok/@ilo-islamabad/documents/publication/wcms_122320.pdf [March 2019].

4 https://paycheck.pk/main/salary/minimum-wages [December 2019].

5 Report: F. Gesualdi and D. Lucchetti, *The Real Cost of our Shoes*, CNMS and FAIR, April 2017.

6 From interview with Dr Martha Chen.

7 Report: C. Mather, *We Are Workers Too! Organizing Home-based Workers in the Global Economy*, WIEGO, August 2010.

8 http://www.wiego.org/sites/wiego.org/files/publications/files/GEC_Study_Executive_Summary.pdf [March 2019].

9 http://www.wiego.org/sites/wiego.org/files/publications/files/GEC%20_Study_II_Executive_Summary.pdf [March 2019].

10 http://www.wiego.org/sites/default/files/resources/files/WIEGO-Myths-Facts-Informal-Economy.pdf [March 2019].

11 http://www.ilo.org/wcmsp5/groups/public/@asia/@ro-bangkok/@ilo-islamabad/documents/publication/wcms_122320.pdf [March 2019].

12 http://www.wiego.org/sites/default/files/publications/files/Sinha-Home-Based-Workers-SEWA-India-WIEGO-PB13.pdf [March 2019].

13 https://www.ilo.org/public/libdoc/ilo/2005/105B09_326_engl.pdf [March 2019].

14 http://www.wiego.org/sites/default/files/publications/files/Sinha-Home-Based-Workers-SEWA-India-WIEGO-PB13.pdf [March 2019].

15 http://www.wiego.org/sites/default/files/resources/files/WIEGO-Myths-Facts-Informal-Economy.pdf [March 2019].

16 P. Markkanen, *Shoes, Glues and Homework: Dangerous Work in the*

Global Footwear Industry, Routledge, 2017, Chapter 2.

17 Ibid., p. 89.

18 Report: *Homeworkers in South India's leather footwear industry*, Homeworkers World Wide, December 2014, http://www.homeworkersww.org.uk/assets/uploads/files/leather-footwear-briefingcomp.pdf.

19 http://www.wiego.org/sites/default/files/publications/files/Sinha-Home-Based-Workers-SEWA-India-WIEGO-PB13.pdf [March 2019].

20 P. Markkanen, *Shoes, Glues and Homework: Dangerous Work in the Global Footwear Industry*, Routledge, 2017, Chapter 3.

21 https://www.news-medical.net/health/What-is-Neurotoxicity.aspx [March 2019].

22 https://www.cdc.gov/niosh/topics/organsolv/default.html [March 2019].

23 Ibid.

24 https://www.cancer.org/cancer/cancer-causes/general-info/known-and-probable-human-carcinogens.html [March 2019].

25 P. Markkanen, *Shoes, Glues and Homework: Dangerous Work in the Global Footwear Industry*, Routledge, 2017, p. 24.

26 https://www.theguardian.com/books/2008/jan/29/fiction.stuartjeffries [March 2019].

27 https://www.gov.uk/government/uploads/system/uploads/attachment_data/file/318348/hpa_Methyl_ethyl_ketone__General_Information_v1.pdf [March 2019].

28 https://www.ncbi.nlm.nih.gov/pmc/articles/PMC4153221/ [March 2019].

29 https://www.gov.uk/government/uploads/system/uploads/attachment_data/file/561046/benzene_general_information.pdf [March 2019].

30 Ibid.

31 https://www.gov.uk/government/uploads/system/uploads/attachment_data/file/659914/Toluene_general_information.pdf [March 2019].

32 https://www.ncbi.nlm.nih.gov/pmc/articles/PMC3084482/ [March 2019].

33 Bangladesh Rehabilitation and Assistance Center for Addicts (BARACA).

34 http://saspublisher.com/wp-content/uploads/2014/07/SJAMS-24A1186-1189.pdf [March 2019].

35 Ibid.

36 https://www.iol.co.za/news/south-africa/glue-loses-high-to-save-street-kid-addicts-53018 and http://thestandard.com.ph/news/-main-stories/207451/street-kids-shift-sniff-from-rugby-to-vulcaseal.html [March 2019].

37 http://www.wiego.org/sites/default/files/publications/files/Sinha-Home-Based-Workers-SEWA-India-WIEGO-PB13.pdf [March 2019].

38 Ibid.

39 https://www.thenews.com.pk/print/420315-11-YEAR-STRUGGLE-FOR-HOME-BASED-WORKERS-RIGHTS-SET-TO-BEAR-FRUIT-THIS-YEAR [March 2019].

40 http://www.ilo.org/wcmsp5/groups/public/@asia/@ro-bangkok/@ilo-islamabad/documents/publication/wcms_122320.pdf [March 2019].

41 Interview with Hannah Reed, senior employment rights officer in the TUC's Economic and Social Affairs Department.

42 *World Shoe Report – World Footwear Production* (2010–2017), Chapter 1.

43 A. Pieper and P. Putri, *No Excuses for Homework*, Südwind-Institut, March 2017.

44 Ibid.

45 WIEGO Organizing Brief No. 7, August 2013.

Chapter Four: Branded

1 https://www.oldbaileyonline.org/browse.jsp?id=t17690906-63&div=t17690906-63&terms=shoemaker#highlight [March 2019].

2 https://www.oldbaileyonline.org/

browse.jsp?id=t17600416-3&
div=t17600416-3&terms=
shoemaker#highlight [March 2019].

3   https://www.oldbaileyonline.org/
browse.jsp?id=t17660903-
23&div=t17660903-
23&terms=shoemaker#highlight
[December 2019].

4   https://www.oldbaileyonline.org/
static/London-lifelate18th.jsp
[December 2019]

5   From interview with Rebecca
Shawcross.

6   https://hbr.org/1992/07/
high-performance-marketing-an-
interview-with-nikes-phil-knight
[March 2019].

7   http://www.iass-ais.org/
proceedings2014/view_lesson.
php?id=33 [March 2019].

8   https://www.emarketer.com/content/
emarketer-total-media-ad-spending-
worldwide-will-rise-7-4-in-2018
[March 2019].

9   Article: J. Schor, 'The New Politics
of Consumption', *Boston Review*,
Summer 1999, http://bostonreview.net/
archives/BR24.3/schor.html [March
2019].

10 https://news.nike.com/news/
nike-inc-reports-fiscal-2018-fourth-
quarter-and-full-year-results and
Forbes real-time calculator: https://
www.forbes.com/profile/phil-
knight/#2c3c67231dcb [March 2019].

11 http://www.consume.bbk.ac.uk/
researchfindings/newconsumers.pdf
[March 2019].

12 J. Schor, *Plenitude: The New
Economics of True Wealth*, Penguin
Press, 2010, p. 40.

13 Ibid., p. 41.

14 https://www.businessoffashion.com/
articles/opinion/op-ed-logomania-
blame-the-hipsters [March 2019].

15 https://www.forbes.com/sites/
kurtbadenhausen/2016/03/30/
the-highest-paid-retired-athletes-
2016/#684ba6431b56 [March 2019].

16 https://www.forbes.com/sites/
kurtbadenhausen/2016/03/30/
how-michael-jordan-will-make-more-
than-any-other-athlete-in-the-world-

this-year/#29ab01973865 [March
2019].

17 https://cleanclothes.org/resources/
national-cccs/foul-play-ii-sponsors-
leave-workers-still-on-the-sidelines
[December 2019].

18 http://www.latimes.com/business/la-fi-
repsneakers-20170905-htmlstory.html
[March 2019].

19 Ibid.

20 Ibid. and http://www.nytimes.
com/2010/08/22/magazine/22fake-t.
html [March 2019].

21 Report: Europol and the European
Union Intellectual Property
Office: *2017 Situation Report on
Counterfeiting and Piracy in the
European Union*.

22 Ibid.

23 http://ficpi.org.uk/wp-content/
uploads/2014/01/Counterfeit-Dont-
buy-into-Organised-Crime.pdf [March
2019].

24 https://www.unodc.org/documents/
counterfeit/FocusSheet/Counterfeit_
focussheet_EN_HIRES.pdf [March
2019].

25 Email interview with Jane Boddington
from the Wollaston Heritage Society.

26 M. Roach, *Dr. Martens – The Story of
an Icon*, Chrysalis, 2003.

27 Ibid., p.24.

28 https://www.theguardian.
com/business/2002/oct/26/
manufacturing?INTCMP=SRCH
[March 2019].

29 http://www.telegraph.co.uk/news/
uknews/1401952/Dr-Martens-gives-
Britain-the-boot.html [March 2019].

30 Ibid.

31 https://www.theguardian.
com/business/2002/oct/26/
manufacturing?INTCMP=SRCH
[March 2019].

32 http://news.bbc.co.uk/1/hi/
england/2896307.stm [March 2019].

33 https://www.designcouncil.org.uk/
news-opinion/power-branding [March
2019].

34 https://www.retail-week.com/fashion/
dr-martens-owner-sets-sights-on-
1bn-sale/7033632.article?authent=1
[December 2019].

35 https://www.highsnobiety.
com/2016/07/22/dr-martens-factory-
tour-cobbs-lane/ [March 2019].

36 https://www.permira.com/news-views/
news/dr-martens-excellent-results-
delivering-on-our-strategy/ [March
2019].

37 https://beta.companieshouse.gov.uk/
company/05678953/filing-history
[March 2019].

38 Ze Frank, quoted in https://heidicohen.
com/30-branding-definitions/ [March
2019].

39 https://www.designcouncil.org.uk/
news-opinion/power-branding [March
2019].

40 http://www.legislation.gov.uk/
uksi/1995/2489/contents/made
[December 2019].

41 Report: F. Gesualdi & D. Lucchetti,
The Real Cost of our Shoes, CNMS
and FAIR, April 2017.

42 Ibid.

43 Ibid.

44 Ibid.

45 https://cleanclothes.org/livingwage/
europe/europes-sweatshops [December
2019].

46 Ibid.

47 From interview with Bettina
Musiolek.

48 Saskia Sassen interviewed by
Shamus Khan, http://publicculture.
dukejournals.org/content/28/3_80/541.
abstract [March 2019].

Chapter Five: A Mile in Refugee Shoes

1 Teffi, *Memories: From Moscow to the
Black Sea*, Pushkin Press, 2016.

2 http://www.un.org/en/development/
desa/population/migration/
publications/migrationreport/docs/
MigrationReport2017_Highlights.pdf
[March 2019].

3 Ibid., p. 11.

4 https://genographic.
nationalgeographic.com/human-
journey/ [December 2019].

5 http://footwearnews.com/2017/
fashion/designers/ferragamo-family-
interview-exclusive-371525/ [March

2019].

6 http://stationmuseum.com/?page_
id=3211 [March 2019].

7 http://www.cbc.ca/radio/
thesundayedition/the-sunday-edition-
december-24-2017-1.4451296/
why-nothing-will-stop-people-from-
migrating-1.4451437 [March 2019].

8 https://www.wsj.com/articles/
eritreans-flee-conscription-and-
poverty-adding-to-the-migrant-crisis-
in-europe-1445391364 [March 2019].

9 https://www.cfr.org/backgrounder/
authoritarianism-eritrea-and-migrant-
crisis [March 2019].

10 Ibid.

11 https://eu.usatoday.com/story/news/
world/2018/05/24/border-walls-berlin-
wall-donald-trump-wall/553250002/
[March 2019].

12 Email interview with Jake Locke,
head of communications at SATRA
Technology.

13 https://thomashyllanderiksen.net/
blog/2018/12/12/overheating-the-tedx-
version [January 2020].

14 https://www.thenational.ae/world/
peshawar-shoe-makers-amused-
by-paul-smith-s-designer-chappals-
1.563165?videoId=5606881154001
[March 2019].

15 https://blogs.wsj.com/
indiarealtime/2014/03/11/how-
paul-smith-sandals-peeved-pakistan/
[March 2019].

16 https://www.theguardian.
com/law/2017/feb/22/
supreme-court-backs-minimum-
income-rule-for-non-european-spouses
[March 2019].

17 http://www.unhcr.org/3b66c2aa10
[March 2019].

18 https://reliefweb.int/report/turkey/
unhcr-turkey-factsheet-october-2017
[March 2019].

19 http://www.reuters.com/investigates/
special-report/europe-migrants-turkey-
children/ [March 2019].

20 From interview with Ercüment
Akdeniz.

21 http://www.reuters.com/investigates/
special-report/europe-migrants-turkey-
children/ [March 2019].

22 https://ec.europa.eu/echo/where/
    middle-east/syria_en [January 2020].
23 https://ahvalnews.com/child-labour/
    there-are-2-million-child-workers-
    turkey-union-says [March 2019].
24 http://www.hurriyetdailynews.com/
    turkish-textile-sector-eyes-bangladeshi-
    workers--73131 [March 2019].
25 https://cleanclothes.org/resources/
    publications/made-by-women.pdf
    [March 2019].
26 https://foreignpolicy.com/2019/01/28/
    investing-in-low-wage-jobs-is-the-
    wrong-way-to-reduce-migration/
    [March 2019].
27 https://www.academia.edu/2069138/
    Sexual_Predators_and_Serial_Rapists_
    Run_Wild_at_Wal-Mart_Supplier_
    in_Jordan_Young_women_workers_
    raped_tortured_and_beaten_at_the_
    Classic_Factory [November 2019].
28 https://www.arabnews.com/
    node/390209 [November 2019].
29 https://www.ilo.org/wcmsp5/groups/
    public/---arabstates/---ro-beirut/
    documents/genericdocument/
    wcms_237612.pdf [November 2019];
    http://www.jordantimes.com/news/
    local/minister-orders-factory-closure-
    after-alleged-abuse-guest-workers
    [November 2019];
    https://www.ilo.org/wcmsp5/groups/
    public/---arabstates/---ro-beirut/
    documents/publication/wcms_556931.
    pdf [November 2019].
30 Ibid.
31 https://www.theguardian.com/
    commentisfree/2018/feb/02/refugee-
    crisis-human-flow-ai-weiwei-china
    [March 2019].
32 http://www.xinhuanet.com/
    english/2018-01/31/c_136939276.htm
    [March 2019].
33 https://www.theguardian.com/
    cities/2018/feb/16/dongguan-spotlight-
    china-factory-world-hi-tech [March
    2019].
34 Ibid.
35 http://www.china-briefing.com/
    news/2013/02/27/dongguan-the-
    worlds-factory-in-transition-part-i.
    html [March 2019].
36 http://www.gsshoe.com/about.html

and http://www.china-briefing.com/
    news/2013/02/27/dongguan-the-
    worlds-factory-in-transition-part-i.
    html [March 2019].
37 https://www.businessoffashion.com/
    articles/opinion/op-ed-chinas-missing-
    factory-inspectors-have-nothing-to-do-
    with-ivanka-trump [March 2019].
38 https://thediplomat.com/2016/06/
    chinas-new-generation-of-urban-
    migrants/ [March 2019].
39 http://siteresources.worldbank.
    org/INTEAECOPRO/
    Resources/3087694-1206446474145/
    Chapter_3_China_Urbanizes.pdf
    [March 2019].
40 Ibid.
41 Translated by Eleanor Goodman,
    http://www.clb.org.hk/en/content/
    obituary-peanut-creatively-cynical-
    world-worker-poet-xu-lizhi [March
    2019].
42 https://thediplomat.com/2016/06/
    chinas-new-generation-of-urban-
    migrants/ [March 2019].
43 http://siteresources.worldbank.
    org/INTEAECOPRO/
    Resources/3087694-1206446474145/
    Chapter_3_China_Urbanizes.pdf
    [March 2019].
44 https://www.rfa.org/english/news/
    china/man-self-immolates-in-beijing-
    after-failing-to-find-school-for-
    daughter-05232016103429.html
    [March 2019].
45 https://www.nytimes.com/2017/12/24/
    world/asia/china-schools-migrants.
    html [March 2019].
46 Ibid.
47 https://thediplomat.com/2016/06/
    chinas-new-generation-of-urban-
    migrants/ [March 2019].
48 Ibid.
49 https://edition.cnn.com/2018/02/04/
    health/china-left-behind-kids-
    photography-intl/index.html [March
    2019].
50 Ibid.

Chapter Six: Hell for Leather

1 https://www.hsa.org.uk/faqs/
   general#n7 [March 2019].

2 https://www.vegansociety.com/whats-new/blog/answering-common-questions-about-veganism [March 2019].

3 https://www.wired.com/2014/06/the-emotional-lives-of-dairy-cows/ [March 2019].

4 https://www.theguardian.com/environment/2014/dec/03/eating-less-meat-curb-climate-change [March 2019].

5 https://leathercouncil.org/introduction-to-leather/what-is-leather/ [March 2019].

6 https://leathercouncil.org/information/statistics-sources-of-information/ [March 2019].

7 M. Joy, *Toward Rational, Authentic Food Choices*, TEDxMünchen, https://www.youtube.com/watch?v=o0VrZPBskpg&vl=en [March 2019].

8 https://www.theguardian.com/environment/2018/feb/02/almost-four-environmental-defenders-a-week-killed-in-2017 [March 2019].

9 https://theintercept.com/2018/10/28/jair-bolsonaro-elected-president-brazil/ [March 2019].

10 http://cicb.org.br/storage/files/repositories/phpJ5Lpan-total-exp-dec18-eng.pdf [March 2019].

11 https://conseilnationalducuir.org/en/press/releases/2018-01-24 [March 2019].

12 http://cicb.org.br/storage/files/repositories/phpyK3Pmm-total-exp-oct-eng.pdf [March 2019].

13 https://e360.yale.edu/features/why-brazils-new-president-poses-an-unprecedented-threat-to-the-amazon [March 2019].

14 https://www.iwgia.org/images/publications/0617_ENGELSK-AISLADOS_opt.pdf [March 2019].

15 https://www.facebook.com/aty.guasu/photos/a.603723143096222/1382401831895012/?type=3&theater [March 2019].

16 http://wwf.panda.org/knowledge_hub/where_we_work/amazon/about_the_amazon/ [March 2019].

17 http://wwf.panda.org/knowledge_hub/where_we_work/amazon/about_the_amazon/why_amazon_important/ [March 2019].

18 http://wwf.panda.org/knowledge_hub/where_we_work/amazon/about_the_amazon/ [March 2019].

19 https://e360.yale.edu/features/why-brazils-new-president-poses-an-unprecedented-threat-to-the-amazon [March 2019].

20 Natural England Research Report NERR043: *Carbon storage by habitat: Review of the evidence of the impacts of management decisions and condition of carbon stores and sources*, 2012.

21 https://jbs.com.br/en/imprensa/releases/jbs-couros-apresenta-tendencias-para-o-mercado-de-couros-na-china-leather-exhibition-2017/ [March 2019].

22 https://reporterbrasil.org.br/2016/09/electroshocks-punching-and-beatings-the-life-of-cows-turned-into-meat-at-jbs/ [March 2019].

23 Ibid.

24 http://www.leathermag.com/features/featurefour-tannery-workers-killed-at-marfrig-plant/ [March 2019].

25 https://portal.minervafoods.com/en/about-us-minerva [March 2019].

26 https://www.reuters.com/article/us-cattle-shipment-santos/brazil-defends-live-cattle-export-after-injunction-temporarily-lifted-idUSKBN1FP2L9 [March 2019].

27 https://www.motherjones.com/politics/2015/10/ship-carrying-5000-cows-sank-brazil/ [March 2019].

28 https://www.reuters.com/article/brazil-slavery/more-than-300-brazilian-companies-busted-for-modern-day-slavery-campaigners-idUSL8N15U3CD [March 2019].

29 https://downloads.globalslaveryindex.org/ephemeral/GSI-2018_FNL_190828_CO_DIGITAL_P-1573046361.pdf [November 2019].

30 https://www.greenpeace.org/archive-international/Global/international/briefings/forests/2017/

Greenpeace-Brazil-Amazon-Cattle-Agreement.pdf [March 2019].

31 https://www.maharam.com/stories/barbe_the-history-of-leather-tanning [March 2019].

32 https://newsmaven.io/indiancountrytoday/opinion/native-american-and-vegan-yes-it-s-possible-i-ve-done-it-for-18-years-JoTkBY5SeEqFxHJgTg6p6g/ [March 2019].

33 https://leatherpanel.org/sites/default/files/publications-attachments/future_trends_in_the_world_leather_and_leather_products_industry_and_trade.pdf [March 2019].

34 https://leathercouncil.org/information/statistics-sources-of-information/ [March 2019].

35 B. Thomson, DeGrowth Canada, http://www.web.net/~bthomson/fairtrade/fair6612.html [March 2019].

36 https://www.publiceye.ch/fileadmin/doc/_migration/CCC/ToughSTORYof_LEATHER_april_2016.pdf [March 2019].

37 http://www.fitreach.eu/sites/default/files/editor/Images/publiacations/Case%20story_Chromium_III.pdf [March 2019].

38 Switzerland Green Cross, *World's Top Ten Toxic Threats in 2013*, https://www.greencross.ch/wp-ontent/uploads/uploads/media_2013_11_05_top_ten_wwpp_en.pdf [March 2019].

39 https://www.theguardian.com/global-development/2012/dec/13/bangladesh-toxic-tanneries-intolerable-human-price & http://www.scielosp.org/scielo.php?pid=S0042-96862001000100018&script=sci_arttext [March 2019].

40 https://www.theguardian.com/world/2017/mar/21/plight-of-child-workers-facing-cocktail-of-toxic-chemicals-exposed-by-report-bangladesh-tanneries [March 2019].

41 https://www.hrw.org/sites/default/files/reports/bangladesh1012webwcover.pdf [March 2019].

42 https://www.thedailystar.net/business/savar-leather-estate-project-delayed-again-1487905 [June 2019]. https://www.thedailystar.net/city/news/pm-opens-savar-tannery-city-two-industrial-parks-1657234 [June 2019].

43 Supreme Court of Bangladesh writ petition document from 6 March 2017.

44 Supreme Court of Bangladesh documents from 10 January 2017–4 July 2019.

45 https://bdnews24.com/media-en/2018/08/28/harindhara-another-hazaribagh [March 2019].

46 http://www.thedailystar.net/business/leather-sectors-exports-cross-1b-second-year-127465 [March 2019].

47 https://thefinancialexpress.com.bd/editorial/making-the-most-of-leather-tech-expo-1542903681 [March 2019].

48 https://www.hrw.org/sites/default/files/reports/bangladesh1012webwcover.pdf [March 2019].

49 https://business.financialpost.com/pmn/business-pmn/toxic-tanneries-polluting-again-at-new-bangladesh-site [March 2019].

50 EU Rapid Alert System for dangerous non-food products, Weekly Overview Report No. 40, https://ec.europa.eu/consumers/consumers_safety/safety_products/rapex/alerts/ [March 2019].

51 http://www.indianet.nl/pdf/DoLeatherWorkersMatter.pdf [March 2019].

52 Ibid.

53 http://ncdhr.org.in/front/dalits_untouchability [March 2019].

54 Ibid.

55 http://www.indianet.nl/pdf/DoLeatherWorkersMatter.pdf [March 2019].

56 https://www.aljazeera.com/indepth/features/2016/08/india-dalit-cattle-skinners-share-stories-abuse-160816122203107.html [March 2019].

57 https://blogs.wsj.com/indiarealtime/2015/08/06/where-you-can-and-cant-eat-beef-in-india/ [December 2019].

58 https://www.hrw.org/news/2019/02/18/

interview-killing-name-cows [December 2019].

59 https://www.reuters.com/article/us-india-cattle-bangladesh feature/indias-push-to-save-its-cows-starves-bangladesh-of-beef-idUSKCN0PC2OW20150702 [December 2019].

60 http://www.indianet.nl/pdf/DoLeatherWorkersMatter.pdf [March 2019].

61 https://www.thehindu.com/todays-paper/10-workers-killed-in-ranipet-tannery/article6843775.ece [March 2019].

62 http://cividep.org/wp-content/uploads/2017/04/Ranipet-Tanneries-CETP-Mishap-Report-compressed.pdf [October 2019].

63 http://www.aplf.com/en-US/leather-fashion-news-and-blog/news/38290/italy-overview-of-tanning-industry-2017 [March 2019].

64 Report: *Did You Know There's A Cow In Your Shoes?*, Centro Nuovo Modello di Sviluppo, November 2016.

65 https://www.publiceye.ch/fileadmin/doc/Mode/2016_CYS_A_tough_story_of_leather_Report.pdf [January 2020]. Please note, the source for the claim of what caused the blast is attributed to a local trade union.

66 Report: *Did You Know There's A Cow In Your Shoes?*, Centro Nuovo Modello di Sviluppo, November 2016.

67 MuSkin is being developed by an Italian company using mushroom caps.

68 The Ananas Anam company have developed Piñatex.

69 https://deborahbirdrose.com/144-2/ [March 2019].

70 http://deborahbirdrose.com/2018/11/23/flying-foxes-on-my-mind/ [March 2019].

Chapter Seven: Getting Wasted

1 http://www.textile-recycling.org.uk/love-your-clothes/ [March 2019].

2 https://www.nation.co.ke/lifestyle/saturday/Making-a-living-off-mitumba/1216-3342796-kgxre6/index.html [March 2019].

3 http://www.cuts-geneva.org/pdf/PACT2-STUDY-The_Impact_of_Second_Hand_Clothes_and_Shoes_in_East_Africa.pdf p.11 [March 2019].

4 https://www.primeugandasafaris.com/day-trips-in-uganda/kampala-tour.html [March 2019].

5 https://africanbusinessmagazine.com/sectors/commodities/rwandas-export-drive-reaps success/ [March 2019]; https://www.reuters.com/article/us-usa-trade-rwanda/trump-suspends-duty-free-status-for-clothes-imports-from-rwanda-idUSKBN1KK2JN [December 2019].

6 https://www.bbc.co.uk/news/world-africa-44252655 [March 2019].

7 https://publications.parliament.uk/pa/cm201719/cmselect/cmenvaud/1952/report-files/195207.htm [March 2019].

8 https://soex.uk/innovations/ [March 2019].

9 https://www.theguardian.com/environment/2009/aug/23/repair-trainers-ethical-living [March 2019].

10 https://www.ibisworld.com/global/market-size/global-footwear-manufacturing/ [January 2020].

11 http://www.ehs.org.uk/dotAsset/8634b481-29ac-458f-b640-07871cd46bb4.pdf [March 2019].

12 Ibid.

13 Ibid.

14 http://www.pnas.org/content/early/2018/07/31/1810141115 [March 2019].

Chapter Eight: The Sewbots Are Coming

1 S. Jones, *Against Technology From the Luddites to Neo-Luddism*, Routledge, 2006; http://www.luddites200.org.uk/theLuddites.html [March 2019]. https://www.smithsonianmag.com/history/what-the-luddites-really-fought-against-264412/ [March 2019].

2 https://www.grammarphobia.com/blog/2010/09/sabotage.html [March

2019];
https://www.etymonline.com/word/
sabotage [March 2019].

3 https://www.trtworld.com/magazine/
will-robots-completely-replace-
humans-from-textile-factory-
floors--14930 [March 2019].

4 https://www.thersa.org/globalassets/
pdfs/reports/rsa_the-age-of-
automation-report.pdf [March 2019].

5 Ibid.

6 Ibid.

7 https://medium.com/@
daveevansap/8-ways-automation-has-
infiltrated-our-lives-and-you-didnt-
even-know-it-2f2fdc36b618 [March
2019].

8 https://medium.com/@thersa/
what-is-the-difference-between-ai-
robotics-d93715b4ba7f [March 2019].

9 http://www.sewbo.com/press/ [March
2019].

10 https://www.youtube.com/
watch?v=MkYczy6xub0 [March
2019].

11 https://www.assemblymag.com/
articles/93672-shoe-manufacturer-
automates-production-in-unique-way
[March 2019].

12 From interview with Jae-Hee Chang.

13 https://www.ft.com/content/585866fc-
a841-11e7-ab55-27219df83c97
[March 2019].

14 https://www.worldfootwear.com/news/
nike-flex-partnership-ends/3573.html
[June 2019].

15 http://manufacturingmap.nikeinc.com/
[March 2019].

16 https://uk.reuters.com/article/
uk-adidas-manufacturing-
idUKKCN0YF1YE [March 2019].

17 http://www.ilo.org/wcmsp5/groups/
public/---ed_dialogue/---act_emp/
documents/publication/wcms_579560.
pdf [March 2019].

18 https://qz.com/966882/robots-cant-
lace-shoes-so-sneaker-production-cant-
be-fully-automated-just-yet/ [March
2019].

19 From interview with Katja Schreiber,
spokeswoman for adidas, in 2016.

20 https://uk.reuters.com/article/
us-adidas-manufacturing-
idUKKBN1XL16U [November 2019].

21 https://techcrunch.com/2019/11/11/
adidas-backpedals-on-robotic-
factories/ [November 2019].

22 https://qz.com/966882/robots-cant-
lace-shoes-so-sneaker-production-cant-
be-fully-automated-just-yet/ [March
2019].

23 From interview with Katja Schreiber,
spokeswoman for adidas, in 2016.

24 https://www.ilo.org/wcmsp5/groups/
public/---ed_dialogue/---act_emp/
documents/publication/wcms_579553.
pdf [March 2019].

25 https://www.thedailystar.net/
round-tables/"target-us50-billion-we-
need-your-support-reach-it"-659905
[March 2019]. Cambodia too: TCF
accounted for over 87 per cent of
the country's total manufactured
exports in 2014: http://www.ilo.org/
wcmsp5/groups/public/---ed_dialogue/-
--act_emp/documents/publication/
wcms_579560.pdf [March 2019].

26 https://www.theguardian.
com/global-development-
professionals-network/2017/apr/06/
kate-raworth-doughnut-economics-
new-economics [March 2019].

27 https://www.project-syndicate.org/
commentary/innovation-impact-on-
productivity-by-dani-rodrik-2016-06
[March 2019].

28 http://www.ilo.org/wcmsp5/groups/
public/---ed_dialogue/---act_emp/
documents/publication/wcms_579560.
pdf [March 2019].

29 https://medium.com/conversations-
with-tyler/a-conversation-with-dani-
rodrik-e02cf8784b9d [March 2019].

30 Ibid.

31 http://drodrik.scholar.harvard.
edu/files/dani-rodrik/files/
premature-deindustrialization.
pdf?m=1435002429 [March 2019].

32 https://www.project-syndicate.org/
commentary/innovation-impact-on-
productivity-by-dani-rodrik-2016-06
[March 2019].
http://drodrik.scholar.harvard.
edu/files/dani-rodrik/files/
premature-deindustrialization.
pdf?m=1435002429 [March 2019].

33 https://www.youtube.com/watch?v=Mkg2XMTWV4g [March 2019].

34 https://foreignpolicy.com/2018/09/12/why-growth-cant-be-green/amp/ [March 2019].

35 Online content from M. Mazzucato, author of *The Value of Everything*, https://www.penguin.co.uk/books/280466/the-value-of-everything/9780241188811.html [December 2019].

36 http://time.com/4504004/men-without-work/ [March 2019].

37 https://www.iseapublish.com/index.php/2017/06/26/automation-expected-to-disproportionately-affect-the-less-educated/ [March 2019].

38 C. B. Frey, T. Berger, and C. Chen, 'Political machinery: did robots swing the 2016 US presidential election?', *Oxford Review of Economic Policy*, vol. 34, no. 3, 2018, pp. 418–42.

39 https://time.com/5723787/chile-climate-change-cop25/ [November 2019].

40 https://www.cnbc.com/2016/07/13/amazon-prime-day-is-biggest-day-for-online-retailer-ever.html [March 2019].

41 https://www.ft.com/content/ed6a985c-70bd-11e2-85d0-00144feab49a [December 2019].

42 https://www.nytimes.com/2015/08/16/technology/inside-amazon-wrestling-big-ideas-in-a-bruising-workplace.html [November 2019].

43 https://www.theguardian.com/technology/2019/jan/01/amazon-fulfillment-center-warehouse-employees-union-new-york-minnesota [November 2019].

44 https://www.newyorker.com/books/under-review/the-deliberate-awfulness-of-social-media [March 2019].

45 https://www.etui.org/content/download/35667/354684/file/working-in-a-modern-day-amazon-fulfilment-centres-in-the-uk.pdf [January 2020].

46 https://www.theguardian.com/business/2018/may/31/amazon-accused-of-treating-uk-warehouse-staff-like-robots [October 2019].

47 https://www.tandfonline.com/doi/abs/10.1080/19424280.2013.799543 [March 2019].

48 https://www.economist.com/science-and-technology/2018/05/24/shoemakers-bring-bespoke-footwear-to-the-high-street [March 2019].

49 https://www.nytimes.com/2017/07/18/us/frances-gabe-dead-inventor-of-self-cleaning-house.html [March 2019].

50 http://lilybenson.com/news/ [March 2019].

51 https://www.theverge.com/2019/3/10/18258134/alexandria-ocasio-cortez-automation-sxsw-2019 [March 2019].

52 https://www.independent.co.uk/news/business/news/finland-universal-basic-income-lower-stress-better-motivation-work-wages-salary-a7800741.html [March 2019].

Chapter Nine: If the Shoe Fits

1 https://www.businessinsider.com/23-giant-companies-that-earn-more-than-entire-countries-2018-7?r=US&IR=T#nikes-profits-in-2017-were-greater-than-cameroons-gdp-16 [March 2019].

2 Gary Younge quoting Benjamin Barber: https://www.theguardian.com/commentisfree/2014/jun/02/control-nation-states-corporations-autonomy-neoliberalism [March 2019].

3 https://www.rdwolff.com/capitalism_is_not_the_market_system [March 2019].

4 J. Stiglitz, *Globalization and Its Discontents*, W. W. Norton & Company, 2002, pp. 5, 21.

5 http://eradicatingecocide.com/our-earth/earth-justice/ [December 2019].

6 https://theconversation.com/why-the-international-criminal-court-is-right-to-focus-on-the-environment-65920 [March 2019].

7 https://www.climateliabilitynews.org/2018/12/26/legal-strategy-climate-lawsuits/ [March 2019].

8   Paper: G. Brown, 'The corporate social responsibility mirage', *Industrial Safety and Hygiene News*, May 2017.

9   Paper: B. Rosenberg, *Working Conditions in Footwear Factories in China; a Brand Attempts Improvements through Corporate Responsibility*, Dept. of Public Health and Family Medicine, Tufts University School of Medicine.

10   Ibid.

11   Department Lecture Transcript: B. Rosenberg, *CSR: What Is It Good For?*, Dept. of Public Health and Family Medicine, Tufts University School of Medicine, October 2010.

12   https://foreignpolicy.com/2017/02/21/saving-the-world-one-meaningless-buzzword-at-a-time-human-rights/ [March 2019].

13   https://edition.cnn.com/2012/05/02/business/eco-business-sustainabilitygrade/index.html [January 2020]; http://www.eiris.org/files/research%20publications/EIRISGlobalSustainbailityReport2012.pdf [January 2020]; https://about.puma.com/en/newsroom/corporate-news/2012/05-07-12-eiris [January 2020].

14   https://www.reuters.com/article/puma-cambodia-idUSL5E8DN8S820120223 [January 2020].

15   https://foreignpolicy.com/2017/02/21/saving-the-world-one-meaningless-buzzword-at-a-time-human-rights/ [March 2019].

16   The Rana Plaza factory contracted to Primark was New Wave Bottoms, on the second floor of the eight-storey building: https://www.primark.com/en/our-ethics/timeline-of-support [December 2019]; https://www.primark.com/en/our-ethics/building-inspection-programmes [December 2019].
Primark paid £6m in compensation. Its parent company, ABF, has a turnover of £7.5b per year. https://www.retailgazette.co.uk/blog/2019/04/primark-half-year-profits-surge/ [December 2019].

17   Research Paper: M. Cowgill and P. Huynh, *Weak minimum wage compliance in Asia's garment industry*, ILO, August 2016, https://www.ilo.org/wcmsp5/groups/public/---ed_protect/---protrav/---travail/documents/publication/wcms_509532.pdf [January 2020].

18   At the time, the eleven Nike executives who left the company denied requests for comment from media outlets. Daniel Tawiah told *The Oregonian/OregonLive* the accusations against him are false: 'I have never bullied anyone – neither directly or indirectly, male or female.' https://www.nytimes.com/2018/04/28/business/nike-women.html [March 2019].

19   http://blogs.lse.ac.uk/management/2018/03/09/taking-metoo-into-global-supply-chains/ [March 2019].

20   http://www.brac.net/latest-news/item/1142-94-women-victims-of-sexual-harassment-in-public-transport [March 2019].

21   http://blogs.lse.ac.uk/management/2018/03/09/taking-metoo-into-global-supply-chains/ [March 2019].

22   https://www.ilo.org/wcmsp5/groups/public/---asia/---ro-bangkok/documents/presentation/wcms_546534.pdf [March 2019].

23   http://www.coha.org/worker-rights-and-wrongs-fair-trade-zones-and-labor-in-the-americas/#_ednref11 [March 2019].

24   https://www.ilo.org/wcmsp5/groups/public/---asia/---ro-bangkok/documents/presentation/wcms_546534.pdf [March 2019].

25   https://www.theguardian.com/environment/ng-interactive/2018/feb/27/the-defenders-recording-the-deaths-of-environmental-defenders-around-the-world [March 2019].

26   https://www.oxfam.org/en/pressroom/pressreleases/2015-12-02/worlds-richest-10-produce-half-carbon-emissions-while-poorest-35 [March 2019].

Chapter Ten: Kick Back

1 400,000 in 2014: https://uk.reuters.com/article/yue-yuen-ind-results/chinas-yue-yuen-h1-profit-falls-48-pct-on-staff-benefits-idUKL4N0QI2YN20140814 [March 2019].

2 https://uk.reuters.com/article/yue-yuen-ind-workers/chinese-shoe-maker-yue-yuen-in-talks-to-resolve-worker-dispute-idUKL3N0N02FX20140408 [March 2019].

3 https://clb.org.hk/content/china%E2%80%99s-social-security-system [March 2019].

4 https://www.youtube.com/watch?v=6Ca-hoozEGE&feature=youtu.be [March 2019].

5 https://uk.reuters.com/article/yue-yuen-ind-results/chinas-yue-yuen-h1-profit-falls-48-pct-on-staff-benefits-idUKL4N0QI2YN20140814 [March 2019].

6 https://www.hongkongfp.com/2016/11/03/guangdong-labour-activist-meng-han-sentenced-1-year-9-months/ [March 2019].

7 https://www.theguardian.com/world/2018/nov/12/ten-student-activists-detained-in-china-for-supporting-workers-rights [December 2019].

8 https://qz.com/827623/throwing-labor-activists-like-meng-han-in-jail-wont-solve-chinas-structural-problems/ [March 2019].

9 http://usas.org/tag/nike/ [March 2019].

10 https://qz.com/1042298/nike-is-facing-a-new-wave-of-anti-sweatshop-protests/ [October 2019].

11 https://www.nytimes.com/1998/05/13/business/international-business-nike-pledges-to-end-child-labor-and-apply-us-rules-abroad.html?mtrref=www.google.com&gwh=A713FDE2B3A78461A9264AAD3250606D&gwt=pay [October 2019]; https://www.business-humanrights.org/en/uk-ethical-consumer-report-puts-starbucks-at-bottom-of-ethical-rating-of-coffee-chains-citing-workers-rights-concerns [October 2019]; https://www.peta.org/blog/mcdonalds-finally-agrees-to-use-less-cruel-slaughter-method-in-2024/ [October 2019].

12 https://www.iea.org/energyaccess/ [March 2019].

13 https://www.marxists.org/archive/marx/works/subject/quotes/index.htm [March 2019].

BIBLIOGRAPHY

Z. Bauman, *Work, Consumerism, & The New Poor* (Open University Press, 2005).

E. Cazdyn and I. Szeman, *After Globalisation* (John Wiley & Sons, 2011).

W. Ellwood, *The No-Nonsense Guide to Globalization* (New Internationalist Publications Ltd, 2010)

F. Grew and M. de Neergaard, *Shoes and Pattens – Medieval Finds from Excavations in London: 2* (Museum of London, 1988).

T. Hoskins, *Stitched Up – The Anti-Capitalist Book of Fashion* (Pluto Press, 2014).

S. Jones, *Against Technology from the Luddites to Neo-Luddism* (Routledge, 2006).

C. McDowell, *Shoes: Fashion & Fantasy.* Thames and Hudson, 1989

P. Markkanen, *Shoes, Glues and Homework: Dangerous Work in the Global Footwear Industry* (Routledge, 2017).

P. Newell, *Globalisation and the Environment* (Polity, 2012).

G. Riello, *A Foot in the Past* (Oxford University Press, 2006).

M. Roach, *Dr. Martens – The Story of an Icon* (Chrysalis, 2003).

J. Schor, *Plenitude: The New Economics of True Wealth* (Penguin Press, 2010).

—— *The Overspent American* (HarperCollins, 1999).

E. Semmelhack, *Shoes: The Meaning of Style* (Reaktion Books, 2017).

M. B. Steger (ed.), *Globalisation – The Greatest Hits* (Paradigm Publishers, 2010).

J. Stiglitz, *Globalisation and Its Discontents* (W.W. Norton & Company, 2002).

J. Swann, *Shoemaking* (Shire Publications Ltd, 2003).

J. H. Thornton (ed.), *Textbook of Footwear Manufacture* (The National Trade Press, 1953).

D. K. Vajpeyi and R. Oberoi, *Globalization Reappraised – False Oracle or a Talisman* (Lexington Books, 2018).

A. Veldmeijer, *Stepping through Time: Footwear in Ancient Egypt* (exhibition guidebook, BLKVLD Uitgevers/Publishers 2017).

J. Waterer, *Leather and the Warrior* (Museum of Leathercraft, 1982).

INDEX